NEW YORK
PRESIDENTIAL
CONVENTIONS

Other Books by R. Craig Sautter

Inside the Wigwam: Chicago Presidential Conventions 1860-1996, (with Alderman Edward M. Burke), Loyola Press/Wild Onion Books, 1996

Philadelphia Presidential Conventions (1848-2000), december press, 2000

The Power of the Ballot (National Urban League Staff Project), 1973

Who Got In? College Bound's Annual National Admissions Survey, editions 1986-2004

Expresslanes Through The Inevitable City (poems), december press, 1990

Smart Schools, Smart Kids (with Edward B. Fiske and Sally Reed), Simon & Schuster, 1991

Floyd Dell: Essays From The Friday Literary Review, december press, 1995

The Wicked City: Chicago from Kenna to Capone (with Curt Johnson), DeCapo Press, 1998

26 Martyrs For These Latter Perilous Days (with Curt Johnson), december press, 2004

NEW YORK PRESIDENTIAL CONVENTIONS

The Pre-TV Era (1839-1924)

R. Craig Sautter

december press

A special issue of December Magazine,
comprising vol. 42, no. 4, 2004

ISBN 0-913204-40-4
Library of Congress Catalogue Card Number 2004095009

Manufactured in the United States of America

Front cover photo: By courtesy of the Statue of Liberty National Monument. **Back cover photo:** Sally Reed. **Photos insert between pages 130 and 131:** *Dictionary of American Portraits,* New York: Dover Publications, 1967. **Last page of insert:** McAdoo, Denver Public Library, Western History Collection, photo by Harry M. Rhoads, RH-5822. Smith, courtesy of the New York State Library/Manuscripts and Special Collections. Davis, courtesy West Virginia State Archives, photo by Sayre, Clarksburg, West Virginia.

Published by december press
Box 302, Highland Park, Illinois 60035
(847) 940-4122

Also available at: www.presidentialconventions.com

CONTENTS

Acknowedgments

Special thanks to Sally Reed and Curt Johnson for advice, assistance, and friendship. Also thanks to the New York Public Library, the Chicago Public Library, particularly periodicals and microfilm departments, the DePaul University Richardson Library, the Northwestern University Library, and the Evanston, Illinois, Public Library.

New York Presidential Politics

In late August and early September 2004, New York hosts its sixth National Presidential Nominating Convention by a major party. The Republicans come to New York City for the first time ever to nominate a presidential candidate. The Thirty-Eighth Republican National Convention is strategically scheduled to position President George Walker Bush against the backdrop of his record in defense of the nation after the tragic events surrounding the deadly surprise attacks of September 11, 2001. Not only will the 2004 Republican National Convention be draped heavily with the multitude of reminiscences of those sad and traumatic events, this assembly will be a rare war-time Nominating Convention, as well as an infrequent Re-Nomination Convention, each with its own histories and peculiarities.

Oddly enough, New York has not been a favored site for Presidential Nominating Conventions. New York now ranks fourth among American cities that have hosted the most National Presidential Nominating Conventions by the two current major parties. Chicago, Baltimore, and Philadelphia all hosted more National Conventions. But the Empire State's early Convention history is a fascinating one, filled with decisions of historical import, and with impact on the ultimate electoral outcome in November. This volume seeks to recover the colorful political characters and decisive debates of those early events that shaped the nation's history.

Infrequency of National Conventions has not stopped New York from a powerful role in selecting the nation's Presidents. Indeed, because New York has been such a prevailing force in party politics, and has been the home to so many potent presidential candidates, the parties may have shied away from bringing their National Nominating Conventions to New York. Throughout the past two centuries, fear that Tammany Hall would somehow swindle the Democratic nomination for one of its allies kept the party away, except in 1868 and 1924. Those raucous Conventions are also recounted in the following chapters. In more recent years, geographical shifts of power and electoral strategy have directed the parties to other cities.

Ever since the early days of the American Republic, New York State has been a powerful springboard to national political prominence, an abundant source of grand presidential talent and aspirations. From the

1

election of Democratic Party co-founder Martin Van Buren, the "Little Magician," as the nation's Eighth President to the landslide Depression victory of aristocratic Governor Franklin Delano Roosevelt, as the Thirty-Second President, New York has supplied the national political arena with decisive and memorable personalities to guide the country's destiny.

New York State became a footnote in the very first presidential election of 1789, when its state legislature was so dead-locked between the forces behind Governor George Clinton and those of Alexander Hamilton that it could not even agree to pick Electors to vote in the first Electoral College. (Rhode Island and North Carolina did not participate, either, because they had not ratified the Constitution.) Because New York and the other two states did not participate in the election (neither did most citizens outside of the state legislatures, something that didn't change until the 1820s), it is inaccurate to say: "George Washington was the unanimous choice as the nation's first President." Nonetheless, Washington was first in the hearts of most of his countrymen, and the only President inaugurated on Wall Street or to serve an official term as President of the United States in New York, the nation's first capital before Philadelphia, then Washington. In 1796, the "congressional caucus" emerged as the mechanism for nominating candidates for President, almost always in secret session. In the 1820's, the caucus system of nominating presidential candidates was replaced by nominations in state legislatures, before that system gave way to Nominating Conventions in the 1830's.

In one of the nation's most bizarre presidential elections, Aaron Burr, born in New Jersey but politically based in New York as Senator, tied anti-Federalist leader Thomas Jefferson for President in the 1800 Electoral College with 79 votes. Electors intended that Burr become Jefferson's Vice President. Both Republicans, as they were called because of their affinity to French radicals, out-polled one-term Federalist President John Adams. The 1800 Electors cast two votes each, but it didn't occur to anti-Adams, anti-Federalists to hold back one vote from Burr to secure Jefferson's victory.

Burr could have been elected President in the House of Representatives where the election was decided, out of spite, had Alexander Hamilton instructed his Federalist allies to cast their votes for Burr instead of Jefferson, both of whom were despised by the Federalists. Patriotism prevailed and Hamilton and his followers voted for the best man, Jefferson. The electoral confusion led to the 1804 passage of the Twelfth Amendment which stipulates that Electors should cast one ballot for President, and another for Vice President. Burr became the nation's Third Vice President. (And of course, he later killed Alexander Hamilton in a duel in New Jersey over another matter "of honor," and was later tried and acquitted of treason for yet another indiscretion.)

2

DeWitt Clinton, George Clinton's nephew, was New York City's mayor from 1803 to 1807, and again in 1810, 1811, 1813, 1814, and 1815. Simultaneously, he was New York's Lieutenant Governor from 1811 to 1813, and then New York Governor from 1817 to 1821 and 1825 to 1828, when he promoted the Erie Canal. In September 1812, the Federalist congressional caucus secretly met in New York City and nominated him for President of the United States to run against James Madison. Clinton also had the support of some Democrat-Republicans, but lost in the Electoral College, 128 to 89.

Although it took nearly half a century before a New Yorker was first elected to the highest office in the land, many from the Empire State played a close second in the Washington corridors of power. The Republic's Fourth Vice President was a New Yorker, Governor George Clinton, who served one term under Jefferson and then another vice presidential term under Madison, who was his opponent. Clinton had been New York Governor from 1777 to 1795 and again from 1801 to 1804. He continued his unsuccessful presidential quest until dying in office as Vice President.

The country's Sixth Vice President was also a New Yorker, three-term Governor Daniel D. Tompkins, a Tammany Democrat, who served two terms under James Monroe. The nation's Eighth Vice President, Martin Van Buren, served under Andrew Jackson, before his elevation by election. The Twelfth Vice President, New York State Comptroller Millard Fillmore, became the Thirteenth President when Zachary Taylor died in office. Former Collector of the Port of New York, the nation's Twentieth Vice President, Chester A. Arthur, became the Twenty-First President when James Garfield was assassinated while walking unprotected through Washington's train station.

Minister to France Levi Parsons Morton, a millionaire New York banker, served Benjamin Harrison, as the Twenty-Second Vice President. Former one-term New York Governor and Twenty-Fifth Vice President Theodore Roosevelt, became the Twenty-Sixth President when William McKinley was assassinated by an anarchist. Upstate Congressman James Schoolcraft Sherman served as the Twenty-Seventh Vice President under William Howard Taft, before dying in office and leaving the post open. Governor Nelson A. Rockefeller, the Forty-First Vice President, became the first appointed Vice President under provisions of the Twenty-Fifth Amendment, when President Richard Nixon resigned, and Vice President Gerald Ford became President and picked the New York Governor as his second.

Although winning the national popular vote three straight elections, New York Governor Grover Cleveland served a split-double term, as the Twenty-Second and Twenty-Fourth President. President Dwight Eisenhower was president of Columbia University in New York

City when he won the Republican nomination in 1952. Richard Nixon, Eisenhower's former Vice President, had retreated from California to New York before winning the 1968 presidential election.

Add to these illustrious names and national personalities, those great New Yorkers who unsuccessfully sought the presidency: New Yorker William Wirt, who was nominated by the Anti-Masonic Party in the first National Presidential Nominating Convention, in Harrisburg, Pennsylvania, in 1831; Senator William Henry Seward, co-founder of the anti-slavery Republican Party, whose forces were out-witted by Lincoln men at the 1860 Chicago Convention; New York Governor Horatio Seymour, who was unexpectedly nominated at Tammany Hall in 1868 (as recounted in this volume); New York publisher Horace Greeley, nominated by Democrats and Liberal Republicans to run against President Grant in 1872, whom he accused of unprecedented corruption.

Additionally, New York Governor Samuel Tilden, winner of the popular vote over Rutherford B. Hayes, was "robbed" of the Electoral Vote in the "Stolen Election of 1876." Former New York Governor and Supreme Court Judge Charles Evans Hughes, the Republicans' 1916 nominee for President lost to Woodrow "He Kept Us Out of War" Wilson. The wildly popular "hero of the tenements" Governor Al Smith (whose 1924 run for the nomination is recounted in this volume) became the nominee in 1928, losing to Herbert Hoover. Wendell Willkie, the "Barefoot Wall Street lawyer" won the Republican nomination in the 1940 "miracle in Philadelphia" to stop F.D.R.'s "third-term."

New York Senator Robert F. Kennedy was storming to the nomination as an anti-war, civil rights candidate when he was assassinated in 1968. Brooklyn Congresswoman Shirley Chisholm ran a symbolic campaign for the 1972 Democratic nomination as an anti-war, anti-racist black woman. Harlem Reverend Al Sharpton campaigned in an articulate but marginal campaign for the Democratic nomination in 2004. Meanwhile, another New York Senator and former First Lady, Hillary Clinton, may be poised for a future run for the presidency. Other New Yorkers are certain to follow.

It was Jimmy Carter, of Georgia, who rediscovered New York as a nominating city in 1976 and who returned in 1980 as a way of reuniting Democrats North and South in the old historic alliance of Andrew Jackson and Martin Van Buren that created the party. Bill Clinton followed suit in 1992. These three National Conventions received worldwide television coverage at the time and now can be found in various television archives, such as at C-Span or the Museum of Broadcast Communications in Chicago. Therefore, they do not merit a book to recover what is not lost and is still recent, which is why this volume concentrates instead on New York's mostly forgotten Pre-TV Era Presidential Nominating Conventions.

Recounted in the following chapters are the early Presidential Conventions of the Liberty and Free Soil parties, held in Upstate New York, which took up the cause of slavery while it was still politically unpopular, and paved the way for eventual Emancipation. Here, too, is an account of the trickery of Tammany Hall in the summer of 1868. The longest and one of the most-bitter Conventions ever took place in 1924 in the old Madison Square Garden, and is recaptured in the final chapter of this volume. It took Democrats 103 ballots to settle on a candidate, and featured a grueling battle between the Governor of the Empire State and one of its former leading citizens. The story of these forgotten New York Presidential Conventions offers enduring lessons for modern readers and surprising insights for political historians.

From the early fights for Immediate Abolition to the Twentieth Century dispute over whether to condemn the Ku Klux Klan; from the struggle whether to promote internal improvements in the states with Federal funds to the impassioned debate whether to abandon the League of Nations, these Conventions served as the nation's center stage for momentous political battles and memorable rhetoric that defined political eras, and are fascinating still.

From New York's forgotten Pre-TV Conventions came heroic nominees such as James G. Birney, the Abolitionist former-slave owner who dedicated himself to Emancipation; Martin Van Buren, the former President who came out of retirement to fight against the party he founded and the spread of slavery; Nathanial Banks, Speaker of the House of Representatives, standing in for another man as the nominee of a secret, anti-immigrant Convention; New York Governor Horatio Seymour, who quelled the New York Draft Riots and presided over the 1868 nomination surprise inside the "Wigwam" of Tammany Hall; and John W. Davis, a Wall Street lawyer who had not only defended J.P. Morgan but labor activists Eugene V. Debs and Mother Jones, and outlasted New York's beloved Governor Al Smith to win the 1924 nomination. Here are some of the stories of New York's Pre-TV Presidential Conventions that made Liberty and Justice the central questions of their times.

The American Anti-Slavery Society Presidential Nominating Convention of 1839

Convention-at-a-Glance

Event: The American Anti-Slavery Society Presidential Nominating Convention
Date: November 13, 1839
Location: Warsaw, New York
New York Governor: William H. Seward, Whig
Number of Delegates: 200
Number Needed to Nominate: A majority
Candidates for Nomination: All anti-slavery leaders
Presidential Nominee: James Gillespie Birney, New York
Age of Nominee: 47
Number of Ballots: One
Vice Presidential Nominee: Dr. Francis Julius LeMoyne, Pennsylvania
Platform Positions: Immediate Emancipation of all slaves, without any compensation to slave owners; Equal Rights for all freed slaves and other black Americans.
Campaign Slogan: "Immediate Abolition"

The American Anti-Slavery Society Presidential Nominating Convention of 1839

"Slavery has corrupted the whole nation."—James G. Birney

New York State hosted its first Presidential Nominating Convention on November 13, 1839, in the small Wyoming County village of Warsaw. Located just north of the great Letchworth Falls of the Genesee River, the isolated outpost was a last stop on the Underground Railroad for escaped slaves seeking freedom across the Canadian border. The seemingly quiet community was also a hotbed of church activism and Abolitionism. Many of the 200 Warsaw delegates were dissident members of the American Anti-Slavery Society, come to western New York to create the first political party dedicated to abolishing slavery from the United States of America. Other organizers and delegates to the Convention were Christian church reformers engaged in what scholars have called "perfectionist politics." They wanted to purify their nation of its most deadly sin and make way for God's Government on Earth. Nurtured by a decade of "Big Tent" revivalism, many at the Warsaw Convention were dedicated to the "entire sanctification" of both individuals and social institutions.

Most of the delegates arrived by horse and carriage from central and western New York where anti-slavery sentiment and evangelicalism were particularly strong. Others journeyed from western Massachusetts, northern New England, and across New York's southern border from Pennsylvania to nominate the first anti-slavery ticket for President and Vice President of the United States of America. As rash as their own declaration of a third political party in support of "Immediate Abolition" seemed to their contemporaries, few of the anti-slavery men and women who ventured to Warsaw could have envisioned that they were about to cast the first decisive votes leading the United States into a bloody Civil War. Nor did these anti-slavery delegates doubt that they would eventually achieve their divine mission of Abolition, because they knew their cause was both "Right" and "Just."

Absent from the Warsaw assembly were anti-slavery men from what was then called the Northwest, even though opposition to slavery had gained a solid foothold in Ohio, particularly where New Englanders had settled. Quaker Abolitionists from the Western Reserve were as quiet as their religion and opposed political action such as this Convention. So were most Abolitionists from the Northeast. The Warsaw delegates were in advance of their own movement by nearly a decade.

Throughout the 1830s, a small contingent of Abolitionists had expressed their moral outrage and religious conviction by organizing churchmen to stand up against the abomination of slavery. They also denounced their own national church denominations for support of the hated institution. Through lecturing to an apathetic public about its immorality, by publishing thousands of anti-slavery pamphlets, by writing local newspapers urging readers on to personal repentance, and by repeated public agitation against human bondage, they had made only small progress. Moral conversion was necessary, most Abolitionists believed, before any political action could succeed. And that had not yet happened.

In recent elections, however, Abolitionists had taken to questioning candidates for public office, finding few willing to vote against the Slave Power in Congress. They also petitioned state legislatures and the Congress itself to take action against slavery. In 1835 alone, Northern Abolitionists flooded Washington with 414,471 anti-slavery petitions. All of them were promptly "tabled." Abolitionists had managed, however, to unleash new bitterness between North and South. In their mind, that was not regrettable.

In December 1835, President Jackson recommended a Federal censorship law to quiet dissent. He wrote Congress: "I must also invite your attention to the painful excitement produced in the South by attempts to circulate through the mails inflammatory appeals addressed to the passions of the slaves—it is nevertheless proper for Congress to take such measures as will prevent the Post-Office Department, which was designed to foster an amicable intercourse and correspondence between all the members of the Confederacy, from being used as an instrument of an opposite character. I would therefore call the special attention of Congress to the subject and respectfully suggest the propriety of passing such a law as will prohibit, under severe penalties, the circulation in the Southern states, through the mail, of incendiary publications intended to instigate the slaves to insurrection."

In 1836, Congress enacted the "gag rule" which prohibited members from discussing slavery at all, because the subject upset them so. The rule asserted: "That Congress possesses no constitutional authority to interfere in any way with the institution of slavery in any of the states of this Confederacy; That Congress ought not to interfere in any way with slavery in the District of Columbia. And whereas it is extremely important and desirable that the agitation of this subject should be finally arrested, for the purpose of restoring tranquility to the public mind...Resolved, That all petitions, memorials, resolutions, propositions, or papers, relating in any way, or to any extent, whatsoever, to the subject of slavery, or the abolition of slavery, shall, without being either further printed or referred, be laid upon the table, and that no further

8

action whatsoever shall be had thereon."

Both President Andrew Jackson, of Tennessee, and his Vice President, Martin Van Buren, of New York, supported choking off Congressional debate for the unity of party and country. Not until 1844, under former President's John Quincy Adams' guidance, was the provision repealed. The gag rule, in turn, fueled an even more radical response from Abolitionists and helped their numbers swell. But the nation's deep racial prejudices endured and pro-slavery forces stiffened. In 1836, the New York State legislature passed its own gag rule.

At the moment of the historic Warsaw gathering, anti-slavery advocates could rely upon but four members of the House of Representatives to carry on their fight. They were led in their resistance by an aging former President, John Quincy Adams, a Massachusetts Whig. Seth M. Gates, of New York, William Slade, of Vermont, and Joshua Giddings, of Ohio, all members of the opposition Whig party, stood by Adams' side.

Whigs themselves were deeply divided on the "slavery question," but ultimately committed to maintenance of slavery as necessary for preservation of the Union, which was sacred to them. Adams, who represented Massachusetts' Eighth District, reflected that there were "two divisions in the party; one based on public principle and the other upon manufacturing and commercial interests."

The American Anti-Slavery Society members who convened the Warsaw Convention claimed that both political parties, Democrats and Whigs, were in the grips of the Southern Slave Power and would remain so as long as slavery endured. Did not anti-slavery supporters have a moral obligation to take their struggle to a new strategic phase of political action, the Warsaw delegates asked?

Yes, slavery was as old as human history and the spoils of war. But that said nothing of morality. Slaves had been regulated by the Code of Hammurabi in Babylon, had built the pyramids of Egypt, were crucial to the economies of ancient Greece and Rome, and were even housed within the Vatican as late as the Fifteenth Century. Slavery was crucial to the colonization of the Americas by the Portuguese, Spanish, and English. From the beginning, African slaves were an important component in the formation of the United States. Introduced to North America by a Dutch slave trader in Jamestown, Virginia, in 1619, slavery spread into Dutch New York in the early 1620s and into Massachusetts in 1636. Not until the philosophical "Enlightenment" of the Eighteenth Century, did public sentiment in Europe and in North America begin to question the morality of the ancient institution.

Meanwhile, rigorous commercialization of the slave trade brought torment and misery to millions of kidnapped Africans. The English Crown even established its own slave trade operation, the Royal African

Company. A rich commercial triangle sent natural resources and manufactured goods from Boston and New York to West Africa where the goods were sold for slaves. These unfortunate human beings, many captured by their fellow Africans, were chained and transported across the Atlantic through the deadly "Middle Passage." In the "West Indies," they were sold for sugar and molasses, which in turn were sold in North America to make rum and other luxuries, and the cycle continued. Most of these dispossessed Africans were shipped to Central and South America where they were literally worked to death. Tens of thousands of others were moved onto the plantations of the American South to work the tobacco fields.

The emergence of cotton planting in the South intensified the cruel demand for slaves. By 1776, when Independence was declared, over 500,000 slaves lived in the Thirteen Colonies. Only 47,000 black Africans were scattered outside the South. Many American revolutionaries assumed slavery would vanish after Independence from their colonial masters. When Thomas Jefferson and John Adams placed a provision eliminating slavery into their first draft of the Declaration of Independence, Southerners in attendance at the Continental Congress angrily threatened to abandon the fight against the British. The offending phrase, one that would have freed millions of human beings and saved the nation more than 600,000 lives in the Civil War some eighty-five years later, was removed without further protest.

The spirit of freedom was further betrayed at the Constitutional Convention of 1787 that legalized slavery in the new nation and treated individual slaves as fractions when it came to voting, from which they were excluded, solidifying the political power of the White South. Article IV, section 11, provided for the return of escaped slaves from state to state. After enactment of the Constitution, many Northern states also passed their own "Black Laws," limiting the freedom of free African Americans.

By the time delegates met in Warsaw, slavery had eaten deeply into the social and moral fabric of the nation and the United States remained almost alone as a slave country among "civilized" western nations. Slavery was already illegal in neighboring Canada and Mexico. The inhumane institution was abolished in France in 1791 after "The Revolution." It was re-established in 1799 in the French colonies because of its profitability, before it would be abolished again in 1848 after another wave of revolution. The British abolished slavery in 1833, although slaves in its West Indian colonies were not freed until 1838. The United States Congress made the foreign slave trade illegal in 1808, when it became "unlawful to import or bring into the United States or the territories thereof from any foreign kingdom, place, or country, any Negro, mulatto, or person of colour, as a slave, or to be held to service or labour." Still, slavery thrived within the boundaries of the United States and one-sixth of the nation's population was enslaved at its founding.

Cotton was king in the American South and its economy was absolutely dependent upon slave labor. The ruthless institution became stronger with the invention of the Cotton Gin. But as panic and depression swept the land in 1837, some anti-slavery advocates persuasively argued that "Slave Labor" was an economic assault on "Free Labor." They pointed out that the national economy's development was hindered by the Slave Power in Congress that prevented internal improvements and blocked higher tariffs that could protect American industry. The Warsaw delegates argued that Abolitionists had no choice but to act in new ways to achieve Emancipation as soon as humanly possible to save slaves as human beings and to save the nation from economic and moral ruin. America must live up to its creed of freedom, they insisted.

The Warsaw Convention was "Called" by three crusading anti-slavery men who were visible throughout the next decade of Abolitionist struggle. Gerrit Smith, age 42, was a graduate of Hamilton College. He had founded an Abolitionist church in his home town of Peterboro, New York, in Madison County, and was also a philanthropist and wealthy landowner who spent much of the 1830s as an anti-slavery agitator. In 1848, he would donate 120,000 acres of his own land for free blacks to create their own community. In 1852, he would be elected to Congress where he carried on the Abolitionist fight. Later, he gave money to help John Brown and advocated violent overthrow of the Slave Power.

Smith's 1837 letter to Rev. James Smylie, of the State of Mississippi, expressed some of his early hostility toward the South. "When I read your quotation from the twenty-fourth chapter of Genesis, made for the purpose of showing that God allowed Abraham to have slaves, I could not but wonder at your imprudence—Abraham's servants held a relation to their master and to society, totally different from that held by Southern slaves. Here we find the most diabolical devices to keep millions of human beings in a state of heathenism, in the deepest ignorance, and most loathsome pollution—Slavery being an abuse, is incapable of reformation."

Smith put out a Convention Call to anti-slavery supporters to launch a third party that could wage battle at the polls. The 1839 national meeting of the American Anti-Slavery Society, held at Albany, commencing August 31, 1839, had been called "to discuss the principles of the anti-slavery enterprise, the mode of political action against slavery, including the question of a distinct party." Members heatedly debated the issue before the meeting broke up in a stalemate. Smith persisted in his argument that anti-slavery advocates had a moral duty to participate in the 1840 presidential election, to vote for anti-slavery candidates, and against pro-slavery defenders. This Warsaw Convention of dissenting American Anti-Slavery Society adherents initiated the process that eventually elevated slavery to the leading electoral issue by 1860.

Smith was joined in his Convention Call by Rochester, New York, newspaperman Myron Holley, an equally passionate anti-slavery organizer. He had been a backer of DeWitt Clinton and was a commissioner on the Erie Canal. Urbane and cultured, Holley was a gentleman and a good speaker. His radical paper, *Rochester Freeman*, was eloquent in its anti-slavery and pro-Abolitionist party appeals. He issued the Call for the Monroe County Convention for Nominations at Rochester, New York, on September 28, 1839, which adopted a series of resolutions that lay the groundwork for the Warsaw meeting and the Liberty Party. As an American Anti-Slavery Society member, Holley campaigned tirelessly for the cause.

By 1838, Alvan Stewart, a lawyer from Utica, who had been one of the New York Whigs' most able speakers, had called for a political Convention to coalesce anti-slavery sentiment. Stewart was a co-founder of the American Anti-Slavery Society and president of the New York Anti-Slavery Society. He was a strong voice for Abolition in upper New York and continued fighting for the cause throughout the next decades.

And at the annual meeting of the New York Anti-Slavery Society at Utica, September 19-21, 1838, William Goodell had written, Myron Holley introduced, and Gerrit Smith eloquently advocated, a series of twenty-two resolutions that "solemnly pledged those who adopted them to vote for no candidates who were not fully pledged to anti-slavery matters." According to Goodell, who was publisher of the *Emancipator*, the resolutions "recognized a moral principle in voting, which, it was afterwards found, could not be acted upon in the existing state of the country, without a new political party. Both parties, then and afterwards, were completely under the control of the slave-holding members." (*The Emancipator* was the official paper for the American Anti-Slavery Society.)

In February 1839, he had strongly urged the executive committee of the New York Anti-Slavery Society to organize an independent anti-slavery party. The committee declined to take action although a distinct minority, as William Goodell, a Liberty Party activist and later historian of the Anti-Slavery movement, said, "had long seen the necessity of strenuous effort to counteract the partisan tendencies of Abolitionists, by inculcating the highest principles of political morality."

However, the dominant Abolitionist leader of the day was notably absent from the Warsaw Convention. William Lloyd Garrison, publisher of *The Liberator*, was skeptical that any political solution could succeed. Political action to abolish slavery within the United States Constitution was futile, Garrison argued, because the Constitution itself was a "slave document" forged in 1787 by Southern slave interests, agreed to by greedy Northern merchants, and enforced by the power of the Federal Government ever since. He called it "the most bloody and heaven daring arrangement ever made by men for the continuance and protection of the most atrocious villainy ever exhibited on earth." America was conceived in the irreconcilable contradiction of freedom and slavery, he charged.

"No Union with Slave Owners," Garrison preached to all who would listen, because slavery was "a damning crime." He also insisted that no Government had moral authority over the Abolitionists. If he favored any political action at all, he supported disunion; breaking the United States into two nations; North and South, Free and Slave. In reference to Southern politicians, he declared, "We would sooner trust the honor of the country and the liberties of the people in the hands of the inmates of our penitentiaries and prisons, than their hands for safe keeping." He advocated taking congressional seats away from the South to force change.

Only moral and spiritual transformation could lead to Emancipation, Garrison proclaimed. Political action only meant compromise and corruption. Abolitionists must remain morally pure. "This political reformation is to be effected solely by a change in the moral vision of the people; not by attempting to prove that it is the duty of every Abolitionist to be a voter, but that it is the duty of every voter to be an Abolitionist," he explained. So believed most religious Abolitionists who opposed political action, which is why the Warsaw delegates were at first only a small faction of the anti-slavery movement. Most Abolitionists were devout Whigs, even though their party did not respond to anti-slavery appeals.

Although opposition to slavery had existed since the nation's conception and most American revolutionaries of 1776 expected slavery to wither away, opponents had gradually become a weak minority voice hushed against the huge influence of Southern cotton powers and slave interests. Garrison had re-breathed fire into the anti-slavery cause and had led the Abolitionist movement during the discouraging decade of the 1830s. He began by founding the New England Anti-Slavery Society in 1831. Two years later in Philadelphia, the nation's "cradle of freedom," Garrison led a coalition of New Englanders who joined with New York mercantilists Arthur and Lewis Tappan, a dedicated Pennsylvania Quaker group, and several free African-American agitators, including former slave Frederick Douglass, to establish the American Anti-Slavery Society.

The Society's "Declaration of Sentiments" proclaimed "every American citizen who detains a human being in involuntary bondage as his property is, according to Scripture (Ex. xxi 16), a man-stealer; That the slaves are instantly to be set free, and brought under the protection of law; That all those laws which are now in force, admitting the Right of slavery, are therefore, before God, utterly null and void; being an audacious usurpation of the Divine prerogative, a daring infringement on the Law of Nature, a base overthrow of the very foundations of the Social Compact, a complete extinction of all the relations, endearments, and obligations of Mankind, and the presumptuous transgression of all the holy commandments; and that therefore they ought instantly to be abrogated.''

Over the next seven years, most often in the face of vociferous, even violent opposition, members of the American Anti-Slavery Society went forth proselytizing against the evils of slavery to an expanding United States that was racist in its core beliefs. Hundreds of local Anti-Slavery Societies and churches soon sprang up in cities and towns across New York, the Northeast, and Northwest. More and more men and women of conscience converted to Abolition and agitated under the Society's banner. Although their numbers were growing rapidly, they were still a small minority.

Individual Abolitionists initially stood alone in their communities, denounced by former friends and foes as dangerous and fanatical radicals. When Abolitionists sent a million anti-slavery brochures to readers in the South, they incited violent reaction. At the request of Southern governors, they were denounced by Northern state legislatures. Their mail was subsequently seized and destroyed, as was pointed out, with Presidential approval. When the Illinois legislature joined in the denunciation of Abolitionism, only six state legislators, including lawyers Dan Stone and Abraham Lincoln, refused to endorse the bill. With each incident of suppression, came new adherents to their Gospel of Freedom.

Abolitionist orators came under constant attack throughout the decade of the 1830s. In July 1834, a racist mob plundered the New York City home of the American Anti-Slavery Society founder Lewis Tappan, before moving on to destroy houses, churches, and schools in the city's small free black neighborhoods. In 1835, Garrison himself was paraded through the streets of Boston with a rope around his neck as a civic warning to desist in his divisive acts.

That same day, delegates to a statewide anti-slavery meeting in Utica, New York, were forced to flee before a raving mob. Then, on November 7, 1837, Abolitionist Elijah P. Lovejoy was shot and killed while defending his anti-slavery press from a mob in Alton, Illinois, stirring wild emotions on both sides of the debate throughout the nation.

A year later, Pennsylvania Hall in Philadelphia, which served as meeting place for the Anti-Slavery Convention of American Women, was burned to the ground by a crazed white stampede. The women escaped unharmed, but the city's official inquiry blamed them for inciting the violence by their very presence.

Despite these dangers, the anti-slavery movement attracted new recruits by the day, and new chapters of the Society sprang up throughout New England, New York, Pennsylvania, Ohio, even way out in Indiana, Illinois, Iowa, and Wisconsin. Converts were convinced by the evangelical tone of the Abolitionist message and the Christian character of the movement's appeal to conscience. Confronted by the horror of the issue, tens of thousands of Northerners came to profess their hatred of slavery. But, they had limited success in influencing national policy or altering the many ways that the nation had grown grotesquely comfortable with slavery and the misery it wrought.

Few of their neighbors found slavery more important than the hot political issues of the day. Angry Democrats and Whigs argued with one another over whether or not to support a National Bank that consolidated financial power and created a common national economy, or whether to undertake internal improvements in the states at Federal expense, or to increase the tariff favored by Northern merchants and opposed by Southern cotton growers. Even with all their agitation, Abolitionists made little headway in achieving their objective of Immediate Emancipation.

While Garrison was skeptical about political action, many other Abolitionists outside of Massachusetts disapproved of his broader radicalism. In their eyes, Garrison had become a Christian anarchist. He questioned the very authority of the church and even argued with details of the *Bible*. He answered only to "a higher authority." What's more, Garrison was not just a pacifist, but he advocated Equal Rights for women and questioned the sanctity of marriage. On this later point of Women's Rights, many of the Warsaw Convention delegates agreed, for their meeting included women in both leadership and supporting roles. And its political successor, the Liberty Party, was the first U. S. political party to run women for public office. It was the first as well to put forward African-American candidates. The escaped slave, Fredrick Douglass, ran under the Liberty Party banner for New York Secretary of State.

Garrison was feared by conservative church and business interests who condemned him for his extremism. But on the question of politics, Garrison was too conservative for the Warsaw delegates who had come to the conclusion that it was time for Abolitionists to nominate anti-slavery candidates for President and other offices, not just to win power, but to raise the slavery issue to the national level and to bring about its end. They intended to set a moral example for other political parties. Smith, Holley, and Stewart argued that only by electing more anti-slavery men and women could Abolitionists ultimately wage an effective battle to change the slavery laws that strangled the nation. Only then could Abolitionists gain enough power to close the hated slave markets in the nation's capital city of Washington. Only then could they prohibit slavery's spread into the newly-settled territories of the Northwest, Southwest, and West. Only then could they challenge the Right of slavery to exist at all as a prerogative of the individual states under the "State Rights" provision of the Constitution.

So, on a crisp November 13, 1839, the political vanguard of the American Anti-Slavery Society and other freedom-loving delegates convened New York's first Presidential Nominating Convention inside the classical white, two-story Warsaw Presbyterian Church. (Warsaw church conservatives were so shocked by the use of their church by its reform members that they expelled the Abolitionists two months later. The reformers, in turn, built The Church of Warsaw, an independent Congregational Church, with an almost identical appearance, on land next to their former brethren.) Mass meetings were common in this old revival country of Western New York and The Church of Warsaw swayed that day with the moral outrage and hopeful forecasts for Abolition.

Beneath the lofty bell tower and stately steeple, delegates first voted whether to launch a third political party to compete with the powerful Whig and Democrats who dominated the nation's political life. It was a momentous decision. They finally agreed with Smith, Holley, and Stewart that a single-issue third party was essential to the eventual success of the anti-slavery cause. They did not expect instant victory, but over time they were confident their moral cause would triumph.

On their next important vote, the delegates enacted a short but powerful platform that called for the "immediate freedom" for all slaves, "without any compensation" whatsoever to slave owners. Their platform also demanded full political Rights for all freed slaves. These were positions that William Lloyd Garrison had advocated for years.

The Warsaw Convention was pleased with the ease of its own power. So next, the Convention agreed to nominate candidates for President and Vice President of the United States to stand for office in the 1840 election. On the First Ballot, this rump Convention of the American Anti-Slavery Society chose as its presidential candidate, James Gillespie Birney, of New York, formerly of Kentucky. Birney served as the tireless secretary of the American Anti-Slavery Society and was author of the: "Letter on the Political Obligation of Abolitionists."

James G. Birney was in New York City at the time of his nomination attending to official business of the American Anti-Slavery Society, but had been on the road for anti-slavery causes for most of the decade and had faced down mobs himself. Myron Holley later reasoned that the Convention had selected Birney because he was, "widely known and generally respected," and he was no politician. That may have been a plus for the delegates, but Birney did not bring the big political name that might have attracted masses of voters. He was, however, a brave and impassioned man. Dr. Julius LeMoyne, of Pennsylvania, was slotted for

Vice President.

Birney stood first among the architects of America's political effort to win Emancipation through the ballot box, and therefore the Warsaw delegates wanted him as their new party's standard bearer. "It is vain to think of succeeding in Emancipation without the cooperation of the great mass of the intelligent minds of the nation," Birney had written. This required political action.

The Warsaw delegates agreed with Birney, against Garrison, when he declared that the Constitution was essentially a "document of freedom." Therefore, Birney insisted, the Constitution would allow an anti-slavery Congress to pass national laws to grant freedom to slaves in the Southern states, if they could elect officials with the courage and moral strength to do it. And Birney believed that the Constitution could protect the Right of free expression by whites in the North, if Abolitionists could only gain electoral power. That Human Rights had a higher claim than State Rights was already established by the Constitution itself and Declaration of Independence, Birney reasoned. He was an able lawyer and advanced constitutional thinker and among the pioneers advocating political action as the only pragmatic way to build an even broader Abolitionist movement beyond the local Anti-Slavery Societies.

When notified of the Convention's action, Birney, who always had a good pragmatic feel for political currents, responded that he was flattered but feared that most Abolitionists were not ready to embrace political action. "While I agree with you entirely that the great anti-slavery enterprise can never succeed without independent nominations," Birney asserted, "I feel assured that the views of Abolitionists as a body do not enough harmonize to make such a measure advisable now."

Birney therefore declined the first Presidential Convention nomination ever offered in New York State. Dr. LeMoyne did the same, writing that he worried that the "bright standard of Emancipation" could be "blurred and smutted at the demand of time serving politicians." Thus, inauspiciously, began the anti-slavery political movement that would eventually culminate in the founding of the Republican Party in 1854, the election of Abraham Lincoln six years later, and finally Emancipation in 1863, the ultimate goal that the Warsaw delegates so diligently sought and fervently believed they could achieve.

The third party people were not deterred by Birney's rebuff. As autumn passed into winter with the approaching presidential election of 1840, Abolitionists intensified their debate over the wisdom of a third party strategy. Another Wyoming County Convention held at Arcade on January 28 through 29, 1840, endorsed the work of the Warsaw Convention. Among its delegates were New Yorkers Myron Holley, Gerrit Smith, Joshua Leavitt, as well as Warsaw pastor Huntington Lyman, and Charles O. Shepard, who became a statewide campaigner.

Reuben Sleeper, of Livingston County, presided. Elizur Wright, Jr., of Massachusetts, also attended.

But the new party activists were cognizant that most Abolitionists still seemed wedded to the two major parties, with the Whigs most favored by those who worked against slavery. This Convention issued a Call for a National Convention to be held in Albany in April to "discuss the question of an independent nomination of Abolitionist candidates for the two highest offices in our National Government, and, if thought expedient, to make such nominations, for the friends of freedom to support at the next election."

"Conscience Whigs," as they would soon be called, were an unwanted force in their own party that was built out of a patchwork of financial conservatives, businessmen large and small, and farmers from both North and South. Most anti-slavery Whigs still believed that a victory by their candidate, William Henry Harrison, of Ohio, over Democratic President Martin Van Buren, of New York, would advance the anti-slavery cause far more than a splinter third party. After all, the "magician from Kinderhook," as the wily Van Buren was sometimes known, had helped fashion the gag rule while presiding over the Senate, as a compromise desired by Jackson.

Whigs thought Van Buren, if re-elected, would continue Jackson's contempt for the law and his vocal defense of slavery. These Whigs taunted the third party sympathizers and believed that to draw votes away from Harrison with a single-issue third party would re-elect Van Buren and promote the hated "Slavocracy" of Southern Democrats to whom the President was politically indebted.

But Abolitionists such as James G. Birney knew that the Whig coalition was built on an implicit pact to protect slavery. The old parties could not be trusted to ever abolish slavery. The Warsaw organizers and delegates had no choice but to move forward with their moral and political crusade.

The First Liberty Party Presidential Nominating Convention and the Election of 1840

Convention-at-a-Glance

Event: First Liberty Party Presidential Nominating Convention
Date: April 1, 1840
Location: Albany, New York
New York Governor: William H. Seward, Whig
Number of Delegates: Seventy-seven from twelve states
Number Needed to Nominate: A majority
Convention President: Alvan Stewart
Candidates for Nomination: Gerrit Smith, New York; James Gillespie Birney, New York
Presidential Nominee: James Gillespie Birney
Age of Nominee: 48
Number of Ballots: One
Vice Presidential Nominee: Thomas Earle, Pennsylvania
Platform Positions: Support of the "Principles of the Declaration of Independence, at the ballot box and everywhere, by every lawful, constitutional, moral and religious influence;" and "Equal Rights" for emancipated slaves and other free blacks.
Campaign Slogan: "Immediate Abolition"

The First Liberty Party Presidential Nominating Convention and the Election of 1840

"Surely the ballot box can never be used for a more noble purpose than to restore and secure to any man his Inalienable Rights."
—Senator Thomas Morris, Ohio

In January 1840, Gerrit Smith, undeterred by James G. Birney's rejection of the Warsaw nomination, called for another "National Convention of Friends of Immediate Emancipation" to be convened that spring in Albany, New York. Smith also had an all- American name for the new group that would be independent of the American Anti-Slavery Society. He christened it the Liberty Party.

Myron Holley, editor of the *Rochester Freeman*, had been agitating for such a meeting for over a year and his paper had created the constituency that answered Smith's summons. William Goodell, who was in attendance at the Albany Convention of 1840 and who later wrote an epic history of the anti-slavery movement, *Slavery and Anti-Slavery: A History of the Great Struggle in Both Hemispheres*, concluded that Myron Holley "came to be recognized as the founder of the Liberty Party." Soon, other county anti-slavery Conventions joined in the Call for a "National Third-Party Anti-Slavery Convention." Societies throughout New England, New York, and Pennsylvania selected delegates to attend the Albany assembly.

The end of March was a bitter time for travel in Upstate New York and the delegates, who ventured by canal or steamer up the Hudson or by train or horseback to the capital of the Empire State met delays and hardship. They persevered, and on April 1, 1840, New York State hosted its second Presidential Nominating Convention. In all, seventy-seven anti-slavery delegates arrived in Albany. But once again both radical and conservative Abolitionists balked. No delegates were sent from the Northwestern states such as Ohio, where the Whigs were strong and their campaign for William Henry Harrison was gaining mirthful momentum. The Trumbull County (Ohio) Anti-Slavery Society, for example, issued a "Solemn Protest against the proposed Convention as uncalled for."

The small but devoted collection of preachers and reformers in Albany got right to business and with the first floor debate reaffirmed their main purpose. Alvan Stewart, the Convention President, called for vigorous debate and then a vote on whether to launch a new political party. By a narrow forty-four to thirty-three vote, the first Liberty Party

Convention decided in favor of waging a national political campaign against slavery starting with the 1840 presidential election. The time was right, a slim majority insisted, and all other methods had failed. It might take years to succeed, but it was their moral duty to participate in the democracy of the American people. It was, as well, a moral duty of all citizens to vote against any candidate who favored any form of slavery, and to vote for any man who would work locally or in Washington to abolish it.

The theological reformers also reasoned that if there were no such men running for office, they were morally obligated to offer such candidates. Liberty Party men and women had no illusion that they could win a first-time election against the powerful "Democracy," as the party of Jackson and his descendents was called, or against the wealthy opposition Whigs. But they knew they had to start a fire that could eventually incinerate the slaveholder's political home. The insidious Slavocracy was gaining power in Congress, not losing it, they warned. Once it controlled the apparatus of the Federal Government, it would make slavery national, not sectional, and all would be lost. The Liberty agitators believed that once Americans faced the facts about their own racism, they would become Abolitionists as well and follow the laws of God and pursue the "Right."

Who should lead this great enterprise of political Emancipation? Who would the Liberty Party nominate to stand for President of the United States in 1840? No Whig or Democrat of repute would attach his name to such a radical political venture as the Liberty Party. No distinguished business man would dare carry its banner. Slave owners in the South and merchants in the North both prospered under the commercial deal that kept slavery vital to national life.

Yet, the Albany Convention had little doubt who it wanted to lead its great moral crusade. He was a man who had calmly stood up to mobs when they swore they would tar and feather him. He had faced down those who wanted to murder him for publishing his anti-slavery paper. Nor was he simply a Northerner pointing his finger at a problem he did not understand. Unlike most Abolitionists, he came from the South itself. A comfortable aristocrat before he risked his life and fortune as an Abolitionist, he was a man who knew slavery because he had been a slave owner, before he had set them free. And he had been disinherited by his wealthy father for his beliefs and actions.

The first Liberty Party Convention then nominated for President the same man who had turned down the Warsaw Convention nomination, James Gillespie Birney, now of New York and secretary of the American Anti-Slavery Society. On the First Ballot, Birney took most of the votes over his esteemed friend and Convention organizer Gerrit Smith. Thomas Earle, a 43-year-old Quaker from Philadelphia, was nominated for Vice

President. Unlike LeMoyne, Earle was ready to carry forward the electoral fight for Immediate Emancipation.

The delegates from twelve states then hammered out their platform, urging voters to "unite as patriots, philanthropists, and Christians, to put down the slavery of all parties, and put up the principles of the Declaration of Independence, at the ballot box and everywhere, by every lawful, constitutional, moral and religious influence." The Liberty Party platform affirmed not only freedom for slaves, but Equal Rights as full citizens after their Emancipation, and for other free blacks. That was truly radical in a society marked by servitude. On this second account, they were even more out of step with popular opinion than on the issue of Emancipation.

"Resolved. That the Liberty Party" will demand the absolute and unqualified divorce of the general Government from slavery, and also the restoration of equality of Rights, among men, in every state where the party exists or may exist:

"Therefore, Resolved, That we hereby give it to be distinctly understood, by this nation and the world, that, as Abolitionists, considering that the strength of our cause lies in its righteousness—and our hope is for it in our conformity to the Laws of God, and our respect for the Rights of Man, we owe it to the Sovereign Ruler of the Universe, as a proof of our allegiance to Him, in all our civil relations and offices whether as private citizen or as public functionary sworn to support the Constitution...." The Liberty Party put a strenuous duty upon all who would be its members.

Birney was in New York City on April 3, 1840, when he was informed of the Convention's decision. Gerrit Smith and William Goodell, another founder of the American Anti-Slavery Society and for the next decade Liberty Party leader and campaigner, urged him to reconsider his decision not to stand for President. Birney finally agreed to let his name be used. The cause of anti-slavery had become his life and he was honored to carry the first Liberty Party banner into political battle. He had held elected office before, and for years had spoken in favor of Abolition before legislatures across the North and South. He was ready to lead the nation out of its moral swamp.

Thus, New Yorker James Gillespie Birney became the first anti-slavery presidential candidate in U.S. history, a direct predecessor of the more cautious and ultimately successful Republican candidate, Abraham Lincoln. Indeed, during the 1840 canvass, the Liberty Party was called variously, the Antislavery, the Abolition, the True Democrat, or the Republican Party, depending upon the region of the country where it ran, and Birney was the electoral pioneer for Emancipation.

Why was James G. Birney given the honor of the Liberty Party's first presidential nomination? Why was he selected to lead this hopeful third party movement? Although he was not a prominent Washington politician, his name had become well known to many across the United States and abroad for his anti-slavery efforts. As a former slave owner who had freed his slaves after recognizing the barbarity of the institution that enslaved millions, he spoke with an undisputed authority. He knew well how the hated practice entangled both slave and slave owner, and morally corrupted even those who idly accepted its racist domination of national life.

Birney's path to this pivotal moment in American history was rather extraordinary. Born into Kentucky's slave-owning aristocracy in 1792, the young gentleman was educated at Princeton, with a young slave at his side. In Nassau Street, he met men who would become influential in the nation's affairs, among them the future Senator and Vice President, George Mifflin Dallas, of Philadelphia, who later served with James Polk. After graduation, Birney became a planter, sat as a member of the Kentucky state legislature, and as a trustee of Centre College in Kentucky. A few years later, after forging through the Alabama wilderness, Birney was elected mayor of Huntsville and then to the Alabama legislature. A successful lawyer, with a loyal family and growing wealth, he faced a bright future of power and prestige.

Then a religious conversion at a Presbyterian revival meeting convinced him to devote his life in service of his fellow man, no matter the personal cost. It was a conversion that redirected his life to intersect with history. He took on President Andrew Jackson and two southern state legislatures in his defense of Indian Rights. He became a lawyer for the Cherokee nation whose land had been usurped by the State of Georgia. He lost its case in a lower court, before taking "Worchester v. Georgia" all the way to the U.S. Supreme Court, winning in 1832.

President Jackson, who had pledged to drive all remaining Indians across the Mississippi, defied the High Court. Of the Chief Justice, Jackson said: "John Marshall has rendered his decision, now let him enforce it." Afterwards, individual Cherokee were violently removed from their land, and in 1838, remnants of the great tribe were driven from its ancestral home by 7,000 soldiers under General Winfield Scott's command. (In 1852, Scott would become the Whig's last viable candidate for President.) Hundreds of Cherokee died on their forced "Trail of Tears" march to hostile lands beyond the Mississippi.

Birney next re-examined his beliefs as a slave-owner. Although he had always been mildly anti-slavery in his sentiments before his religious conversion and like other Kentuckians expected the institution to gradually die out, he soon undertook dynamic personal action in opposition to slavery. He argued on the floor of the Alabama legislature in favor of Christian charity toward Negro slaves. He promoted gradual Emancipation, literacy laws, and vocational training to prepare slaves for their freedom. But after Nat Turner's 1831 slave insurrection in Virginia, the Deep South became more repressive toward slaves and their white sympathizers. Alabama passed laws forbidding blacks from learning to read or assembling in all but small groups while working. Discussion of anti-slavery proposals among whites was no longer permitted. New state militias were mobilized and armed.

Birney began to hear threats of violence from whites who opposed any scheme to reduce absolute power over their "property." In 1832, Birney had accepted a position with the American Colonization Society which was working to return free blacks and former slaves to Liberia, West Africa. He traveled across the South speaking to state legislatures and churches advocating "colonization" as a way of doing Justice to those who had been stolen from the African continent, and of preserving peace and preventing insurrection in the South. His articles were published in sympathetic newspapers across the South and caused him notoriety. His one-time political hero and future presidential opponent, Henry Clay, was titular head of the American Colonization Society. Privately, Birney saw colonization as a first step in "the extermination of slavery."

His neighbors saw him as a danger and hostility toward Birney escalated. In 1833, for the safety of his family, he took them back to Kentucky, hoping to make impact on the slave situation in the Border States. By the time he reached his old home, Birney realized that "colonization" was no solution at all, but simply a way for slave owners to divert attention away from the real moral and religious evil. In 1834, he resigned from the Colonization Society, arguing that the society had been ineffective. From 1820 to 1830, the society had spent nearly $100,000 to send just 1,200 persons back to Africa. He became convinced that slavery was a sin and destroyed not only blacks, but whites who exploited their labor and stole their lives. He was no longer content to accept its evil influence.

That same year, Birney freed his own Kentucky slaves and urged all he knew to do the same. He then hired them back for wages and paid for their education. He explained his position in letters that reached the newspapers in Kentucky and Ohio. He was branded an Abolitionist by his opponents and defiantly accepted the label. He now favored Immediate Abolition. As a former slave-owner, his words gave power to the Abolitionist cause and he soon became known as the leading Southern Abolitionist.

Birney continued to agitate for change among his neighbors and the churches of Kentucky. But afraid of alienating their congregations, few ministers embraced his ideas. Even members of his family cooled toward him. Yet, he found allies as he lectured and wrote letters to newspapers advancing the anti-slavery debate on moral and legal grounds. After he co-founded the Kentucky chapter of the newly-founded American Anti-Slavery Society, he received more threats and more papers rejected his articles.

In 1835, Birney traveled to New York City for the first time to attend the Second Annual American Anti-Slavery Society meeting. There, he introduced a resolution declaring that for "the permanent safety of the Union, it is indispensable that the whole moral power of the Free States should be concentrated and brought into action for the extermination of slavery among us." The rhetorical resolution passed unanimously.

Birney rode home to Kentucky by stage and on horseback, lecturing on Abolition in small towns and churches along the way with a calm and legal precision that converted his listeners to the cause of Emancipation. Back in Kentucky, he wrote more articles on the moral, legal, and constitutional contradictions of slavery. His *Letter to the Church . . . on . . . the Duty of Immediate Emancipation* argued that slavery was maintained by violence in violation of the spirit of the Gospel; stole the fruits of labor from one group who had done no wrong and gave them to others who had not earned those benefits; stupefied the minds and consciences of its victims and its benefactors; and bred indolence among slave-owners and contempt for their fellow beings. Voluntary peaceful action must be taken to end slavery, he exhorted time and time again to a growing body of disciples. If the nation heeded not, Birney darkly prophesized: "The thing must come to a head, and when it does, it will burst over the land with tremendous and desolating violence."

The opposition Birney faced was overwhelming. He was denounced by most Kentucky papers, even those running his columns, and by churches in the Deep South as a "race traitor." His friends tried to protect him by explaining that Birney had lost his senses, but they wondered why he had forsaken his bright future. His wealth was in danger as well. He was accused of trying to incite insurrection among the slaves. The last straw came when he launched his own anti-slavery paper to overcome the censorship he faced with his articles. Threats against his life and his family increased again. Because he was tipped off several times, he avoided tar and feathering. Finally, his friends and family implored him to leave. Birney sadly concluded that he could no longer accomplish anything for Abolition while remaining in his beloved home State of Kentucky.

In 1835, Birney moved across the Ohio River to Cincinnati, "Queen City of the West," to launch his paper, *Philanthropist*. Through this organ, his anti-slavery sermons eventually reached millions of people throughout the North. Ohio mobs immediately plotted to tar and feather him. Local papers assailed the new publisher and even the Mayor and

Sheriff of Cincinnati urged him to leave town, blaming him for the turmoil. One evening, Birney and his eldest son William walked unnoticed into a large mass meeting that was planning to smash his press and loot his home. Seated before him on stage were both the rabble of the town along with a Judge and other leading Cincinnati citizens.

When Birney dramatically disclosed his identity to them, someone shouted, "Kill him." But he was granted a hearing. His calm and reasonable speech in favor of Liberty lasted nearly an hour and temporarily tamed the lions. He even converted some in the audience to greater tolerance and was allowed to leave unharmed. But when he put out the first edition of his paper, the threats of violence turned into action and the press Birney used was destroyed by a mob and his newly printed papers burned. He escaped harm only because he was out of town delivering an Abolitionist lecture. One of his sons stood on the front porch of his home with a shotgun and held off the angry group which then looted the homes of free blacks instead; one reason that some blacks weren't all that enthusiastic about Abolitionists.

Like so many slave families in the South, Birney's own family lived in fear of attack by night. But the publisher refused to abdicate. He expanded his fight for Abolition to include defense of his constitutional Right to Free Speech and Press. He published again, denouncing the mobs that plagued him and other dissenters. "Must we trample on the Liberty of the white men here because they have trampled on the Liberty of black men in the South?" he inquired. "Must we forge chains for the mind here, because they have forged them for the body there? Must we extinguish the Right to speak, the Right to print in the North, that we may be in unison with the South? No, never."

Again the mobs struck, destroying his new printing equipment. Meanwhile, Birney's fight for the *Philanthropist*'s survival was avidly followed by the readers of other Northern papers. Finally, Cincinnati citizens rallied to his defense and eventually the violence ebbed. Birney intensified his crusade, riding on horseback, week after week, from community to community, making his plea. Very often, he was pelted by eggs and stones. Unfazed, he persisted, becoming among the best known and most respected anti-slavery voices in the land. The *Philanthropist* survived to become one of the most-read Abolitionist papers. "We fight, not with the courage of despair," Birney wrote, "but with the calmness of certain victory; with the strength of those who feel that their power is from the Almighty; with the weapon of Truth prepared by him who is the friend of Truth, for the destruction, the final and utter destruction of its adversary, error."

His troubles were not over. In 1837, Birney was arrested in Cincinnati for harboring a fugitive slave under the provisions of the Ohio Fugitive Slave Law that reinforced a similar Federal statute. A mulatto woman whom he had hired as a maid when she escaped across the Ohio River was forcibly removed from his home. To defend her, Birney hired young Salmon Portland Chase, who twenty-three years later would become Lincoln's Secretary of the Treasury, then Chief Justice of the Supreme Court. Working all night together they fashioned defense arguments based upon provisions of the 1787 Ordinance of Northwest Territories which forbid slavery. Their appeal was fruitless and an Ohio court declared the girl a fugitive slave, returning her to slave hunters who immediately took her South to be resold. Birney was fined $50, which he refused to pay.

Abolition slowly took hold in Ohio. Anti-slavery crusaders such as Joshua Giddings, a lawyer from the Western Reserve, was elected to the House of Representatives, where he served from 1838 to 1861. Thomas Morris was sent to the U.S. Senate, where he served from 1833 to 1839. Morris declared: "Moral power is sufficient for this work, but that moral power must operate by means that can make it effectual. Political action is necessary, and that action can only be effectually exercised through the ballot box. And surely the ballot box can never be used for a more noble purpose than to restore and secure to any man his Inalienable Rights."

In the summer of 1837, the national office of the American Anti-Slavery Society asked Birney to move to New York City to take charge of the organization that was being split by internal debates between the followers of Garrison and the more traditional church voices. Birney accepted the offer and moved his family to Brooklyn. He immediately began lecturing across the Northeast on behalf of the Society, telling all who listened that its purpose was "re-animation of the Republican principles of our Constitution." He called on Congress to end the slave trade that still thrived despite its illegality and to free the slaves of Washington D.C. Should the South leave the Union, he warned, it would bring ruin upon itself. His mostly widely read work, *The American Churches, the Bulwarks of American Slavery*, was published in 1840.

Unfortunately, years of sacrifice had taken a heavy toll on his wife, Agatha, who died in New York soon after her arrival, at age 39. She succumbed to the stress of Birney's commitments, plus birth of eleven children, five of whom died before her. At age 48, Birney whose income was limited and whose remaining wealth had been spent on the cause, sent his children off to separate schools and continued his crusade in loneliness. His own health was far from robust.

In 1840, these personal hardships did not prevent James G. Birney from finally accepting the presidential nomination of the new Liberty Party. It was his greatest honor. He became the first presidential candidate in the history of the United States to advocate the total Abolition of slavery. Unless the United States and individual men

27

associated with slavery soon repented, Birney predicted, damnation and a terrible war would surely follow.

He, however, did not plan on campaigning. In 1840, it was still deemed below the dignity of presidential candidates to stoop to the level of personal appeal for votes, although near the end of the fall canvass the Whig nominee, William Henry Harrison took to the stump, becoming the first presidential candidate ever to campaign for himself. Rather, Birney campaigned with his pen. In letters to supporters and Abolitionist papers, he argued that neither Harrison nor the Democratic President Martin Van Buren would do anything to eliminate slavery. Moreover, the ascendancy of Southern power in Congress threatened to extend slavery across the entire nation unless it was checked. He cited the gag law and the fact that the U.S. mail refused to carry anti-slavery newspapers as evidence of its insidious effect. Birney also blamed the panic of 1837 and the resulting economic hard times on the slave system that promoted "expense, waste, credit, and procrastination."

Then, Birney withdrew from the active campaign altogether and departed for England to participate in the World Anti-Slavery Convention and to carry the Abolitionist cause to an even larger international stage. He stayed abroad from May until November, returning only after the 1840 election was over. With little hope of actually winning the contest, the Liberty Party didn't bother to establish a national campaign organization or strategy. Instead, it left that work to scores of local Abolitionist societies and churches in the various states and to the individual conscience of voters.

The Liberty Party drew supporters from the rural working class, farmers, mechanics, their wives and daughters, who stood as moral exemplars to their communities. Many Liberty leaders were reform pastors of Abolitionist churches, practicing the doctrine of "entire sacrifice" in an effort to sanctify the political process. Among the Liberty campaigners of 1840 were James C. Jackson, Luther Lee, Reverend Thurston, and Luther Myrick, a reformer who challenged all human hierarchies. They sought to reform church and state. As the first "Gideon's Army" in U.S. political history, they campaigned not just for Birney, but for "God's moral Government on Earth." The Liberty Party provided Christian voters with an electoral alternative to supporting the sin of slavery, and a way to purge themselves of complicity in its evil. But with the enduring effects of economic depression, few could contribute money to the Liberty campaign.

Four years earlier during the 1836 election, the new Whig Party had put up anti-Jackson candidates on a regional basis because they could not agree on a single national leader. Their strategy was to deny a majority of Electoral votes to New Yorker Martin Van Buren, Jackson's Vice President, and thereby force a run-off in the House of

Representatives. The Whigs (who took their name from the Conservative party in England) planned to coalesce around an alternative candidate, as had happened during the 1824 election that selected John Quincy Adams over Jackson. But in 1836, they failed to force a run-off and Van Buren was elected.

Changing strategy, the Whigs held their first National Presidential Convention in a Lutheran Church at Harrisburg, Pennsylvania, in December, 1839, much more hopeful of victory. Their party touted patriotism and the sanctity of the American Union, a national bank, higher tariffs, and internal improvements in the states paid for by Federal funds. Henry Clay, William Henry Harrison, and General Winfield Scott were the leading candidates contending for the nomination, with Clay the most popular among the delegates. But Clay, who had been in the national spotlight for over two decades, had many enemies. Additionally, members of the Anti-Masonic Party that had been strong in New York and Pennsylvania in the early 1830s, had now joined the Whigs, and Clay was a Mason.

At first, the Whigs seemed as divided as they had been four years earlier. To make progress, the Convention appointed a nominating committee made up of three delegates from each state, which was required to vote as a unit. Professional politicians, such as Thurlow Weed, editor of the Albany, New York, *Evening Journal*, were able to manipulate this group. The committee recommended Harrison, despite Clay's superior skills and popularity on the Convention floor. On the assembly's Fourth Day, the entire Harrisburg Convention ratified William Henry Harrison, of Ohio, who had shown best among the 1836 Whig regional candidates, as its nominee. The final vote read 148 for Harrison, 90 for Clay, and 16 for Scott. Clay responded with the famous quote that would serve as his political epitaph: "I would rather be right than President."

Harrison, whose father had signed the Declaration of Independence, was born to Virginian aristocracy. But he had spent most of his adult life enduring the hardships of the frontier. He served in the Indian campaign of the Northwest Territory from 1791 to 1798, and that year was appointed Secretary of the Territory. In 1800, he became Governor of the Territory of Indiana, holding that post until 1812. In 1811, he defeated the combined Indian forces led by the great Shawnee chief Tecumseh, whose medicine man brother "The Prophet" was killed at the Battle of Tippecanoe. A year later, Harrison commanded an expedition at the Battle of the Thames in which Tecumseh was killed. During the War of 1812, Harrison directed the army of the Northwest, rising to the rank of Major General in 1813. From 1816 to 1819, he served Ohio in the U.S. House of Representatives. From 1825 to 1828, he represented Ohio in the U.S. Senate before serving a year as U.S.

Minister to Colombia. He was a clerk for a local Ohio court when he was nominated for President.

Harrison was chosen as the Whig nominee for 1840, in part, because he was "available." That meant he had been out of national office long enough that most people did not know his views on the current topics, and he had few political enemies. While he was far less talented than Clay, Harrison was religious, kind, humorous, and incorruptible. His military background allowed his supporters to depict him as a great general on a white horse, just like George Washington. In the 1840 campaign, Harrison was cast as the folk hero, "Old Tippecanoe," to appeal to the "Common Man," whose vote had formerly gone to Jackson. To protect Harrison from attacks, the Whig Convention adjourned without passing a platform. Harrison was its platform.

The other party in that election, the Democracy, as the Democratic Party was then called, held its quadrennial Convention in Baltimore, where it had met since 1832, first gathering in a Baltimore saloon. (The first U.S. Presidential Nominating Convention was held by the Anti-Masonic Party at Harrisburg, Pennsylvania, in 1831. The Democracy quickly took up the Convention idea.) Baltimore was favored as its Convention city, in part, because it was not far from Washington.

The 1840 Baltimore Democratic Convention lasted two days, May 5 through 6. William Carroll, of Tennessee, served as Permanent Chairman and Van Buren was unanimously re-nominated. Despite the economic depression, Van Buren had remained loyal to Jackson's policy of opposition to a National Bank and had kept the Democrat Party unified. During Jackson's reign, paper money pushed out gold, land speculation was rampant, prices and wages soared. It all crashed in the Panic of 1837 upon Van Buren. The President, an optimist who was quick to humor, was seen as a kind of political magician for his ability to pass legislation. But he could not undo the depression that cast its deathly shadow over the nation. Yet since he held a firm hand over party apparatus, his re-nomination was certain. (Van Buren popularized the cryptic saying "O.K." when he approved something in writing. "O. K." may have stood for "Old Kinderhook," the name of his New York home town.)

Strangely, the Democratic Convention nominated no vice presidential candidate to serve with Van Buren. Richard Mentor Johnson, of Kentucky, Van Buren's sitting Vice President, stirred so much opposition that he was not re-nominated. He had been hand picked by Andrew Jackson in 1836 as a reward for his loyalty. But he was hated in much of the South because his common-law wife was a slave and because he raised his mulatto children not as slaves but as free Kentuckians whom he educated. Before he was seriously wounded at the

Battle of the Thames, Johnson had killed the Indian chief Tecumseh. Johnson also had led the legislative fight to end the practice of prison for debtors. The Baltimore Convention thought that if Van Buren were reelected, the U.S. Senate would appoint a new Vice President.

To overshadow the Democracy at the start of the campaign, Whig strategists called a corresponding Convention for its young members and packed the streets of Baltimore with over 100,000 youthful demonstrators for Harrison. The Democracy was caught off guard by use of its own brash campaign tactics. Damage was done. From the beginning, Van Buren fought an uphill battle during economic depression to hold on to office. He was ridiculed by Whig orators and called effete, aristocratic, remote, and unworthy of the "Man of the People" laurel Jackson had worn before him. During the campaign, Pennsylvania Congressman Charles Ogle rhetorically charged, "This Democratic President's house is furnished in a style of magnificence and regal splendor that might well satisfy a monarch." Van Buren was mocked for his immaculate style.

In turn, the Baltimore *American*, a Democratic paper, ridiculed Harrison. "Give him a barrel of hard cider and settle a pension of $2,000 a year on him, and my word on it, he will sit the remainder of his days in a log cabin by the side of a sea of coal fire and study moral philosophy." That barb was turned into the Whig battle cry by Thurlow Weed, who had helped to secure Harrison's nomination. Weed who emerged as a major Whig publicist during the fall campaign, not only used his own paper to counterattack, but he founded *The Log Cabin*, a party sheet dedicated to Harrison's victory. Weed named young Horace Greeley, already publisher of the struggling *New Yorker*, as *The Log Cabin* editor. They printed 100,000 copies of each issue.

After marrying, Harrison had lived in a five-room log cabin at North Bend, Ohio, but by 1840 it had expanded into a twenty-two room mansion. Weed and Greeley refashioned the image of the retired aristocrat into a man of the people and fueled Harrison's famous "Log Cabin and Hard Cider" campaign. At many Whig rallies, a log cabin was erected in a single day as a symbol of the party's strength and loyalty, and barrels of hard cider quenched the thirst of those who marched in old Tip's parade.

The 1840 election was the first in which almost all white men were finally eligible to vote, whether or not they owned property. The Whigs, who were more formidable campaigners, took advantage of the new mass politics. Scores of communities hosted Whig Conventions of their own to endorse the nomination. Crowds at Whig rallies were calculated by the acre, with supporters covering a *reported* 100,000 acres in the largest gathering at Dayton, Ohio. "Now join the throng and swell the song; Extend the circle wider," they sang. Picnics, parades, badges, songs, poems, chants, newspaper, cartoons, and pamphlets wildly celebrated "Tippecanoe and Tyler too;" the Tyler referring to John Tyler, of Virginia. (He had once defeated Harrison's father in a Virginia state election.) Harrison was singing their tune as well. "All the measures of Government are directed," he declared late in the canvass as he became the first nominee to campaign for himself, "to the purpose of making the rich richer and the poor poorer."

"Cold water may do for the Locos," Whigs playfully sang of Democrats, "or a little vinegar stew; But give me hard cider and whiskey, And Hurrah for Old Tippecanoe!" Whigs even rolled a giant ten-foot-high ball, made of rope, thread, paper, leather, and all sorts of items, down the road from community to community from Kentucky to Baltimore to "keep the ball rolling" for the party. Preservation of the Union was the religion of Whigs North and South. Slavery was barely mentioned. Of Van Buren, Whigs chanted, "Farewell old Van, you're a used up man."

Democrats were demoralized and divided. At the 1840 Ohio Democratic state Convention to endorse President Van Buren's nomination, former Senator Thomas Morris stood in defense of the anti-slavery movement when it was bitterly denounced in Convention debate. Democratic orators had called the Liberty Party nothing "but ancient Federalism under new guise," and accused it of being "but a branch of the Federal Whig Party." They charged that "the political action of anti-slavery societies is only a device for the overthrow of Democracy." They also claimed that Harrison was the "Northern Abolitionist candidate." Morris, in turn, was roundly condemned by his fellow Democrats as a "rotten branch that ought to be lopped off." Ohio Democrats agreed with the national party that slavery should not be abolished in the District of Columbia without consent of the voters of Virginia. That fall, Morris denounced Van Buren and declared for the Liberty Party.

As Birney had predicted, most Abolitionists were not ready to engage in political action for a third party. They preferred to carry out their fight on religious and moral grounds or to vote Whig. But as Gerrit Smith had said, both parties were pro-slavery, because "the South will enter into none but the pro-slavery parties." The supporters of Garrison who believed no human Government had authority over them, also refused to participate in the Liberty Party canvass. Other Abolitionists simply hoped that Harrison would not disappoint them, despite his record of trying to push slavery into the Northwest Territories. They refused to "throw away" their vote for Birney. Harrison, they said, would restore the National Bank that had been closed by Jackson, and back high tariffs to help American industry and business expand. Harrison supported Henry Clay's American System, designed to protect American industry in the North with high tariffs, create a reliable market for Southern cotton, while funding internal improvements for the West.

After a decade of vibrant growth as a national organization, Abolitionists were suddenly in disarray. The Ohio Anti-Slavery Society, meeting in May, broke down the middle over whether its members should support the Liberty ticket over anti-slavery Whigs or Democrats. The same divisions appeared in Michigan, Indiana, and Illinois in the West. Still the Liberty Party managed to put together a slate of Electors in those states. That same month, the annual meeting of the American Anti-Slavery Society was torn asunder in New York City. Garrison brought scores of supporters from Boston and grabbed control of the Convention, even electing a woman to the national board. His bloc denounced political participation. The third-party men, including Birney, defeated in vote after vote on the Convention floor, bolted and formed The American and Foreign Anti-Slavery Society. The split was fatal to the electoral strength of the new Liberty Party and to the future of the American Anti-Slavery Society.

As the fall campaign gathered steam, some Liberty supporters drifted back to the Whigs because of their opposition to Annexation of Texas, their support of the tariff, or state issues that drew their allegiance. Others with Abolitionist sympathies stuck with the Whigs because they figured the third party would be eventually absorbed anyway. Some simply saw slavery as too narrow a political plank and stuck with the all-purpose Whig party or the Democracy. At the same time, Whig papers, afraid of the drain on their party, stepped up their attacks on the Liberty Party as a front for Van Buren. They accused Birney of "mad folly." And, they unleashed the most boisterous populist campaign yet seen in American politics.

Come November, Harrison won the popular contest, gaining 1,275,390 votes in nineteen states to Van Buren's 1,128,854 votes from seven states. Two-thirds of the South went for the Whigs, and so did every Northern state except New Hampshire and Illinois. Even Andrew Jackson, who came out of retirement to campaign for Van Buren, couldn't save Tennessee for the President. The Electoral College total was a rout. Harrison collected 234 votes to just 60 for the incumbent President.

In the end, Birney and the Liberty Party attracted only 6,797 votes nationally from the estimated 70,000 eligible voters who belonged to the various Anti-Slavery Societies. In Ohio, Birney took only 903 out of 274,000 votes. New Yorkers cast 2,809 Liberty Party votes. Van Buren lost his home State of New York. Gerrit Smith also lost his Liberty Party bid to become New York Governor. The Liberty Party managed to nominate Electors in most states, but failed to let voters know who those Electors were, or to distribute properly prepared ballots to their potential voters on Election Day. In its first electoral venture, the Liberty Party of 1840 was reduced to a protest party plagued by amateur mistakes. Despite the poor showing, Liberty Party leaders still believed they would win a majority by 1848.

William Goodell concluded that most Abolitionist voters "too readily persuaded themselves that the candidate of their own party, though but slightly or ambiguously pledged (to act against slavery), or even if not pledged at all, would probably do more for the slave, if elected, than the candidate of the other party, whatever his anti-slavery reputation or his pledges might be . . . This delusion and its effects began, at length, to afford candidates an excuse for not answering the questions of Abolitionists."

Goodell added, "It was hoped that by the organization of a distinct political party, this delusion might be dispelled, and Abolitionists would honor their principles at the polls. Though a minority, they could exhibit correct example, and thus preserve their integrity, and thus increase their moral power." Thereby, the Liberty Party of 1840 stood as a faint light of hope for the slowly growing anti-slavery sentiment that would burst forth in fire to illuminate the American political landscape in the decades to come.

Harrison, the new Whig President upon whom the anti-slavery Whigs cast their hopes, caught pneumonia at his inauguration in March 1841, and died at age 68 after only a month. His last words: "May the principles of Government be carried out." He was the first U.S. President to die in office. The pro-slavery former Virginia Senator John Tyler, who had wept after Clay's defeat at the Harrisburg Convention, became the new President.

Tyler was a Jeffersonian Democrat in all but name and had been selected to appeal to State Rights defectors from the Democrats. He backed a pro-slavery agenda. Anti-slavery Whigs were devastated. The party soon split wide open after President Tyler vetoed a Whig bill to re-establish the National Bank in September 1841. With the exception of his Secretary of State, Daniel Webster, Tyler's entire Whig Cabinet resigned in protest. The enthusiasm of millions of new voters dissipated in bitter disappointment.

The Second Liberty Party Presidential Nominating Convention and the Election of 1844

Convention-at-a-Glance

Event: Second Liberty Party Presidential Nominating Convention
Date: August 30, 1843
Location: Buffalo, New York
New York Governor: William C. Bouck, Democrat
Convention Chairman: Leicester King, Ohio
Number of Delegates: 1,000 from twelve states
Largest Crowd: 5,000
Number Needed to Nominate: A majority
Candidates for Nomination: Judge William Jay, New York; James Gillespie Birney, Michigan
Presidential Nominee: James Gillespie Birney
Age of Nominee: 52
Number of Ballots: One, unanimous
Vice Presidential Nominee: Former Senator Thomas Morris, Ohio
Platform Positions: Return to the Revolutionary Principles of the Declaration of Independence; Equal Rights for emancipated slaves and other free blacks.
Campaign Slogan: "Immediate Abolition"

The Second Liberty Party Presidential Nominating Convention and the Election of 1844

"We are coming, we are coming! Freedom's battle is begun!"—Liberty Party song

In the chaotic wake of the 1840 election and the death of President Harrison, the Liberty Party gained new support from bitter Whigs who felt betrayed by the elevation of John Tyler to the presidency and his pro-slavery actions. In 1844, one issue loomed above all others; the Annexation of Texas. Almost immediately after Harrison's death, the young Liberty Party mobilized against Tyler's threat to bring about the broadest expansion of slavery in the nation's history.

One Liberty convert was Salmon Portland Chase, the future Chief Justice of the Supreme Court. Chase later wrote: "I supported Harrison because I imagined that his administration would be less pro-slavery than Mr. Van Buren's. As soon as I discovered my mistake, I was ready to concur in an independent movement and was one of the first who took an active part in organizing the Liberty Party in Ohio."

By 1843, the Annexation of Texas, a territory that had broken free from Mexico to become an independent Republic in 1836, was the most pressing issue facing the United States. Traded away to Spain in 1821 in exchange for part of Florida, Texas had its original boundaries set at the Sabine River. Under Sam Houston's leadership, Anglo colonization transformed the territory before it won its Independence. But Mexico, at British urging, took a new interest in the area as a buffer against the expanding colossus to the North. From a military point of view, Mexico had reason to keep Texas independent. Critics of Tyler warned that Annexation was likely to lead the United States into war with its southern neighbor and enhance the Slave Power in Congress.

The Texas issue had been so hot that neither Presidents Jackson nor Van Buren sought to solve it. But President Tyler put the issue in the hands of his Secretary of State John Caldwell Calhoun, of South Carolina, who began negotiations. Conscience Whigs opposed Annexation and war as unworthy tools of national expansion for a moral nation. The situation seemed so dire to former President John Quincy Adams that he wrote in his diary on April 22, 1844: "The treaty for the Annexation of Texas to the Union was this day sent to the Senate; and with it went the freedom of the Human Race."

Expansionism was running quick in the young Republic's blood.

36

Western men wanted "more land for his beautiful pastures," observed one New Jersey legislator. And "Cotton Whigs," who supported slavery, were enthusiastic about Texas, especially since expansion seemed to fulfill the nation's "westward destiny." Even so, many Northern Democrats were apprehensive or opposed to Annexation, as were Conscience Whigs. The fault lines in the old parties were beginning to show strains around fundamental differences and would break asunder into pro-slavery/anti-slavery parties within a decade. However, Tyler's Texas Treaty failed in the U.S. Senate, where it withered under the blistering assault of Whigs Henry Clay and Daniel Webster who upheld the faith of anti-slavery advocates.

Could the Whig coalition hold onto the national power base it built in 1840 after such a disastrous first term? Could the old Democracy reclaim the throne? Could the nation cleanse its slavery-stained soul? The political stakes had never been higher in a presidential election. The hoopla and exuberance of the 1840 campaign were gone. Bitter passions over Annexation grew hotter as the presidential campaign unfolded. Under the stress of this debate, the Liberty Party held its Second National Convention at Buffalo, a year before the election. (That Summer, Buffalo also hosted the National Negro Convention.)

On August 30, 1843, over 1,000 delegates from twelve states and another 4,000 to 5,000 Liberty Party supporters crammed together on the public square before the Buffalo Court House, pushing closer under the shade of a giant canvass tent, probably an "Oberlin Big Tent" used for religious revivals during the preceding decade. The Liberty crowd was like no other before it in the politics of the United States. African Americans, such as Samuel Ringgold Ward, an Abolitionist preacher who campaigned for the party throughout the next decade, were members of the Liberty movement. So were women, some holding Liberty leadership roles. Both groups were evident at the amazing Buffalo assembly.

This time around, the Liberty Party was more sophisticated. Each state delegation was granted voting strength equal to its Electoral count, plus two at-large delegates. Leicester King, president of the Ohio Anti-Slavery Society and Liberty's candidate for Governor in Ohio, was elected Convention Chairman. At one point during the proceedings, Liberty orator Henry Highland Garnett, incited the crowd, "In case of servile war . . . would you take up arms for the Negro?" The assembly roared, "Yes! Yes!"

James G. Birney, the 1840 presidential candidate, had called for "an open Convention." He expected Judge William Jay, son of the nation's first Chief Justice of the Supreme Court and head of the New York City Anti-Slavery Society, to be selected to lead the party in 1844. The delegates thought otherwise. Under no compulsion to select him, they unanimously re-nominated Birney on the First Ballot. The Southern

Abolitionist would be their leader. Thomas Morris, the former anti-slavery Democratic Senator from Ohio, was selected as the party's vice presidential candidate.

Delegates then adopted a 3,000-word platform, the longest of the nineteenth century, drafted by Salmon P. Chase reaffirming "Immediate Abolition" as Liberty's preeminent goal. The platform called for a rededication to the "Revolutionary Principles of 1776." It also claimed that since both Liberty candidates originally hailed from the South, (Birney was from Kentucky; Morris from Virginia) that their party should be called "national," not "sectional," as critics charged.

After the 1840 election, Birney, whose wealth and health were broken by his long struggle for Abolition, had gathered his family and left New York State to become a log cabin farmer in the wilderness near Saginaw, Michigan. In 1842, he ran unsuccessfully for Michigan Governor on the Liberty ticket and was involved in other complicated electoral efforts in that state that allowed some to view him as a front for the Democrats, which he denied. Party loyalties were in flux. He was notified of his Liberty nomination for President by Leicester King, the Convention's chair, and again accepted the honor. This time, the Liberty Party built a local base for the national campaign.

Birney's former idol, Henry Clay, was nominated for President by the Whigs at their National Convention at Baltimore that opened on May 1, 1844. (He had been running for President since 1824.) New Jersey Senator Theodore Freylinghuysen was tapped to be his Vice President. Clay was a formidable opponent, the most "gallant" and powerful politician of his era. A self-educated lawyer born in Virginia, the handsome young red-headed Kentuckian first served in that state's legislature from 1803 to 1806, then as U.S. Senator from 1806-07, and from 1810 to 1811. His greatest legislative accolades came as a member of the U.S. House of Representatives from 1811 to 1814, 1815 to 1821, and again 1823 to 1825. Upon his arrival in Washington, he was immediately elected Speaker of the House and became one of its most brilliant and persuasive leaders.

"The Great Compromiser," as he was called late in his career, along with Daniel Webster and John C. Calhoun, was author of the "Missouri Compromise" of 1820. That agreement silenced the slavery debate for over a decade by admitting Missouri as a Slave State that was balanced by admission of the Free State of Maine. Although Clay professed to be for the gradual elimination of slavery, Abolitionists believed his Compromise guaranteed the steady spread of the despised institution into new states formed from the Louisiana Purchase. Many Southern politicians hated him as well.

In the 1824 presidential election, Clay stood as candidate for the National Republicans. When that race was thrown into the House of

Representatives, "Harry of the West" lent his support to John Quincy Adams, of the East, in exchange for the promise of office, it was alleged. Both Adams and Clay denied the accusation. Adams then defeated Andrew Jackson, even though Jackson had won the popular vote. Adams in turn appointed Clay as his Secretary of State, an office he held until 1829. Clay became the Whig presidential nominee in 1832, losing to Jackson. In 1840, he lost out to Harrison at his party Convention. Now again in 1844, he represented the Whigs. Clay initially opposed the Annexation of Texas. Once again, most Abolitionist Whigs stuck with their party as the best hope of limiting slavery.

Former President Martin Van Buren was still popular in 1844 and his comeback bid had been endorsed early in the campaign by twelve state Democrat Conventions. Despite the fact that the economic depression begun under his tenure lingered, the old political leader still ruled over the Democracy he had created with Jackson. Their party was essentially a coalition of rural Southern and Northern interests, neo-Jeffersonian Republicans, entrepreneurs and laborers, bound together by deal-making. It was an electoral convenience sealed by a pledge to work for the general interests of the populace. Since 1828, the "Common Man" had replaced state legislatures in electing Presidents. Both Democrats and Whigs sought his support in various ways.

Van Buren's forceful opposition to Annexation of Texas proved fatal to his campaign. When the Fourth National Democratic Convention convened on May 27, 1844, at the Odd Fellows Building in Baltimore, with Hendrick B. Wright, of Pennsylvania, as its Permanent Chair, a fight ensued for the nomination. Van Buren was checkmated by the powerful John C. Calhoun, leader of the State Rights faction who staked his claim of the nomination on his work to advance Annexation.

Future President James Buchanan and Missouri Senator Thomas Hart Benton also claimed delegate support. But Van Buren had lost his base of patronage and the dominant Southern bloc at the Convention was able to dump the former President on the Ninth Ballot. In exchange, they were forced to abandon their leader, the South Carolinian Calhoun, for a younger James Knox Polk, of Tennessee. Van Buren had his chance and lost, many Democrats said. It was time to reestablish the party with new vitality. Van Buren's "betrayal" would be vindicated four years later in the election tallies of 1848.

Instead of Van Buren, the Democracy returned to Jackson's home State of Tennessee to nominate the best young debater in the South's arsenal, James K. Polk. Birney's Princeton friend, George M. Dallas, was slotted to become Polk's Vice President, after New York Senator Silas Wright received the nomination, but declined. The Democracy's boisterous platform demanded "the Whole of the territory of Oregon . . ." from England and "the re-Annexation of Texas." Democrats referred to it as "re-Annexation," because they contended Texas was originally part of the Louisiana Purchase and should never have been sold to Spain for Florida in the first place. Polk's greatest qualifications in the eyes of Democrat delegates were his avid support of slavery, his unbending belief in "Manifest Destiny," and his willingness to Annex Texas and Oregon. The 1844 Democracy coined as its slogan, "Fifty-Four Forty or Fight" to highlight Oregon's plight.

Polk was born in North Carolina in 1795 and studied at its university before moving West to be admitted to the Tennessee bar in 1820. He soon jumped into national affairs, serving in the U.S. House of Representatives from 1825 to 1839, the last four years as Speaker of the House. He was an able leader of Jackson's legislative program for the people, favoring low tariffs that made everyday goods more affordable. When Congress was out of session, Tennessee families traveled from miles around for picnics where they listened to his orations. He knew how to entertain as well as debate. From 1839 to 1841, Polk returned to serve as Tennessee Governor, before losing two elections for the same office. Polk had been campaigning for the presidency since 1841, saying that the Whigs had won in 1840 through "ridiculous, unmeaning, and disgusting pageants." With the skilled political help from the old Jackson machine, he emerged as the "Dark Horse" victor at the Baltimore Convention after both Van Buren and Calhoun were stymied. Polk pledged to serve a single term.

Initially, the Whig press, expecting to run against Van Buren, ridiculed the Democracy's mysterious decision. Polk's nomination meant certain victory for Clay, Whigs assumed. Clay was not lulled into complacency. When informed of Polk's nomination, he turned pale and privately predicted his own defeat. He recognized the political skills of his opponent, who had succeeded him as Speaker of the House.

The gaiety of the Whig's 1840 campaign was long gone. With so much hanging in the balance, the 1844 campaign proved a dirty one, featuring reckless assaults on the character of all three candidates. Whigs attacked Polk as "an ultra slaveholder" who would spread its evil further into the territories. The former President campaigned for him, so critics called Polk, "Jackson's tool." Democrats shot back that Clay was a "moral degenerate" who spent his days gambling and nights with unsavory women. Each of these attacks was reshaped and amplified by campaign orators for the momentary delight of villages, towns, and cities across the land.

Clay was eager to expand his support in the South. So despite declaring against Annexation of Texas to the satisfaction of Conscience Whigs, he courted Cotton Whigs as well. In a letter to an Alabama friend, Clay hinted that he might approve of Annexation, if it could be done without injuring the Union. His letter was published and set off a firestorm within his own party. Would he or wouldn't he stand against the admission of Texas? Clay, bruised by the rebuff of his ambitious tactics, denied backing away from his opposition to Annexation, leaving voters uncertain where he stood. Whigs were thrown into a tizzy.

Meanwhile, Elizur Wright, of Massachusetts, convinced Birney that he must actively campaign for the Liberty Party. In October, the old Abolitionist agreed, and became the second presidential candidate, after Harrison in 1840, to campaign for himself. He delivered reasoned speeches across Massachusetts from Boston to Northampton before visiting New Haven, Connecticut, and swinging back through New York from Albany to Syracuse and Rochester. He visited Geritt Smith's hometown of Peterboro, and also Batavia before venturing to Buffalo where the Liberty tent had echoed with cheers for his name in nomination. Meanwhile, Liberty Party orators who fanned out to Abolitionist churches across the North reminded voters that both Polk and Clay were slave-owners, no matter what they said, and asserted that as President either one would promote slavery in the territories.

Finally in November, Birney arrived home in Michigan to address three crowds in Detroit. In addition to his pleas against slavery, he warned Liberty voters against the evils of using war to achieve territorial expansion. He believed a nation should defend itself when attacked, but a war of expansion was a betrayal of the nation's moral principles, Birney admonished. His speeches were always preceded by the old hymns of Abolition and new campaign songs with verses such as: ''We are coming, we are coming! Freedom's battle is begun!''

Wright managed Birney's campaign schedule and publicity. In addition to the grueling series of speeches, Birney prepared his own attack pamphlet entitled, ''Headlines in the Life of Henry Clay,'' in which he detailed Clay's service on behalf of the Slave Power in Congress. Birney listed his various duels and alluded to his ''immoral'' gambling, drinking, and womanizing.

Birney was also a target. By mid-campaign, Whigs sensed that he posed a real threat to their own hopes. John Quincy Adams wrote of Birney at the time that he ''suffers persecution obliquely, and loss for the cause of Liberty for which he is entitled to respect and gratitude; but he is the sport for envious, bitter, ambiguous, and malignant passions, and his head is turned by the greatness thrust upon him of a party candidacy for the presidency.'' Adams called Birney's party the ''Abolition Liberty Party'' and said Birney was ''like a spark upon a barrel of gunpowder.''

Other Whigs stepped up their attacks on the Liberty candidate, falsely accusing him of being a secret front for Catholicism. Some charged he was a British agent. Even Garrison tried to settle an old grudge by attacking his former Abolitionist cohort, alleging that Birney had ''conspired to betray the anti-slavery cause,'' had tried to ''gag the anti-slavery women of the United States in public meetings," and had sought "to destroy the American Anti-Slavery Society, by withdrawing from it in a spirit of hostility, and giving his support to a rival association."

Throughout the contest, both Democrats and Whigs attacked Birney as a "spoiler," a "fanatic," an "anarchist" trying to take votes away from their candidates to elect the other. Gerrit Smith countered that, "expediency is not the rule of Right, but the Right the rule of expediency." Abolitionists were trying to wreck the political process, critics chimed in unison. Liberty leader Alvan Stewart reported that being a Liberty supporter was like being "a man attacked from without, in his own house, who fights for existence, and not conquest." Late in the campaign, Whigs circulated a fake letter that seemed to prove Birney was fronting for the Democracy. He didn't have time to set the record straight.

In the end, Clay should have adhered to the traditional vow of silence during the campaign. In part, his ambiguity on Texas cost him the election. In November, Polk won the popular contest 1,339,494 votes to Clay's 1,300,004, a margin of just 39,490. In the Electoral College, the Democracy prevailed over the Whigs 170 to 105.

However, the Liberty Party decided the contest. Besides alleged voter fraud in Louisiana that robbed Clay of six Electoral Votes, pro-slavery Democrat James Knox Polk became the Eleventh President of the United States because the anti-slavery Liberty Party siphoned away 62,300 votes, a huge surge over four years earlier. In New York, Birney attracted 15,812 voters, while Clay received 232,482 and Polk won with 237,588. The Liberty vote, coming mostly from former Whigs, pushed New York's 36 Electoral votes back into the Democrat column. Liberty voters made the difference in Michigan as well. The two Liberty strongholds gave Polk the national victory.

Although the Liberty Party garnered only 2.3 percent of the national vote, that was more than the margin of victory by Polk. New York Whig editor Horace Greeley forever blamed Clay's ambiguous stand on Annexation for the hateful loss. Most Whigs, including Abraham Lincoln out in Illinois, who stumped widely for his beloved leader, were heart-broken at another defeat for their "valiant Clay." John Quincy Adams wrote, "It is the victory of the slavery element in the Constitution of the United States. The depression and despondency of the Whig Party at the issue of the Presidential election in the State of New York is beyond all example or precedent."

The consequences of the election were swift. By joint resolution of the new Democratic Congress that came in with Polk's election, Texas was admitted into the Union as a Slave State, under Tyler's leadership even before Polk's inauguration in March 1845. With the threat of force at his back, Polk then brought the Oregon Territory into the Union, up to the 49th instead of the 54th Parallel.

Then in 1846, probably at Polk's instigation, the nation launched a bloody, two-year war against Mexico that ended with its complete and humiliating defeat, and the westward expansion of the United States through California. As a result, the United States stretched from "Sea to Shining Sea." Indeed, more territory was acquired by the expansion of the United States through the territories and cultures of other people under the single term of James Knox Polk than by any other President except Thomas Jefferson and his Louisiana Purchase of 1803. The expansion did not diminish, but rather intensified, the question of slavery in the deeply-divided Union.

The Liberty League Presidential Nominating Convention of 1847

Convention-at-a-Glance

Event: The Liberty League Presidential Nominating Convention
Date: June 8-10, 1847
Location: Macedon Locke, New York
New York Governor: John Young, Whig
Convention Chairman: William Goodell, New York
Number of Delegates: Several hundred
Number Needed to Nominate: A majority
Candidates for Nomination: Gerrit Smith, New York
Presidential Nominee: Gerrit Smith
Age of Nominee: 50
Number of Ballots: One
Vice Presidential Nominee: Elihu Burritt (who declined and was replaced at a later Rochester Convention by Charles C. Foote, Michigan)
Platform Positions: Immediate Abolition and Universal Reform; opposition to all monopolies, including government enterprises such as the post office; the eventual abolition of the army and navy to defend the nation's honor without fighting; elimination of the tariff in favor of free trade; opposition to secret societies; direct taxation on individuals, including slaves, to force Emancipation; and distribution of public lands to landless men.
Campaign Slogan: ''Immediate Abolition''

The Liberty League Presidential Nominating Convention of 1847

"You blame members of the national Congress because they defer voting for Emancipation, for fear the Union will be dissolved, and the country plunged into civil war. But, you will not vote for Emancipation . . ."—William Goodell

The Liberty Party had increased its popular appeal during the 1840s only a little as a percentage of the total vote. But Liberty had succeeded in placing the slavery issue on the national agenda. And it had inflicted great damage on one of the major political parties, the Whigs. Ironically, the "political tornado" of President Polk's unintended election in 1844 ultimately meant the spread of slavery, not its Abolition. Many Liberty members felt they had to broaden party appeal by addressing more than one issue in order to win. Others thought they should form a coalition with another party to gain the electoral strength to take on the Slave Power. As the 1848 election approached, internal divisions splintered the Liberty Party.

Liberty also became leaderless when its two-time nominee, James G. Birney, worn out by two decades of tireless Abolitionist agitation, wrote his friends that he would seek public office no more. Injured in a fall from his horse while working on his farm, he now preferred simply to become "one of the rank and file" of the Liberty Party. As the election drew closer, several Liberty leaders, including anti-slavery crusader and theologian William Goodell and New Yorker Henry B. Stanton, expressed fears that the national Liberty committee was stalling a Call for a National Convention. Even worse, they suspected the national committee was planning to dissolve the party altogether to unite with the Whigs in an unholy coalition. The Liberty leadership had already agreed to "defer a presidential nomination in 1847, leaving it to the next year, to see what course would be taken by prominent men in other parties," William Goodell reported.

Many Liberty activists did not trust any of the other parties to fulfill their promises even if they won. So, William Goodell issued a Convention Call himself. And when the splinter party met, he named it the Liberty League. Several other multi-issue Liberty leaders, including James G. Birney, fearing their party was slipping away, seconded Goodell's Call. Huntington Lyman, the Warsaw pastor, joined the universal reformers. The Liberty Leaguers held views reminiscent of Garrison's program of broad institutional reform.

"Slavery was only to be overturned through the destruction of minor monopolies and aristocracies subsidized and sustaining it," William Goodell explained. "The forces needed at the ballot box to overthrow slavery consisted to a great extent, of the masses of men who feel that they have wrongs of their own to be redressed, and who could have no confidence in a Liberty Party not committed to universal equality and impartial Justice to all."

The Liberty Leaguers assembled on June 8, 1848, at Macedon Locke southeast of Rochester in Wayne County, and nominated Abolitionist stalwart Gerrit Smith for President. Elihu Burritt, the "learned blacksmith," was promoted for Vice President (but after Burritt declined, Charles C. Foote, of Michigan, was made the vice presidential nominee at another Convention held at Rochester). Alvan Stewart and other party founders attended the Convention and worked for Smith through November. Birney was absent, but also supported the ticket with articles in the Abolitionist press, a role he had long mastered.

While keeping Abolition the one and true object of the party, the Liberty Leaguers wrote a platform they hoped would also appeal on other voter issues. As a "universal reform" party, calling for change on several fronts, it opposed all monopolies including the post office. The platform called for the eventual abolition of the army and navy, so that the nation could learn to defend its honor without fighting. It came out for free trade. It denounced secret societies, as had the Anti-Masonic Party of 1831 that also had its origins in Western New York. It called for direct taxation on individuals, and for taxes to be levied on slaves to force quicker Emancipation. And it advocated distribution of public lands to landless men, the limitation of land ownership, and free suffrage, including for women.

The Liberty League Convention stimulated state Liberty Leagues in Massachusetts, Ohio, and New York. Opponents of the Liberty League complained that it had spread its focus too thinly and the appeal of universal reform was limited. More crucially, other political realignments were taking center stage as the memorable 1848 election approached. But Gerrit Smith kept up the agitation for Emancipation, along with other reforms.

The Third Liberty Party Presidential Nominating Convention of 1847

Convention-at-a-Glance

Event: The Third Liberty Presidential Nominating Convention
Date: October 20, 1847
Location: Buffalo, New York
New York Governor: John Young, Whig
Number of Delegates: Hundreds
Number Needed to Nominate: A majority
Presidential Nominee: Senator John P. Hale, New Hampshire
Age of Nominee: 41
Number of Ballots: One
Vice Presidential Nominee: Leicester King, Ohio
Platform Positions: Abolition of slavery and civil rights for emancipated slaves.
Campaign Slogan: "Immediate Abolition"

The Third Liberty Party Presidential Nominating Convention of 1847

The actions of the Liberty League prompted the Liberty Party's national committee to finally call for another National Presidential Nominating Convention to be held in Buffalo a year before the election. Some Liberty Leaguers joined in, hoping New York's Gerrit Smith would be nominated, and that the breach in the party might be quickly repaired. The national committee running the Convention had other ideas. On October 20, 1847, the remnants of the Liberty Party nominated U.S. Senator John P. Hale, an Independent Democrat from New Hampshire, for the presidency. Leicester King, of Ohio, was selected to run for Vice President.

Hale, who was born in 1806 in the Granite State, was first elected to Congress in 1842 as a Democrat. He had refused to vote for the Annexation of Texas, even though he was instructed to do so by his state legislature. They withdrew his re-nomination. In 1846, he won a Senate seat as a Free Soil candidate, the first in that body. He would serve in the Senate as a Free Soiler until 1854, when he was re-elected as a new Republican, holding that office until 1865, when he would be appointed Minister to Spain.

Then in November, 1847, the Liberty Party held an endorsement

Convention in New York City where it ratified the nomination of Hale and King. A Liberty Party splinter group held another small Buffalo Convention on June 15, 1848. It endorsed Liberty League candidates of Smith and Foote. Still another Liberty Party Convention was held September 28, 1848, which endorsed the Liberty League's platform. As the Liberty Leaguers feared, by the time the election rolled around most of the Liberty Party members had defected to the new Free Soil movement that was gaining strength across New York State, New England, and the Northwest, even though it only favored stopping the spread of slavery in the territories and not Immediate Abolition everywhere in the nation.

Then, a month before the election of 1848, Liberty Party nominees, Hale and King withdrew, throwing their support behind the Free Soil cause in a more unified assault on slavery. At least if the new party didn't win, the Free Soil movement would fragment the old parties around the slavery issue. Goodell added, "The enemies of the Liberty Party, Whigs, Democrats, non-resistants, and Garrison Abolitionists, rejoiced greatly at its supposed 'death and burial.'"

A. A. Gutherie, of Ohio, had been among those disappointed by the fact that the Buffalo Convention went outside of the Liberty Party to nominate Hale. But he wrote, "To one at the time, it did seem that the people had become thoroughly awake, both to the Rights and their duties, and that party attachments are no longer to prevent a manly, fearless, assertion of the Rights of the free North to take control of the Government, and to wield it in favor of Liberty."

However, that moment of optimism quickly passed after the election of 1848, and Gutherie confessed, "I am constrained to admit that the high hopes then formed have faded away and left the sad conviction that the people of the Free States are yet to learn lessons of deep humiliation, before they will rise to the true position and dignity of freemen."

The Liberty Party, that had brought the great cause of Abolition into electoral politics, ceased to be a factor after 1848. In 1852, Gerrit Smith was elected as a Free Soil candidate to Congress from the Twenty-Second District of New York. He was still calling for Voting Rights for "all persons, the black as well as the white, the female as well as the male." He served one term and later became a financial backer of John Brown's violent attempt to spark a slave insurrection and civil war. Brown was hanged; Smith escaped prosecution by seeking refuge in a mental sanitarium.

In August, 1852, true-believers from the Liberty and Free Soil parties, met in Pittsburgh, Pennsylvania, to unanimously nominate Senator John P. Hale for President, and George W. Julian, of Indiana, for Vice President, to run against Whig Winfield Scott and Democrat Franklin

Pierce. The final Liberty platform opposed the "Compromise of 1850," supported the Abolition of slavery, welcomed immigrants, pushed for more Federal funds for homesteading, and for river and harbor improvements.

Other Abolitionists nominated Gerrit Smith in both 1856 and 1860 under the label of the Radical Abolitionist Party. Both Goodell and Smith continued their campaign for universal reform throughout the rest of their lives. Local Liberty Party candidates also ran campaigns from 1840 until the 1860 election. In 1855, Frederick Douglass was nominated as the Liberty Party's candidate for New York Secretary of State. In 1857, another African American, James McCune Smith, was nominated for the same spot as a Liberty man. The Abolitionist Congregational preacher, Samuel Ringgold Ward, sometimes called "The Black Daniel Webster" for his eloquence, was nominated as a Liberty candidate for the state Assembly. Local Liberty Conventions nominated women for local offices as well.

When the anti-slavery Republican Party held its first Presidential Nominating Convention in Philadelphia in 1856, Liberty men were numerous among them. In Philadelphia and in later Republican National Conventions, Gerrit Smith, Salmon Chase, and other early third-party Abolitionists and Liberty men were warmly celebrated for their pioneering electoral work and their banners flew high over Republican Convention halls. The Liberty men had endured the torments of hostility alone for most of a decade. Finally, their call for an end to slavery was catching fire across the North. In history's ultimate judgment, they were the pioneers of racial Justice and for the universal sanctity of freedom that eventually transformed the United States into a more humane nation.

In the end, the Liberty Party's one-issue focus and association with radical Abolition prevented it from attracting the broad support it needed to win a national victory. But the Liberty Party's greatest achievement was breaking the ground for anti-slavery electoral politics that ultimately freed the nation. Its bold electoral initiative culminated, in part, in the election of Republican Abraham Lincoln and the Civil War that at last forced a constitutional solution to slavery. After the Civil War, some Liberty men and women, including William Goodell, joined the Prohibition Party, expanding their notion of "perfectionist politics" with pursuit of another "hopeless cause" that ultimately came to fruition decades later in the United States of America, the land of ever-changing idealism.

The Free Soil Convention and the Election of 1848

Convention-at-a-Glance

Event: The Free Soil Convention
Date: August 9-10, 1848
Location: Buffalo, New York
New York Governor: John Young, Whig
Convention President: Charles Francis Adams, Massachusetts
Number of Delegates: 466 from eighteen states
Largest Crowd: 40,000
Number Needed to Nominate: A majority
Candidates for Nomination: Charles Francis Adams, Massachusetts; Congressman Joshua R. Giddings, Ohio; Senator Jon P. Hale, New Hampshire; Associate Supreme Court Justice John McLean, Ohio; Former President Martin Van Buren, New York
Presidential Nominee: Martin Van Buren
Age of Nominee: 65
Number of Ballots: One
Vice Presidential Nominee: Charles Francis Adams
Platform Positions: The "National Platform of Freedom" declared the Free Soil Party would "maintain the Rights of Free Labor against the aggressions of the Slave Power;" pledged to prevent the spread of slavery to the territories; denounced all compromises with the South over slavery; called for Congress to abolish slavery where it had the constitutional power to do so, such as in the City of Washington; demanded "freedom for Oregon;" as well as "free postage, retrenchment of the expenses and patronage of the Federal Government, the abolition of all unnecessary offices and salaries, and the election by the people of all civil offices."
Campaign Slogan: "Free Soil, Free Speech, Free Labor, Free Men"

The Free Soil Convention and the Election of 1848

"The Convention . . . may . . . be productive of more important consequences than any which has gone before it, save only that which formed the Federal Constitution."—Former President Martin Van Buren

On August 9, 1848, as revolution raged across Europe overthrowing the old Royal tyrannies, a new Free Soil Party in the United States held its founding Convention in Buffalo, New York, with high hopes of over-throwing the tyranny of slavery that was strangling its own nation. As many as 40,000 anti-slavery supporters poured into the Erie County seat which, like Warsaw, also served as a northern station on the Underground Railroad.

The 466 Free Soil delegates who arrived in the thriving city were elected from congressional districts in the eighteen states that sent representatives, including the Slave states of Delaware, Maryland, and Virginia. The delegates, and as many spectators as could fit, crammed together beneath the canvas shade of a "Big Tent," the kind used during the religious revivals that had swept upstate New York and New England a decade earlier. The surrounding crowd overflowed across the city's well-groomed public square, where four years earlier the Liberty Party had drawn 5,000 followers for much the same purpose. Across the street, towered Buffalo's ornate City Hall, a white, two-story structure with six tall Greek columns facing the avenue. The classical civic trophy was topped with a stately copula, befitting the wealthy merchant city facing west on Lake Erie at the gateway to the inland empire, youthfully optimistic and dedicated to Liberty.

Political operatives from three political parties crowded together with a real sense of excitement. Most were ending a life-time of political ties with their old parties to take the radical step of creating a new political party that would again take up the battle cry of the American Revolution for the Rights of Man. They were above all dedicated to preventing the spread of slavery that had rotted the soul of their Republic, a menace since the nation's formation. If the Slave Power triumphed in Congress, slavery would infect the West, then the North until it was legal in all but a few states.

Why was a new Free Soil Party necessary in 1848? The answer lay, in part, in the complicated currents of national politics of the time. To begin with, during late winter, President James Knox Polk announced he had accomplished enough in office and reaffirmed his promise not to run for a second term. Polk had waged a bitter but victorious war with Mexico and he had reaped its rewards in terms of praise and honors in Washington. Like his mentor, Andrew Jackson, Polk had worked for the "Common Man," and had vastly expanded the territory of the nation. He was content to end his distinguished political career that had taken him from Tennessee all the way to Speaker of the House of Representatives and presidency of the United States, the only Speaker to be so elevated. That was enough for a Tennessee backwoodsman.

Polk's term had been controversial. Texas was admitted to the Union as a Slave State a month before his March inauguration by President Tyler and the Democratic Congress that was elected with Polk's victory and sworn into office in January. Two years into his term, President Polk ordered Major General Zachary Taylor to take a position in Texas just south of the disputed Rio Grande, inside Mexican territory. That provoked a Mexican counter-attack which became Polk's pretense for war. In the two-year-long conflict that ensued, U.S. forces easily decimated their proud but weak neighbor to the south in a slaughter that sickened many U. S. citizens, including one junior officer and future President, Ulysses S. Grant. He called it, "One of the most unjust wars ever waged by a stronger against a weaker nation." Through the spoils of war, James Knox Polk fulfilled his party's promise of "Manifest Destiny." But after four years of intense work, Polk, who had been sick much of his life, sensed his own vulnerability and stepped aside. Within three months of leaving office, he was dead of cholera at age 53. Among his last requests was that after his wife's death, his slaves should be freed. Unfortunately for them, that moment came many years thereafter.

Polk's decision not to run meant the race for the presidency was wide open. Both Democrats and Whigs felt they could win the November election and advance their competing visions. The Democracy stood for restricted Federal and banking power and State Rights. Whigs promoted protective tariffs, a National Bank, and internal improvements paid for by the Federal Government. The anti-slavery Liberty Party that had thwarted the 1844 election of Whig Henry Clay lurked as a wild card in 1848, although the radical minority party seemed in recent disarray.

Suddenly, a fourth coalition formed calling itself the "Free Soil Party." The odd collection of Free Soil delegates in Buffalo that August represented an uneasy political union formed from among the deserters of all three parties. They had been bitter opponents. Now they were determined allies.

The first group, dissident Democrats from New York, was the dominant driving force behind the Buffalo Convention. During the Mexican War which had ended in February 1848, they had stood against their own President. Now they worked for passage of the "Wilmot

Proviso," a bill introduced by northern Pennsylvania's Democratic Congressman David Wilmot, which sought to prohibit slavery in the new territories of the Southwest that were the spoils of the Mexican War. President Polk threatened to veto the Proviso if it ever reached his desk, and the Southern-dominated United States Senate refused even to consider it.

Most recently, these New York Free Soil Democrats known as "Barnburners" had been rebuffed at the Fifth National Democratic Convention held May 22 through 25, 1848, at the Universalist Church in Baltimore, city of the party's first four Conventions. The dissidents were called "Barnburners," because like the hard-headed New York Dutch farmer, they'd rather "burn down the barn to get rid of a rat" than compromise with slavery.

(Jackson had picked up on the Convention idea after the Anti-Masons convened the first U.S. Presidential Nominating Convention at Harrisburg, Pennsylvania, in 1831, nominating William Wirt, of New York. In 1832, Jackson used the Convention as a way to take nominating power away from the state legislatures that had taken the power away from the secret Congressional Caucuses, to give more apparent democratic power to the people.)

But in Baltimore in 1848, the radical New York faction was shortchanged on the number of delegates it received and poorly treated in platform deliberations. Polk and the national party were in league with the conservative New York "Hunker" faction. Worst of all, from the radical New Yorkers' perspective, was the nomination of Senator Lewis Cass, of Michigan, for President over James Buchanan, of Pennsylvania, and Levi Woodbury, of New Hampshire, on the Fourth Ballot of the Baltimore Convention. No Northern Senator better served the interests of the South. William O. Butler, of Kentucky, was selected to run for Vice President. The Convention liked Cass and touted his long Senate service. He, too, had fought in the War of 1812 with General Harrison in the successful defense of Detroit, and had served as President Jackson's Secretary of War, then as Minister to France. In the future Lewis Cass would become Secretary of State under President Buchanan. But in aiming for the 1848 nomination, Cass had curried Southern support by working for the Annexation of Texas. He was generally viewed as a Northern apologist for slavery. That made him a "Northern man with Southern principles," something anti-slavery Northern Democrats such as the radical New Yorkers despised.

Senator Cass advocated "squatters' sovereignty" to solve the slavery issue in the territories. He wanted to simply let each new territory "democratically vote" on the heated issue when they petitioned for Statehood. His doctrine was renamed "popular sovereignty" by Stephen A. Douglas in the 1850s and led to civil war in Kansas.

The Barnburners, however, followed the lead of Congressman John Van Buren, eldest son of the former President. "Prince John" as he was sometimes called, had been born in 1799, had served as a member of the state Assembly in 1831, and then in Congress from 1841 to 1843. He was currently the district attorney for Ulster County. In protest against Cass' nomination, Van Buren's faction abstained from voting.

At Buffalo, the Barnburners were joined by the older New York "Locofocos," radical urban labor Democrats from the 1830s who had supported Martin Van Buren, and were ready to campaign for him again.

The Barnburners stood opposed by the Hunkers, the conservative Democrats who "hunkered down" in defense of the South. Hunkers supported the Northern business powers that traded with slave-owners and those who favored concentrated economic power. They had opposed President Van Buren's attempts to create an independent Treasury. They vigorously opposed the Wilmot Proviso. Their refusal to give up economic ties to the Southern slave economy ultimately split the New York Democracy.

After the Baltimore Convention nominated Cass, the Barnburners "bolted" from the Democracy they had helped build and began planning to create the Free Soil Party. When they arrived back in New York City, they held a giant anti-Cass rally in City Hall Park. Then in June, the Barnburners gathered upstate for a Convention at Utica. John Van Buren, Benjamin F. Butler, who had been Van Buren's law partner and Secretary of War, and Preston King, (who served in Congress from 1843 to 1847, and would become a Republican U.S. Senator from 1857 to 1863), dominated the passionate affair.

Near the end of the Utica Convention, famed attorney David Dudley Field, who had just led codification of New York's common law, read a letter from former President Martin Van Buren. The former President denounced the Baltimore Convention and its candidate, Cass. The Baltimore Convention had illegally excluded New Yorkers and therefore the true New York Democracy was not bound by its platform or candidate, the elder Van Buren charged. An animated crowd cheered almost every word. They had always been for Van Buren, the "little magician" from Kinderhook. Now in this new battle for Human Rights, the old warrior was their champion again.

Despite his declaration "never again to be a candidate for public office," the Utica Convention nominated the 65-year-old former President as its candidate for the Buffalo Free Soil Convention in August. Henry Dodge, of Wisconsin, was nominated to be his vice presidential nominee. Dodge, the Democratic Governor of Wisconsin, soon to be its Senator, declined. The Utica Convention resolved to bring all the opponents of slavery in the territories together in Convention in August.

The venerable Abolitionists from the Liberty Party made up the second group in the 1848 Free Soil coalition. They were the first to take the slavery issue to the U. S. electorate. But they had run poorly in two presidential elections, even though they had decided the outcome of the last one. Many of their members were anxious for results and cared little for ideological purity, so they defected to the Free Soil movement in a pragmatic search of a better chance of winning at the ballot box and striking a blow against slavery.

"Conscience Whigs," mostly from New England and Ohio, were the third group in the Buffalo Free Soil coalition. They had seen the slavery issue rebuffed by their own party in the last two presidential elections. They were led by the son of a former President of the United States and grandson to another, Charles Francis Adams. He had political advantages few others in the nation possessed. Born in 1807, Adams had written an influential essay entitled "A Whig of the Old School" in 1835. He had served in the Massachusetts Senate from 1835 to 1840. Adams gave prestige to the Conscience Whigs and led them into the new alliance.

Adam's retreat from Whiggery had been slow and difficult. Three years earlier, in January, 1845, Adams and other Conscience Whigs had met in Boston's Faneuil Hall (named after the Boston Merchant Peter Faneuil who donated it) to urge President Tyler not to admit Texas into the Union as a Slave State. The Unitarian reformer William Ellery Channing stood before them and bellowed: "I now ask whether as a people, we are prepared to seize on a neighboring territory to the end of extending slavery? I ask whether as a people we can stand forth in the sight of God, in the sight of nations, and adopt this atrocious policy? Sooner perish! Sooner our name be blotted out from the record of nations!" But protests in New England did little to sway the President. With a new Congress, Tyler had ushered Texas into the Union as the twenty-eighth state. The power of the slave bloc in Congress increased. Some Southern strategists even dreamed of cutting the giant state into five separate states with ten pro-slavery Senators.

When the Mexican War broke out in April 1846, Adams founded and edited the *Boston Daily Whig* which argued against the spread of slavery through conquered territories. Among Adams' young advisors were Charles Sumner, the future U. S. Senator, and Henry Wilson, a future Republican Vice President under Ulysses S. Grant. Sumner, born in 1811, was Harvard educated. He would be elected to the U.S. Senate as a Free Soiler in 1850, and later ran as a Republican, serving until 1874. Sumner called Polk's war a "slave owner's conspiracy." Adams called it a "crime" and asserted that his explanation of its origin was a "lie." The paper condemned fellow Whigs who voted to fund the Mexican conflict, accusing them of betraying the high-minded ideals of the Whig party.

At the 1846 Massachusetts Whig Convention, the party had finally split over the strength of its anti-slavery plank. While most Massachusetts Whigs opposed slavery, Adams and other Conscience Whigs wanted stronger denunciations. And they wanted direct action to prevent its spread to the territories. The Cotton Whigs would not agree to drastic moves against their Southern allies. In the 1846 election, Adams and Sumner opposed Whig Congressman Robert Winthrop, the official party candidate, because he voted appropriations for Polk's war. Mainstream Whigs called Adams and his friends "Abolitionists" and "traitors to the true political faith."

In Congress, most Whigs had supported the war appropriations even if they were uneasy with Polk's clear provocation against Mexico. And most Whigs believed that no new territories should be added through war. But in the end, the dissenters to the war were few. They included "the lonely Whig from Illinois," one-term Congressman Abraham Lincoln, who demanded to know from President Polk the exact "spot" where the Mexicans had attacked, implying that that spot was not on U.S. but Mexican soil. He became known as "Spot Lincoln." Because of his anti-war polemics, Lincoln proved so unpopular back in Illinois that he could not run for re-election. The future President left politics for a decade, until the outbreak of warfare in Kansas brought him back to the anti-slavery fight.

Adams and the other Conscience Whigs vowed, "No more slaveholders," such as Harrison or Clay. Adams initially favored Senator Thomas Corwin, of Ohio, for the 1848 Whig nomination. Corwin had been a Whig Congressman from 1831 to 1840, until he was elected Governor. He failed to be re-elected, but was sent to the U.S. Senate as a Whig from 1845 to 1850, when President Fillmore appointed him Secretary of the Treasury. He would oppose Fillmore's signing of the "Compromise of 1850." Corwin remained Adams' candidate for a while. However, Adams eventually decided against Corwin because, although he voted against the Mexican War, he was too weak an opponent of slavery, and he was not likely to stop Taylor.

Adams was firmly opposed to the Whig front-runner, Mexican War hero Major General Zachary Taylor, who was an absentee Mississippi plantation slave owner. Taylor had become a national hero for leading the U.S. forces that defeated Santa Anna at Buena Vista in the first battle of the Mexican War. But he resented Polk's provocation against Mexico and the 700 dead soldiers under his command that the war inflicted. Taylor also blamed Polk's Secretary of War, former New York Governor William Marcy, for the unnecessary conflict. And he seethed over the President's refusal to allow his men to join the final push to victory in Mexico City. Polk sensed Taylor's presidential potential and did what he could to derail the popular General.

But Whigs who mentioned Taylor''s name saw him as the most "available" candidate because of his sudden war popularity. They were eager to regain power in Washington. After the war, General Taylor, who had never even voted for President, would not say whether he was a Whig or Democrat. He simply asserted that he was above party, and for the good of the Union. The Democratic-led Annexation of Texas as a Slave State was the unintended outcome of the Liberty Party's 1844 success, and that gave Adams and other Whigs pause. They did not want to simply elect another Democrat. For a time, Adams looked for an alternative to leaving his old party. But after losing a battle in defense of the Wilmot Proviso at the 1847 Massachusetts Whig Convention, Adams began actively working to create a new anti-slavery party. He knew his actions ultimately ended any chance that he would become the third Adams to serve as President.

Meanwhile, on September 4, 1847, Zachary Taylor was nominated for President by the National American or "Know-Nothing" Party at a secret Philadelphia Convention. The xenophobic party only endorsed candidates who favored its America-first policy of limiting immigrant and foreign influence in national affairs. Taylor was known in some circles as "a man of prejudices rather than opinions." The General returned to New Orleans and a hero's welcome on December 3, 1847, before moving to his "Spanish Cottage" located on his plantation near Baton Rouge. In January 1848, the Tennessee legislature called for Taylor to become the Whig nominee. On February 2, 1848, the Treaty of Guadalupe-Hidalgo ended the Mexican war. Mexico ceded the rest of Texas, New Mexico, and upper California to the United States, in exchange for $15 million, a relatively paltry sum for so vast a region. The burning question was whether the new territory would be opened to slavery. The acquisition was a huge political victory for Polk and his Democracy that they hoped would attract voters in the next election.

In February 1848, John Quincy Adams, who had returned to the House of Representatives after his presidency, died on its floor fighting the Slave Power. (By that time, fourteen Abolitionists occupied seats in Congress.) Charles Francis Adams inherited his father's moral authority, and that he lay upon the Free Soil movement. Now the younger Adams was freed from the party father and son had once cherished.

On June 7, 1848, the Whig Party held its National Convention in the Philadelphia Museum Building, popularly known as the "Chinese Museum" because of an exhibit it once housed. Among the 15,000 delegates and supporters was a future President, Abraham Lincoln, on his way home from Congress. The Whig nomination fight pitted the 1844 nominee and former Senator, Henry Clay, of Kentucky, against General Winfield Scott, of Virginia, who had taken Mexico City in the recent war, as well as Senator Daniel Webster, of Massachusetts, and Major

General Zachary Taylor. Taylor was so non-partisan that he had received votes for the same office at the Democratic National Convention the month before the Whigs met, although in a letter to a friend he had admitted that he was a "Whig" but not an "ultra-Whig."

On the Fourth Ballot of the Whig's Philadelphia Convention, the Taylor forces, predominantly from the South, surged to victory. New Yorker Millard Fillmore, a Whig party founder and long-time supporter of Clay's "American System" of checks between industry and agriculture, was selected for the vice presidency to balance the ticket in traditional Democratic fashion. Whigs were so confident that they had a winner in General Taylor that they didn't adopt a platform beyond words of praise for their nominee. Taylor was the platform. That fall, New York Senator William Henry Seward managed Taylor's campaign. Lincoln campaigned for Taylor, as he had for other Whigs over the years.

After the slave-owning Taylor was nominated and Whigs didn't bother to adopt a platform, Adams said the Whigs should cease to exist as a "party of principles." Weeks after the Philadelphia Convention adjourned, on June 28, 1848, more than 7,000 Massachusetts Conscience Whigs gathered in Worcester, under the leadership of Adams and Sumner, to declare Free Soil ideals. They listened to an impassioned plea by Ohio Congressman Joshua Reed Giddings urging them to attend the Buffalo Free Soil Convention. Some Whigs were not yet convinced this was the best option. For one thing, it was rumored that the Whig's old enemy, Democrat President Martin Van Buren, could become the Free Soil nominee. But by the end of the Worcester Convention, the two rebellious states of Ohio and Massachusetts vowed to join forces.

On top of all of this anti-slavery turmoil, another revolutionary event took place in Upstate New York a month before the Buffalo Convention. On July 10, 1848, the Seneca Falls Women's Convention, the first Women's Rights assembly, fused the issues of anti-slavery with a new Emancipation plan for half of the nation's inhabitants. Lucy Stone, Lucretia Mott, and Elizabeth Cady Stanton, wife of Liberty Party founder William Stanton, organized the new movement for equal political Rights, equal education, vocational choices, wages, and equitable divorce and property laws. Their actions set off a seventy-year battle that transformed social relationships throughout the nation and the world. Radical change was in the air that feverish New York summer of 1848.

August 9, 1848, the first day of the Free Soil Convention, was hot and humid in Buffalo. Tired delegates and supporters arrived at the Big Tent after a raucous night of torchlight parades and old-fashioned oratory in the city's luxurious hotel lobbies and numerous saloons. Exactly at 8:30 a.m., Judge Stevens of Indiana, a former Liberty Party leader, banged his gavel to establish order over the restless throng. Delegates sat on chairs in the front facing boisterous supporters who tightly squeezed together on wooden benches, with others crowded around the edges in standing room only. The loud chorus of voices was slow to respond to the Judge's orders, but eventually they came to a lull.

The Convention's first order of business was to elect a President. That decision had already been made behind the scenes by the Convention's organizers during the days leading up to the assembly. Charles Francis Adams was selected to guide their momentous affairs. He had arrived for organizational meetings on August 8, strategizing with New York Democrats Preston King and Benjamin Butler, Liberty men Chase, of Ohio, and Joshua Leavitt, of New York. Whig Giddings was there as well. Adams' presence at the Convention gave it prestige and stature. He had initially resisted taking the post of Convention President since he was not a strong public speaker. But he eventually was convinced that he had an obligation to represent the Whigs.

As Adams stood before the assembly, many noticed the band of black crepe pulled around his arm in memory of his father John Quincy. The aura of "Old Man Eloquence," as the former President was called for his forceful orations against slavery, hovered over his son Charles Francis as he addressed the historic Convention. "Fellow Citizens," Adams began after taking the gavel. "It is a matter of deep and heartfelt gratitude to me that I have been selected as an unworthy instrument to preside over the deliberations of this great body." Decorum was always the order of the hour with Adams. "Fellow Citizens, you have all assembled here today out of pure devotion to a principle.

"I regard the Wilmot Proviso as, in substance, a struggle between right and wrong; as a contest between truth and falsehood, between the principles of Liberty and the rule of slavery." The Convention burst into cheers of approval. "Now fellow citizens," Adams' voice rang out earnestly, "is the accepted time when we all come together to note what our position is and how far the Government has drifted from the ancient landmarks which our fathers set up. Now is the accepted time when we are taking a new observation of the national ship. . . ." Adam's thin voice grew stronger. "The question before us is one which involves the proposition whether we shall adhere to the solemn principles of the Declaration of Independence; whether we shall deduce Government from the consent of the governed; and whether we shall make Government a system which promotes Justice or which sanctions slavery in the new territories of the West." The crowd echoed, "Yes, yes, that is the question."

"Fellow Citizens," Adams sternly continued, "the eyes of the whole country are upon our action this day, and there are many ill-disposed persons who are greedily looking for some manifestation of distraction and dissention and division, which shall succeed in defeating, as far as any human power can defeat it, the success of our movement.

Looking at the results of their own Conventions, in which they have presented the mortifying spectacle of nothing but division, they do really suppose that we who come here are in just the same position. . . ." The assembly laughed. "They do not understand that we come here and say . . . everything for the cause, nothing for men." The applause at the end of Adams' oration was thunderous and long sustained.

An exulted Adams rested as he looked out across the large crowd saluting his message. The former political enemies who gathered in Buffalo as Free Soilers were more sophisticated than the political idealists, religious zealots, universal reformers, ministers, and Abolitionists who had dominated the Liberty Party Convention four years earlier. (Unlike in the Liberty Party, there were no Free Soil women under the Big Tent.) Free Soilers were mostly professional politicians and operatives who knew how to win elections for their parties, and how to run a state, or a country. Tested political realists, they wanted to create a more effective anti-slavery party that also would appeal to voters with a strong platform on a variety of national issues. That fact made their platform an important bargaining tool that could solidify the coalition.

As Adams surveyed the Free Soil delegates that August morning, he saw many Liberty men. These included, the sparse records recall, Harding, of Indiana; Treadwell, of Michigan; Owen Lovejoy, of Illinois, brother of the martyred Abolitionist; Codding and Holton, of Wisconsin, along with Booth, editor of the *Milwaukee Freeman*; Lewis, Smith, Paine, Guthrie, and Townshend, of Ohio, also defected from the Liberty cause and brought their battle to a new Free Soil banner. Other Liberty men in the crowd included Gamaliel Bailey, who edited James G. Birney's old paper, The *Philanthropist*, Samuel Lewis, and Stanley Mathews, of Ohio; Joshua Leavitt and William Jay, of New York; Nathaniel Colver and Elizur Wright, of Massachusetts; Austin Willey, of Maine. He saw Negroes in the immense crowd as well.

Adams also spotted the Free Soil Democrats before him, led by Brinckerhoff, Gillet, Chandler, and Sawyer, of Ohio; Wright, of Indiana; Christiancy and Wilson, of Michigan; Isaac Arnold, a future Republican Congressman from Chicago; Crocker and Wilson, of Wisconsin; Miller, of Iowa. Young Samuel Tilden, a protégé of Van Buren who would become New York's Governor and the 1876 Democratic presidential nominee, worked with John Van Buren to hammer out the principles around which the Free Soil Party would go forward. Adams also spied New Yorkers William Culent Bryant, editor of the *New York Evening Post*, and Senator John Adams Dix, who would become Buchanan's Secretary of the Treasury and eventually New York Governor.

Likewise, Adams gazed upon his fellow Conscience Whigs in the crowd including Briggs, Vaughn, and Hamlin, of Ohio; and Julian and Cravens, of Indiana. Thousands of others, even more obscurely remembered in the early and sparse records, stood at their sides cheering loudly in a wild scene of rare unity among political rivals. Throughout the Buffalo Convention, delegates sang and shouted, clapping together as though they were attending a religious revival. Despite their different political histories and philosophies, all of the Free Soilers chanted their unifying slogan: "Free Soil, Free Speech, Free Labor, Free Men."

("Free Soil, Free Speech, Free Labor, Free Men." Eight years later in 1856, that slogan would be taken up by the new Republican Party at its first National Presidential Nominating Convention in Philadelphia and converted to: "Free Soil, Free Speech, Fremont," in support of the "Pathfinder" John Charles Fremont, the Republicans' first presidential nominee.)

Next, the Free Soilers voted to assign the 466 actual delegates sent from Congressional Districts, or appointed at-large from each state, to serve as a smaller Committee of Conferees. The Committee would craft a platform upon which they all could agree and then pick a Free Soil nominee for President. The larger Convention would then ratify its work if it agreed. After Adams' speech, smaller working committees dispersed to the local Universalist Church and various hotel lobbies and rooms to do their initial work. The Committee of Conferees reconvened that summer evening under the Big Tent, where Salmon P. Chase was elected chairman of the smaller body. Chase had been at the forefront of the Liberty effort since 1841.

Under the Big Tent that afternoon, the remaining anti-slavery men were treated to a series of fiery orators, with Adams presiding. The crowd applauded their fine phrases and determination to save their nation from moral and economic ruin. Speaker after speaker denounced the practices and character of the national administration, the nominees of their opponents, the evils of Polk's Mexican War and the spread of slavery into the territories. The orators, polished and unpolished, prepared and extemporaneous, extolled the Wilmot Proviso as the only Just resolution of the conflict that had brought so many new states and territories into the Union. They promised to prosecute the Free Soil crusade at every polling place of every town and hamlet in their respective states until the threat of slavery was extinguished from the new territories of the land of the free.

The Convention was especially eager to hear from Joshua Giddings, the Ohio Abolitionist pioneer from the Western Reserve. Giddings had been so politically alone in Congress that he was driven out of the House of Representatives by other members for violating the gag rule prohibiting any discussion of slavery. But he was resoundingly re-elected and returned to carry on the fight. Now the House of Representatives was beginning to listen to the former Whig. The crowd under the Big Tent shouted his name as he rose to speak extemporaneously. Reporters called the applause "deafening."

"Friends, countrymen, and fellow citizens," the Ohio crusader began. "I know of no sublimer spectacle that could be presented to the eye of the Patriot, Statesman, or lover of Mankind, than to see a people assembled in mighty Convention, for the maintenance of their own unalienable Rights . . . ." Giddings recalled that slavery had been established in Jamestown, Virginia, the same year that their "puritan fathers established human Liberty upon the wild New England shore. And these antagonistic principles have been spreading and widening, and pursing out, and bearing fruit from that day to the present. And while New England has been, with devotion to her country, her God, and to Mankind, endeavoring to extend her principles of Liberty," the Congressman expostulated, "the Southern states have been eagerly and energetically engaged in extending and perpetuating human degradation and slavery." The crowd roared in agreement.

Giddings was bitter. "And that institution existed when it was first brought upon the southern shores of these states precisely as it is now sought to be established in California and New Mexico . . . In violation of heaven's high decree, the white man seized his fellow colored man and compelled him to submit to his will . . . by the bowie-knife, the scourge, the whip, and the dread instruments of torture, he will establish slavery there unless prevented by the law," he warned.

Giddings then turned to the current electoral contest as if he were in a lobby of the Capitol building conferring with fellow insiders. "Of General Cass I will not speak. He has been a political opponent of mine, and is now. Of General Taylor I can only remark that I know not enough of him to say any thing in his favor or to speak evil of him. I can only speak of his principles and those of the old Whig party." The crowd laughed. He then praised Henry Clay for opposing the extension of slavery in the election of 1844 and he condemned the Southern Whigs who abandoned him to help elect Polk. Again Giddings reminded his audience, that just months earlier, the Whigs had turned away from Clay for Taylor. Giddings noted Clay "lies low, smitten down by the ruthless Slave Power, which has never spared any however exalted, whom it suspected of a willingness to recognize the principles embodied in the Declaration of Independence."

Someone in the crowd shouted out Van Buren's name. Giddings responded, "Well, gentlemen, you know that I opposed Martin Van Buren with all my powers. I left no stone unturned in '40 to defeat his election. Martin Van Buren rejected Texas in '37. She was then at war with Mexico. In '44 the slaveholders of Mississippi interrogated him upon this subject, which with them was the transcendent question of all others, and he declared his opposition to the Annexation of Texas in '44. This is a matter of Truth and history, and I declare it to be the brightest spot in his political life. There was in that act a perfect consistency, and a perfect adaptation to his present position as I understand it.

"You will understand that I am not an advocate of Martin Van Buren for the presidency. He is not my choice, but if he shall be fairly selected candidate of this Convention, then, I say I shall be for him. . . ." Giddings was again interrupted by resounding applause. "Whoever is put forth, I will regard as my political brother. . . ."

While the Free Soil spellbinders were holding sway under the Big Tent, the Committee of Conferees, composed equally of former Liberty, Whig, and Democratic representatives, worked on a platform that would bind them all together as a true political entity. Dignified and effective, old Benjamin F. Butler, Van Buren's representative, was appointed to chair the platform committee.

The Liberty men were represented on the committee by the sophisticated anti-slavery lawyer, Salmon P. Chase, who had worked with James G. Birney a decade earlier in Ohio on fugitive slave cases. The 40-year-old Chase would be elected to the U. S. Senate from Ohio as a Free Soiler and serve until 1855, when he would be elected Governor of Ohio on the Free Soil/Democratic ticket. He would be re-elected as a Republican in 1857, and then sent to the U. S. Senate in 1860, as a Republican, before being appointed as Lincoln's Secretary of the Treasury, and eventually Chief Justice of the Supreme Court. Joshua Leavitt, publisher of *The Emancipator*, and Henry B. Stanton, both American Anti-Slavery Society colleagues of Birney, also spoke for the Liberty men during the platform deliberations.

Congressman Preston King and Benjamin Butler led the Democratic contingent on the committee. Various caucuses meeting in City Hall and the hotels put forward planks for a provisional document. Chase and King drafted the final language. The Committee of Conferees then worked late that first night under the Big Tent to finish and unanimously adopt the platform.

The next morning, August 10, thousands of Free Soil men of the entire Convention happily endorsed the document after Chase read its provisions from a wooden podium. "Whereas, We have assembled in Convention, as a union of Freemen, for the sake of Freedom, forgetting all past political differences in a common resolve to maintain the Rights of Free Labor against the aggressions of the Slave Power, and to secure Free Soil for a Free People," its preamble began.

"And whereas, The political Conventions recently assembled at Baltimore and Philadelphia, the one stifling the voice of a great constituency entitled to be heard in its deliberations [referring to the Barnburners], and the other abandoning its distinctive principles for mere availability [referring to Taylor and the Whigs], have dissolved the national party organizations heretofore existing by nominating for the

Chief Magistracy of the United States, under slave-holding dictation, candidates neither of whom can be supported by the opponents of slavery extension without a sacrifice of consistency, duty, and self-respect," Chase intoned. The large body agreed by its ovation.

"And whereas, These nominations so made furnish the occasion and demonstrate the necessity of the Union of people under the banner of Free Democracy [a phrase that reflected the strength of the Barnburners who had taken the lead in organizing this extraordinary affair], in a solemn and formal declaration of their independence of the Slave Power, and of their fixed determination to rescue the Federal Government from its control," Chase paused to let the logic of the propositions sink in and then continued.

"Resolved, therefore, That we, the people here assembled, remembering the example of our Fathers in the days of the first Declaration of Independence, putting our trust in God for the triumph of our cause, and invoking His guidance in our endeavors to advance it, do now plant ourselves upon the National Platform of Freedom in opposition to the Sectional Platform of Slavery."

However, unlike the Liberty Party that stood for Immediate Abolition, the first Free Soil plank proposed "no interference by Congress with slavery within the limits of any state." Thus, they declared that slavery depended upon state law alone, as stipulated by the U. S. Constitution, and conceded that Congress had no power over slavery in the states. Northern states already had repudiated slavery. So would Southern states, someday, but it must spread no further into the territories, the Free Soilers declared.

(This was the position taken six years later by the new Republican Party founded in 1854, and the position subscribed to by Abraham Lincoln when he ran for President in 1860. They reasoned that as immoral as it may be, slavery might exist in the individual states of the South, as long as those states so legislated, because that was how the Constitution was constructed. That was the compromise without which there would be no "United States." Free Soilers, like Whigs and Democrats from which they were drawn, were loyal to the Constitution and Union above all civic values. Ultimately, only Civil War would offer Lincoln the legal escape from the constitutional dilemma, since a Constitutional Amendment to abolish slavery would never pass the South. Only war powers granted the President under the Constitution could be used to abolish slavery, Lincoln understood, as a necessary step to military victory.)

The second plank of the "National Platform of Freedom," however, recounted the efforts of Jefferson and the Congress to keep slavery out of the territories, including the Ordinance of 1787 that prohibited it from the Northwest Territory, proving that, "it was the settled policy of the nation, not to extend, nationalize or encourage, but to limit, localize, and discourage slavery; and to this policy, which should never have been departed from, the Government ought to return."

The third plank reaffirmed the great national purposes "to establish Justice, promote the general welfare, and secure the blessings of Liberty." These clear affirmations satisfied the Liberty men in attendance and across the nation, who mostly abandoned their old party for this new one. The new Free Soil Party also denounced all attempts to compromise over the slavery issue in Congress, as had been done with the Missouri Compromise of 1820, and as would occur again two years later with the Compromise of 1850. They began from where they were in the choices that faced the nation.

The Federal Government had no power to deprive anyone of life, Liberty, or property without the due process of law. Therefore, the Free Soil National Platform of Freedom declared Congress could not institute slavery in new sections of the nation. Further, Free Soilers maintained that Congress had the duty to abolish slavery where it possessed the power to do so, such as in the City of Washington. It emphasized that Congress had no more power "to make a king than to make a slave."

The Free Soil platform also demanded "freedom for Oregon" from the British. Inclusion of Oregon in the Union was the basis of the appeal in Polk's slogan "48/40 or Fight" that rallied Democrats in 1844. But those particular boundaries had been compromised away with the British as a condition of peace. Free Soilers also believed in Manifest Destiny, but that destiny had to be one of freedom for all.

The Free Soil platform then passed onto other issues that party founders hoped would broaden its appeal among voters. "We demand cheap postage, retrenchment of the expenses and patronage of the Federal Government, the abolition of all unnecessary offices and salaries; and the election by the people of all civil officers in the service of the Government, so far as the same may be practicable." These were issues particularly important to Democrats. The party implied it favored the election of U.S. Senators, a prerogative at the time delegated to state legislatures, and an idea that didn't become law for over half a century. Free Soilers, like the Democrats, stood in opposition to a growing Government bureaucracy.

To attract Whigs and Western men, the new party declared in favor of Clay's "internal improvements" of harbors, rivers, and canals, which in the past the Democracy had simply held to be unconstitutional. Additionally, Free Soilers called for passage of a homestead law to help settlers move west. To further attract Whigs, the platform extolled "early payment of public debt and the tariff for revenue." The tariff, the platform affirmed, protected American industry, even though it boosted product prices, and it created Government revenue which reduced any need for taxes. But it should not go much further in protecting special economic interests, a concession to Democracy. On most of the traditional policy questions, former Democrats gave in to former Whigs, perhaps anticipating a pay off in the presidential nomination.

Wild cheering by delegates and spectators greeted Chase as he read each provision to the full Convention, indicating that the first step in solidifying their alliance had been successful. Again and again, the frenzied crowd roared, "Free Soil, Free Speech, Free Labor, Free Men."

Many in the assembly wept as Chase read the momentous document that declared the ideals of their new political party. From the press tables, newsmen sent telegraph dispatches to newspapers across the land reporting the Free Soil provisions, some with ebullience, others with wary caution. Most established party papers responded with scorn.

Once the platform was unanimously endorsed by the delegates and saluted by the Free Soil men inside the Big Tent on the morning of August 10, attention turned to the question of the presidency. Each faction had a preferred candidate for nomination as the party's first standard-barer. In the Committee on Conferees, possible nominees had been debated previously.

Chase upset the Whigs by withdrawing the name of Associate Supreme Court Justice McLean. Prior to the Convention, Chase, who was McLean's son-in-law, had urged the respected jurist to allow his name to be submitted for the Free Soil nomination. Finding little enthusiasm on the Judge's part, Chase decided to announce that McLean did not wish to have his name considered. His decision disappointed Adams and the other Whigs in Buffalo who saw McLean as the only viable alternative to Van Buren.

(It would be the same with McLean at the 1856 and 1860 Republican National Conventions. The aging Justice had many admirers, especially after his dissenting vote in favor of freeing the escaped slave Dred Scott in 1857. After the Free Soil Convention, he told Adams that he would have accepted the nomination if it had been extended. Adams suspected that Chase, who harbored presidential ambitions himself throughout his career, simply did not want McLean to win the office. Ultimately, the old jurist never strayed from the bench.)

Abolitionist Henry B. Stanton presented a letter from U. S. Senator John P. Hale, of New Hampshire, saying he endorsed the Convention and its work. Hale wrote that he was ready to submit to its will, whatever that may be. Candidate letters to political Conventions were common ways for potential nominees to directly communicate with delegates; but decorum and modesty prevailed. Hale was passionately favored by most of the Liberty men. In fact, Hale already had been nominated for President by the Liberty Party in 1847, along with Leicester King, of Ohio, for Vice President. But Democrats and Whigs at the Free Soil Convention feared Hale's outspoken Abolitionism on the floor of the U.S. Senate would drive away voters.

The names of Congressman Joshua R. Giddings, the early voice for Abolition in Congress, and Charles Francis Adams were put forward for the presidential honor by various members of the committee. Benjamin Butler then argued that Martin Van Buren would offer the party's best hope because of his experience as President. He avoided the fact the nation suffered a terrible depression during his one term.

A year earlier, the New York Barnburners, who hosted this Convention and were numerous at the Buffalo confab, had been pushing their former Governor Silas Wright for the presidency as a Democrat. As a U. S. Senator, Wright was nicknamed "the Cato of the Senate," because of his stoic, moral rectitude. He had been elected New York Governor in 1844, and that year turned down the Democratic nomination for Vice President. But he had died suddenly. Barnburners blamed his political "murder" on the Hunkers who had betrayed him during his lost 1846 gubernatorial re-election campaign. In fact, the New York State Convention a year earlier had broken into riot over Wright's "murder." James Wadsworth, an upstate aristocratic rebel from Livingston County, had jumped upon a table beside that Convention's podium and yelled out, "Silas Wright might be dead, but we can still do Justice to his cause."

Then at an October 26, 1847, mass meeting of 4,000 in a field outside Herkimer, New York, the Barnburners had endorsed the Wilmot Proviso and declared their independence from the state Democratic Party. Congressman John Van Buren had stood out at the meeting with his organizational and speaking skills. When the Barnburners met again in Utica in June 1848, they turned back to their old hero, Martin Van Buren, who was by then converted to the anti-slavery cause. All the passion for Wright and over the events of the past year poured out in Buffalo in the Barnburners' effort to secure the nomination for "Little Van."

Some of the Whigs at Buffalo, and many more in the distant states that they represented, were reluctant to support the former Democrat President under any conditions. Van Buren was their long-despised political enemy. They could not forget that for the sake of party unity between Democrats North and South, Van Buren had promised to veto any law freeing the slaves of Washington D. C. And as Jackson's Vice President presiding over the Senate, he had helped pass the hated gag rule.

Now with national conditions changed, Martin Van Buren renounced both positions. His recent 15,000-word treatise tracing the constitutional authority of Congress to prohibit slavery in the territories had inspired anti-slavery activists. Southern Democrats insisted Congress had no power to deny slavery in those new areas of the nation. Van Buren and the Barnburners vehemently disagreed. They argued that Slave

Labor and Free Labor could not exist side by side. Van Buren wrote that free workers "are unwilling to share evils of a condition so degraded and the deprivation of the society of their own class. . . . " His manifesto contained the entire Free Soil argument. Free men could not tolerate slavery among them.

The 65-year-old Van Buren himself was skeptical about this new fourth party. He feared a schism in the Democratic Party would simply elect a Whig rather than a Democrat. Yet, he no longer wanted any part of Polk, his Southern allies, or the "doughfaces," who were the Northern men with Southern principles like the Democracy's candidate, Senator Lewis Cass, who offended him. And Cass had been one of those who blocked Van Buren's attempt to regain the nomination at the 1844 Democratic Convention in Baltimore. To deprive his rival of the presidency by splitting the Democrats might have been one of Van Buren's motives and satisfactions.

To convince the reluctant in Buffalo, David Dudley Field then read the delegates on the Committee of Conferees an August 2, 1848, letter from Van Buren to the Convention. First, the former President recounted how his name had been endorsed against his will by the Utica Convention. But, second, he pointed out that "the using of my name was necessary to enable the ever faithful Democracy of New York to sustain themselves in the extraordinary position into which they had been driven by the injustice of others. . . ."

The former President then wrote of the business at hand. "The Convention, of which you form a part, may, if wisely conducted, be productive of more important consequences than any which has gone before it, save only that which formed the Federal Constitution. In one respect it will be wholly unlike any political Convention which has been held in the United States since the present organization of parties. It will, in a great degree, be composed of individuals, who have all their lives been arrayed on different sides of politics, state and national and who still differ in regard to most of the questions that have arisen in the administration of the respective Governments, but who feel themselves called upon, by consideration of the highest import, to suspend the rival action upon other subjects, and unite their common efforts for the accomplishment of a single end—the prevention of the introduction of human slavery into the extensive territories of the United States now exempt from that great evil, and which are destined, if properly treated, to be speedily converted into a wilderness of free minds."

Van Buren continued, "I need not say how cordially I concur in the sentiment which regards this great object as one sacred in the sight of Heaven, the accomplishment of which is due to the memories of those great and Just men, long since, we trust, made perfect in its courts, who laid the foundations of our Government, and made, as they fondly hoped, adequate provision for its perpetuity and success, and indispensable to the future honor and paramount welfare of our entire confederacy." He then wrote that if they wished to pick another as their nominee, "it would be most satisfactory to my feelings and wishes."

In the Committee of Conferees deliberations, the Liberty men were happy enough with the strong anti-slavery platform to yield to the Democratic majority on its candidate. But Van Buren had been a lifelong enemy of the Adams family. However, Charles Francis had already declared his principles above men. Despite Whig hesitancies, Van Buren got their nod and that of the Committee, primarily, they thought, because his presidential stature would gain the attention of the entire nation.

Although an alleged deal had been made for Van Buren, Liberty delegates in the Committee on Conferees were still greatly enthusiastic for Senator Hale. And Ohio Whigs spoke fondly in favor of Giddings. But when the first informal Free Soil ballot was taken, 244 delegates rose in support of Van Buren. Hale drew a spirited 183 votes. Giddings trailed with 23 votes. Adams attracted 13 and 3 votes went to Ellsworth. The Committee on Conferees then unanimously recommended Van Buren. Next the Committee made Adams its vice presidential nominee. He was the choice of nearly everyone. "He's the man for this day and time," an old farmer told author and lawyer Richard H. Dana, a co-founder of the party.

On the evening of August 10, 1848, back under the Big Tent, Chase rose to inform the entire Convention of thousands that the Committee of Conferees had unanimously decided upon former President Martin Van Buren to represent the Free Soil Party at the polls in November. His announcement was greeted with excited cheering. Then, Joshua Leavitt, "one of the blackest of the Abolitionists," as his opponents said, stood up to recount the history of the Liberty Party in a solemn testimony. He recited the importance of its goals. Then the Liberty man moved to make Van Buren's Free Soil nomination unanimous. Leavitt hailed Van Buren as "our glorious old man in the battle against the Slave Power."

Many in the crowd wept at the passion of the old Abolitionist's explanation. Samuel Lewis seconded Leavitt, and the entire Convention unanimously endorsed his nomination with wild cheers. Celebration broke loose and the names of Van Buren and Adams were heralded again and again in rousing cheers. Hats were thrown high and banners bearing Van Buren's name were unfurled. Free Soil slogans rang through the Big Tent. The old political wounds were forgotten and a new movement for freedom was launched.

The melding of dissident Liberty men, anti-slavery Whigs, and Democrats into a Free Soil Party was complete. The Convention adjourned. A giant parade of banners streaming, drums beating, and supporters shouting, "Van Buren and Free Soil, Adams and Liberty" marched out of the Big Tent into the streets of Buffalo. That evening, torchlight parades wound through the main streets in raucous celebration. In the hotel lobbies and city saloons exuberant participants loudly boasted that they could win the national election in November by converting other Whigs and Democrats everywhere in the North to their cause. They then dispersed to hold Free Soil ratification Conventions in their home states.

Two weeks later, Martin Van Buren sent his letter of acceptance to the officers of the Buffalo Convention. He again declared in favor of freeing the slaves of Washington and avowed his support for the Wilmot Proviso. His words were widely quoted in newspapers across the North. But his reception was far from friendly. The Free Soil ticket was denounced by Whigs such as Massachusetts Governor Briggs and Harvard President Edward Everett (who later became Secretary of State under Millard Fillmore and a Republican Senator). Daniel Webster trusted Zachary Taylor more than he did his arch enemy Van Buren and stuck with the party he had helped form. Whig stump speakers had a field day hurling Adams' earlier printed denunciations of Van Buren back in his face.

Newspapers such as the Buffalo *Commercial Advertiser*, a Whig paper, reminded readers that as President, Van Buren had opposed internal improvements and was likely to let them down. The Buffalo *Daily Courier*, a Democratic voice, called the Convention "a political monstrosity." President Polk denounced Van Buren for splintering the Democratic Party he had created with Jackson, and for crushing the election hopes for Senator Cass. "Mr. Van Buren is the most fallen man I have ever known," Polk bitterly proclaimed upon hearing of his nomination. The Convention also unleashed the ire of Southerners who were already talking about secession.

Word of the Buffalo Convention's outcome spread quickly and rallied anti-slavery voters across the North and West. Free Soil converts, old Democrats, Whigs, and Liberty men held their own ratification Conventions in towns and cities across the country. Charles Sumner wrote: "Henceforward, protection to Man will be the true American system . . . The old and ill-compacted party organizations are broken and from their ruins are now formed a new party, the Party of Freedom."

Chicago hosted a large meeting for Illinois Free Soilers on August 22. Ohio Free Soilers endorsed the nominations of Van Buren and Adams at a Cincinnati mass meeting that drew thousands on August 25. Two Free Soil meetings a day reputedly were held in Ohio all the way to the November election. In preparation for Wisconsin's first presidential election, Milwaukee held its endorsement Convention on August 26. Other mass rallies convened at Indianapolis, and Ottawa, Illinois, on August 30. In September, New York's Senator John Adams Dix accepted the state Free Soil nomination for Governor, a post he would eventually occupy from 1873 to 1875. Thousands more traveled to Ann Arbor, Michigan, on September 20, and to Iowa City at the end of the month. With each meeting, the hopes of Free Soil advocates rose, and the concerns of both Democrats and Whigs grew. Political uncertainty escalated and new political shifts were occurring that would carry the nation into Civil War twelve years later.

Electoral slates were organized by the experienced Free Soil politicians in a way that the Liberty Party could never manage. In all states that sent delegates to Buffalo, ballots endorsing the Free Soil ticket were printed and ready for voters. Eight years earlier, state Liberty Party enthusiasts had often failed to print party ballots, and that failure cost thousands of votes for their cause on Election Day.

The 1848 campaign was a memorable one. In October, Liberty nominee Senator Hale withdrew to make way for Free Soil candidate Van Buren. However, other Liberty men, who were purists on the issue of Immediate Abolition, could not tolerate the Van Buren nomination. And they wanted the November debate on slavery to center on the South where the crime was worst, not simply in the sparsely populated new territories. They clung to Liberty League nominee Gerrit Smith.

The *Democrat*, owned by Chicago Democratic Congressman "Long John" Wentworth, seemed to warm to the Free Soil call in late summer. But Wentworth, who turned out to be a party jumper himself when the Republicans came along, ultimately protected his position in Congress by endorsing Cass. The battle of the old parties to hold onto their constituencies intensified throughout the fall in state after state.

At first, some Whig papers believed that the Free Soil movement was fracturing the Democracy more than their unstable party, and encouraged the Free Soil split of the Democrats. "Cheering indeed it is to Whigs," concluded the *Chicago Journal*. But as the Free Soilers gained momentum, Whigs too feared that they might hurt Taylor. They took to proclaiming that their Whig nominee, a Mississippi slave owner, was opposed to the extension of slavery. (Indeed, that turned out to be the case.) The *Milwaukee Sentinel* also reminded readers of Birney's 1844 "crime" which had deprived their beloved Henry Clay of the presidency. The paper sternly warned voters against falling for the same Abolitionist "third party swindle."

Whigs charged Van Buren with consorting with "long-haired and wild-eyed Abolitionists." Daniel Webster laughed that "the leader of the free soil party" had once headed the "free spoil party." But Sumner on the stump argued, "It is not for the Van Buren of 1838 that we are to vote, but for the Van Buren of today; the veteran statesman, sagacious, determined, experienced, who, at an age when most men are rejoicing to put off their armor, girds himself anew and enters the lists of champions of Freedom."

Meanwhile, the Michigan Whig central committee cautioned that, "Every Whig vote given to a third candidate helps to elect Cass. . . ." It also claimed the Whig Party was the "true free soil party. . . ." Ultimately, most Whigs who had not attended the Buffalo Convention could not vote for Van Buren under any circumstance. As Giddings bitterly wrote to Sumner during the campaign, "There is a large class of Whigs, however, that would come to the support of almost any man who will not support him."

Yet, as many as seventy newspapers in the Northwest took up the Free Soil cause. Hope among its supporters continued to increase throughout the fall canvass. As a result, the campaign became as raucous and acrimonious as any presidential contest in the nation's short history. Personal attacks on the candidates were the standard fare. "He who still for Cass can be, is a Cass without the 'C,' " Whig jokesters such as Lincoln laughed. Van Buren's Democratic detractors called him a "traitor" to the great Democracy of Jackson and Jefferson, and a "hypocrite" on the issue of slavery, about which he had done nothing when he had the power to act. Orators of both parties recounted his past anti-Abolitionist pronouncements. Nervous Northern Democrats tried to cut the ground under Van Buren with electoral slogans like "Cass and Free Soil."

On Election Day, November 7, 1848, the first in which all states voted for President on the same day, fifteen states declared for Taylor and the Whigs and fifteen for Cass and the Democrats. But General Taylor emerged victorious with 1,360,099 popular and 163 Electoral votes to Senator Cass's 1,220,544 popular and 127 Electoral votes. The Free Soil Party won a total of just nine votes in Virginia, and none in the other Southern states.

But as the Liberty Party had done four years earlier, the Free Soilers brought their influence to bear on the outcome, this time fatally wounding the Democrats. Van Buren's 291,263 Free Soil votes gave the election to Taylor and the Whigs, just as Liberty Party votes for James G. Birney had elected the Democrat Polk. Van Buren and the Free Soil Party failed to win a single Electoral vote. But in New York State, they split the Democratic majority and that was enough to block Cass from the presidency. New York Democrats tasted the bitter tang of Whig Hamilton Fish's election as New York Governor.

Once again, New York decided the election. Van Buren polled 120,510 to Cass' 114,318, while Taylor tolled 218,583 and took the state. Whigs also won in Fillmore's home county of Erie where the Free Soilers had met in Convention, with 7,606 votes to 3,364 for Cass. Van Buren and Adams finished last with only 2,359 Erie votes.

Even in defeat, the anti-slavery forces showed they were on the march. In Ohio, the Free Soilers tallied 35,354. But Cass won, in part, because more Whigs than Democrats defected to the Free Soil Party. Free Soilers pulled three times more Illinois voters than the Liberty Party had done four years earlier. Wisconsin had the highest proportion of Free Soil voters in the West, with 28 percent. Wisconsin also elected former Liberty man, Charles Durkee, as its Free Soil representative to Congress.

Cass lost in Massachusetts, and a strong Free Soil turn-out took 29 percent of the vote. Taylor gained only a plurality. He was given the Electoral votes by the Whigs in the Massachusetts state legislature. Elbridge Spaulding was sent to Congress from Boston. (Adams eventually served in Congress from 1859 to 1861, before being appointed by Lincoln as U.S. Minister to England trying to keep the British neutral during the Civil War.) The Free Soil Party did even better in Vermont.

Besides taking a tenth of the electorate and raising the slavery issue higher onto the national agenda, the Free Soil Party won nine Congressional seats in Northern states and hence increased the power of the anti-slavery coalition in Congress. In coming elections, the Free Soilers would take over the state legislature of Massachusetts. Activists such as John Van Buren and Charles Francis Adams were invigorated by the growing strength of the anti-slavery movement and vowed that the 1848 Free Soil effort was only the beginning in their crusade for freedom. But that would not be the case. Most Free Soil activists and voters slipped back to their original parties.

Taylor, the nation's twelfth President, surprised those who thought he was in the grasp of the Slave Power. He endorsed the Wilmot Proviso, in spirit, by prohibiting the spread of slavery into the new territories acquired from Mexico. He was a Southern man with Northern principles. But tensions were rapidly increasing. On January 21, 1850, a decade before actual war, Congressman Thomas L. Clingham, of North Carolina, proclaimed the South's "right of session," if the Federal Government tried to interfere with slavery. President Taylor treated all calls for session by the South with scorn. But the great divide between North and South was widening.

To repair the breech, Daniel Webster, Henry Clay, and John C. Calhoun carried on negotiations which ultimately became the Compromise of 1850. Their agreement would prohibit the slave trade in the nation's capital, the City of Washington, although it did not outlaw slavery there. President Taylor refused to sign their compromise. He opposed most of the provisions that favored the South. A nine-state Southern Convention added to the tensions with a call to extend the Missouri Compromise all the way to the Pacific, hence spreading slavery through the lower region of the proposed State of California. To make matters worse, Texas threatened to extend its claim into the newly acquired New Mexico territory, until President Taylor threatened to send in troops to repulse the Texans. Unfortunately, two years after assuming office, Taylor became sick with cholera after eating cherries at a July Fourth celebration. He died on July 9, at age 65.

Millard Fillmore then became New York's second United States President. Fillmore had started his career as a teacher in Buffalo while he studied law. He had helped establish the city's free public school system, the first in the nation to drop any tuition charges. He'd been elected to the state Assembly in 1828 as an Anti-Mason, a movement that sought to root out secret influences of Government. Later, he became a founding member of the Whigs. Elected to Congress for seven terms, beginning in 1832, Fillmore eventually served as Chair of the Ways and Means Committee. He had voted against tabling Abolitionist petitions. For state political reasons, he ran for and was elected New York State Comptroller in 1847. Then, as Taylor's Vice President, he had presided over the Senate for two years with dignity and skill, and those attributes served him well in the presidency.

But Fillmore's most enduring act as President was to sign the series of bills that became known as the Great Compromise of 1850, which Taylor had resisted. To quiet the anti-slavery sentiment of the North, the final compromise called for the suppression of the slave trade in the nation's capital and admission of California to the Union as a Free State. It also suggested Cass's popular sovereignty as a way for settlers of new states to solve the question of slavery.

In return, the South was provided with a promise that the North would enforce the Fugitive Slave laws. The act provided for a $1,000 fine and six months in prison for aiding an escaped slave, plus another $1,000 in damages to the slave owner. It also established enforcement commissions with the right of "posse comitatus." Fillmore, who had stood in opposition to slavery, faced a terrible dilemma. In 1850, the Slave States were threatening rebellion if he didn't sign. Clay and Webster finally convinced him that civil war would be a worse choice than their compromise. Fillmore finally agreed. In so doing, he signed his own political death warrant and covered his name with dishonor, Abolitionists felt. Man hunters in search of "escaped slaves" infested the North. With Fillmore's signature, the national crisis passed and eleven years of peace followed before civil war broke loose across the land. However, the compromise set off fierce protests in the North and ruptured the Whig Party, making it impossible to elect another Whig President.

Fearing a future of civil war, Fillmore issued one presidential address in which he denounced the "misdirected and pernicious zeal" of the Abolitionists. Rather, he called for freeing and colonizing all the nation's slaves in either Haiti or Africa, at U.S. Government expense. If that was not done, Fillmore predicted, a race uprising like that which had occurred in Santa Domingo, was almost certain. The old Buffalo politician feared that would result in "the utter extermination of the black race." That last prediction was suppressed before Fillmore delivered his message.

While the Free Soil Party fell short of its goal, it ultimately helped bring California and Oregon into the Union as a Free States, brought about the repeal of the Black Laws of Ohio, was responsible for fifteen party members entering the House of Representatives, electing Senators Chase and Sumner, and giving control of the state legislatures to Free Soilers in Massachusetts, New York, Ohio, and Wisconsin. Above all, the Free Soil Party had pushed the issue of slavery closer to the top of the national agenda and accelerated the disintegration of the nation's two leading political parties.

The North American (Know-Nothing) Party Presidential Nominating Convention and the Election of 1856

Convention-at-a-Glance

Event: The North American (Know-Nothing) Party Presidential Nominating Convention
Date: June 1856
Location: Secret location in New York City
New York Governor: Myron H. Clark, Fusion-Republican
New York City Mayor: Fernando Wood, Democrat

Number of Delegates: Secret
Candidates for Nomination: John Charles Fremont, California; Speaker of the House Nathaniel Prentiss Banks, Massachusetts; and perhaps others unknown
Presidential Nominee: Nathaniel P. Banks
Age of Nominee: 40
Vice Presidential Nominee: William F. Johnston, Pennsylvania
Platform Positions: Secret; but generally, protection of the Rights of American-born citizens over immigrants; Americans electing Americans; a twenty-one-year residency requirement to hold any public office; prohibition against slavery in the territories.
Campaign Slogan: "100 Percent American"

The North American (Know-Nothing) Party Presidential Nominating Convention and the Election of 1856

"Americans must rule America."—American Party platform

In the Spring of 1854, President Franklin Pierce, of New Hampshire, and his Democrat-dominated Congress passed the Kansas-Nebraska Act which broke the Nebraska Territory in half and allowed each section to determine by democratic vote, a policy known as popular sovereignty, whether or not the territory would apply to the Union as a Free or Slave State. The effect was to overturn the Missouri Compromise of 1820 that had outlawed the extension of slavery north of latitude 36 degrees and 30 minutes. Anti-slavery sentiment had grown rapidly over the decade since the Liberty Party first ran James G. Birney for President in 1840. Riots broke out in Northern cities protesting the Kansas legislation. Senator Stephen Arnold Douglas, of Illinois, who introduced the bill, grimly joked that he could travel on a train from Boston to Chicago at night by the light of his own burning effigy.

Both North and South financed settlers to pour into Kansas as homesteaders to vote on a state constitution. The pro-slavery forces won the election and established a Government at Lecompton with a pro-slavery constitution. Kansas was consumed by uncontrolled violence. An anti-slavery government was also established at Topeka. Two Governors, two legislatures, and two militias, one pro-slavery, the other anti-slavery, engaged in the first skirmishes of civil war. The young and handsome Democratic President Franklin Pierce, who had been elected in a landslide in 1852 as the voice of "young America," sent troops to enforce the results of the pro-slavery state election as prescribed by law. His popularity in the North dissolved and his chances for re-election disappeared.

Then, on February 24, 1854, the Republican Party was founded in Ripon, Wisconsin. The new party, a coalition of former Whigs, Free Soilers, and anti-Nebraska Democrats, spread like wildfire across a dry prairie. In the mid-term congressional election that autumn, Democrats lost thirty-one seats to a coalition of Republican, National-Americans, and temperance crusaders. Even before they held their first Presidential Nominating Convention in Philadelphia two years later, the new Republicans were optimistic they could win the presidency in 1856 and stop the spread of slavery into the territories.

Another surging group was the Order of the Star Spangled

77

Banner, popularly known as the "Know-Nothings" or National American Party. Know-Nothings, who were upset because President Pierce appointed a Catholic to his Cabinet, voted in large numbers in 1854 against the Democrats. The name "Know-Nothings" first appeared in Horace Greeley's *New York Tribune* on November 10, 1853. The term was coined because members responded, "I Know Nothing" when asked about their secret organization. The Know-Nothings decided to run a candidate for President in 1856. The party was notoriously anti-Catholic and anti-foreigner at a time when rioters were burning Catholic churches in U.S. cities to protest the foreign immigrant invasion.

The "nativist" movement had been gaining momentum for years. In New York City, Samuel F. B. Morse, painter and later inventor of the telegraph, had unsuccessfully run for mayor in 1836 supported by the Native American Democratic Association. He received just seventy-seven votes. The anti-immigrant impulse was further fueled by a fierce public reaction to an 1840 law proposed by Whig Governor William H. Seward, Lincoln's future Secretary of State, to supply public school funds to foreign-born students and teachers so they could learn in their own tongue. Anti-Catholic secret societies sprang up almost overnight and within a few years there were over fifty in New York City alone. On election night 1842, an anti-Catholic mob looted Irish sections of the city and stoned the residence of Bishop Hughes.

In the 1844 mayoral contest, James Harper, a publisher and nativist, had been victorious, with the help of fellow publisher Thurlow Weed, a Whig. A majority of nativists were also elected to the New York City Common Council that year. (New York mayoral elections took place every year from 1834 until 1852, when two-year terms began. Four-year mayoral terms became the rule in New York City with the 1905 election.)

The nativist movement was further stimulated by a massive influx of Irish immigrants from 1845 to 1850. Nearly half-a-million had fled the "old sod" in search of a new beginning. Once here, they were met by the anti-Catholic, American Protestant Union, which was founded in New York City in 1845. In the mid-1840s, an anti-Catholic was elected mayor in Boston as well, and Massachusetts chose a nativist Governor for three consecutive terms. New York and Pennsylvania sent nativists to Congress. In New York, Know-Nothings were first publicly known as the Order of the Star-Spangled Banner, founded in 1850, a top-down organization, with secret oaths, handshakes, and slogans. Among the oaths, members vowed to vote against all foreigners and Catholics.

After the Whigs were decisively defeated in the 1852 election, many party members, particularly Southern Whigs, signed up with the National Americans. That year, former President Millard Fillmore was denied the Whig nomination. General Winfield Scott, the Whig nominee, then lost the presidential election, winning only four Northern states after declaring his Abolitionist sympathies. Fillmore, who began his political career as an Anti-Mason, moved to take over the National American Party. His followers worked their way into the various Know-Nothing lodges across the country, which were top-down organizations, bringing the doctrine of patriotism and sanctity of the Union to go along with nativism, thus giving the lodges new vitality and direction.

On George Washington's birthday, February 22, 1856, the National Know-Nothing Lodge emerged from secrecy to meet in Philadelphia in preparation for the presidential election. Local lodges sent 227 delegates from twenty-seven states to nominate a candidate for President and to advise lodge members how to vote. The Know-Nothing assembly reaffirmed allegiance, "to the Federal Union, as the palladium of our civil and religious liberties." It also declared, "Americans must rule America" and that native-born citizens should be selected for all state, Federal, or municipal offices and Government employment. The party sought to make, "a continued residence of twenty-one years an indispensable requisite for citizenship." And it called for "excluding all paupers or persons convicted of crime from landing upon our shore, but no interference with the vested Rights of foreigners."

The National American Party Convention in Philadelphia also declared "opposition to the reckless and unwise policy of the present administration in general management of our national affairs . . . as shown in an insolent and cowardly bravado toward the weaker powers, as shown in reopening sectional agitation by repeal of the Missouri Compromise . . . as shown by the corruptions which pervade some of the departments of Government . . ."

So far, the delegates had agreed in their xenophobia. But when it came to the question of what to do about slavery in the territories once the issue had been broached, the National American Convention suddenly split asunder. Many delegates from New York, New England, Pennsylvania, Ohio, Illinois, and Iowa bolted from the meeting, leaving behind the pro-slavery majority. They determined to reconvene in New York and proclaim their anti-slavery sentiments.

The National Americans remaining in the City of Brotherly Love renamed themselves the American Party and called for, "the unequaled recognition and maintenance of the reserved Rights of the several states," which meant the perpetuation of slavery, and "the cultivation of harmony and fraternal good will between the citizens of the several states, and to this end, the non-interference by Congress with questions pertaining solely to the individual states . . . ." The American Party Convention then nominated Millard Fillmore as its presidential candidate, and named Andrew J. Donelson, of Tennessee, as its candidate for Vice President.

The "National Democracy," as the Democratic Party now called itself in contrast to the "sectional" Republicans, held its Presidential

Nominating Convention at Cincinnati in early June, 1856, the first National Democratic Convention outside of Baltimore and the first in the "West." A standoff developed between delegates supporting President Pierce, Senator Stephen A. Douglas, of Illinois, and James Buchanan, of Pennsylvania. On the Seventeenth Ballot, that Convention finally nominated Buchanan for President, and named Kentucky Congressman John C. Breckinridge as his running mate. Buchanan had served five terms in the House of Representatives and in the Senate from 1834 to 1845, before President Polk appointed him Secretary of State. President Pierce had made Buchanan U.S. Minister to Great Britain, so he was out of the country during the recent Kansas/Nebraska turmoil and therefore had a slight advantage over the other candidates, a kind of Democratic "availability."

The new Republican Party kicked off its presidential quest in Philadelphia on June 17 through 19, 1856, meeting in Musical Fund Hall in Broad Street. The new party called for restoration of the Missouri Compromise, prohibition of slavery and bigamy in the territories, immediate admission of Kansas to the Union as a Free State, opposition to admission of Cuba to the Union because it practiced slavery, and Federal funding of internal improvements including a transcontinental railroad, old Whig positions.

During that same June week, the Northern faction of the National American Party reconvened in secret Convention somewhere in New York City to nominate its own candidates. It became known as the North American Party. Many North Americans were sympathetic with the Republican cause. They wanted to nominate whomever the Republicans nominated. In fact, the decision of whom the Republicans would nominate had been made shortly before the First Republican National Convention by party elders in a meeting at the Maryland home of Francis P. Blair, an old friend of Andrew Jackson's and publisher of the influential *Washington Globe*. The word was passed to delegates who enthusiastically endorsed their choice for President.

(Many of the Free Soil Democrats who attended the 1848 Buffalo Convention ultimately became founders of the Republican Party. At the 1856 Republican National Convention in Philadelphia, Republican delegates devotedly gave up their seats to veterans of the 1848 Free Soil Convention. And David Wilmot, an anti-slavery Democrat and author of the famed Wilmot Proviso, was later to serve as the Temporary President of the 1860 Chicago Convention that nominated Lincoln. Horace Greeley claimed he named the party, but others including Joseph Medill had suggested the Republican tag as well.)

The new Republican founders eliminated the influential New York Senator William H. Seward and anti-slavery crusading Ohio Governor Salmon P. Chase as potential candidates because they were believed to be too Abolitionist by voters to win a general election. Even though they were party founders, they were passed over. Supreme Court Justice John McLean was crossed out because he was too old. Instead, following the precedent of Franklin Pierce's youthful campaign of 1852, the powerful group selected a young explorer who manifest the spirit of America's western "destiny," a national hero whose exploits blazing a trail to California had been followed by newspaper readers east of the Mississippi. John Charles Fremont, California's first Senator, known as "the Pathfinder" for his daring exploits, became the first Republican candidate for President.

Greeley and Thurlow Weed, New York's leading former Whigs and Republican co-founders, relayed this and other information to the North Americans who were meeting in New York City. The two powerful newspaper publishers kept in close touch with both the Know-Nothing and Republican Conventions and helped relay messages back and forth between New York and Philadelphia.

The North American Party responded. They too wanted to nominate John C. Fremont for President to stand against Buchanan and the Democracy, and against their former society fellow, Millard Fillmore. Their followers were many and word of the secret society's Convention choice would bring out thousands of voters for the Republican candidate. The North Americans sent their message to the Philadelphia Convention offering to work in concert. Their letter of June 17, 1856, was hand-delivered to the First Republican National Convention in Philadelphia.

The letter was read the next day by Edwin Denison Morgan, the Republicans' new national chairman and future New York Governor and Senator, to the 558 Republican delegates and thousands of spectators. As a Whig state Senator, Morgan had introduced the legislation establishing Central Park. The Northern Know-Nothings' letter announced that a committee appointed by the North American Convention wanted to confer with the Republican Convention upon candidates for the offices of President and Vice President. They wanted to keep correspondence going, "in the same spirit, with a perfect unanimity of sentiment . . . to give joy to the heart of every lover of freedom throughout the land, and strike terror to the hearts of his enemies." The letter was signed by George Law.

De Witt C. Littlejohn, of New York, stood up inside the ornate Musical Hall, where the Republicans had just convened, to support the North American gesture. He knew that like the Democrats themselves, the Know-Nothings had already courted Fremont, who was living at 56 East Ninth Street in Greenwich Village, to become their presidential candidate. Fremont had turned the Democrats down because they insisted that he support the Fugitive Slave Act. But he was known to have nativist opinions, especially concerning Chinese immigration in California. "It is only right that the great party represented by the North American Convention should have one candidate on the ticket nominated by the Republican Convention," Littlejohn declared.

Republican Congressman Joshua Giddings, of Ohio, rose to object. "It pains me to be compelled to oppose that motion," he exclaimed, explaining that the Republican Convention Call had been open to all who opposed the expansion of slavery and that if special communications were conducted with the Northern Know-Nothings, they should be conducted with those representing citizens of foreign birth as well. Giddings' motion carried the day and official communications with the North Americans ceased. Republicans were more worried about carrying the foreign vote with them, and a coalition with the Know-Nothings meant trouble with new citizens.

Later that day, balloting for the first Republican nominee began and the 43-year-old Fremont won an informal poll with 359 votes to 190 cast for the 70-year-old Justice McLean. The Convention was ready to make the nomination unanimous when Ohio's Giddings suddenly stood again to discuss the correspondence with the North American Convention. Although he thought the Republican Convention was open and special communications with any group might cause problems, he said, his friends had convinced him to reconsider his earlier motion.

Mr. Littlejohn, of New York, responded, "I do not propose to receive the communication because of any particular sympathy I have with the Know-Nothings, but I believe if they do not cooperate, James Buchanan will ascend to the presidency . . . ." He was thinking of the Know-Nothings' strength in New York and Pennsylvania. Littlejohn added, "The communication does not imply we wish to exclude foreigners. Certainly not."

Thomas D. Elliot responded. "I have just been given the pleasure of casting all of Massachusetts' votes for the nomination of John C. Fremont. I hope this Convention does nothing to lessen the strength of the Republican Party in Massachusetts." Connecticut's former Governor Cleveland reminded the Republican Convention that the North American Convention was made up of those who bolted the Philadelphia National American Convention in February, and that they held anti-slavery views. The Republican Convention had invited them, he said, and they had responded. Now it was their duty to receive them.

Owen Lovejoy, brother of the martyred Illinois Abolitionist, responded with anger. "We did not invite them. If this Convention receives the Know-Nothings as a body, that demagogue, Stephen A. Douglas, will tickle the senses of the foreign born in Illinois, and Illinois will be lost. Let the North Americans come as individuals. Let them answer the call of freedom as individuals and Illinois will be saved." The Republican Convention applauded his logic.

Mr. Gazzam, of Pennsylvania, defended the Pennsylvania Know-Nothings, saying that they had become an open party that constituted the bulk of the Republican Party in his state. Judge Hoar, of Massachusetts, whose words carried weight, said he saw no harm in admitting them as a group. Mr. Sherwood, of New York, argued that if they did not admit the North Americans, it was akin to inviting a man to dinner and then kicking him out on the street. The North Americans wanted to confer about platforms and candidates.

The Convention buzzed with debate on the floor. Finally, Pennsylvania's Governor Ritner tried to bring attention back to Fremont and the Convention formally voted 520 for Fremont, 37 for McLean, 1 for Seward. Then the decision was made unanimous. The next day the Republicans nominated William Lewis Dayton, a former Senator from New Jersey, for Vice President over a one-term former Whig from Illinois, Abraham Lincoln, who was not in attendance. Lincoln later quipped that the delegates must have confused him with another Lincoln from Massachusetts. They had not.

Before the final vote on the vice presidential nominee, Judge David Wilmot rose to read another communiqué from the North American Convention in New York asking for a Republican committee to be formed with which it could communicate. The Republican Convention complied by appointing a committee headed by its behind-the-scenes leader, Francis P. Blair, to negotiate between the groups.

The North Americans also wanted to nominate Fremont. But Greeley and Weed, who were sympathetic to their cause and probably members of their secret society, convinced them that they should not nominate Fremont for fear of a backlash that could hurt his chances. Instead, at their urging, the North Americans nominated Nathaniel Prentiss Banks as a stand-in for Fremont, and William F. Johnston, of Pennsylvania, for Vice President, with the understanding that Banks would step aside after both Conventions were over and that the North Americans would vote for the Republican nominee Fremont, who was a friend of Banks. In fact, Banks had been involved in the unsuccessful attempt by Democrats to recruit Fremont as their presidential nominee.

Nathaniel P. Banks, just 40-years-old at the time of the North American Convention, had been elected as a Democratic member of Congress in 1852 and re-elected as a member of the National American Party. He became Speaker of the House of Representatives on February 2, 1856, after an epic two-month struggle. Banks was pitted against William Aiken, of South Carolina, and the House was deadlocked for weeks while Democrats, Whigs, Republicans, and Know-Nothings struggled to name a new leader. Finally, after 133 ballots, anti-slavery forces coalesced behind Banks, and he became the new Speaker, the first ever elected solely with votes from one region of the nation. Banks would become a Major General during the Civil War and serve as Massachusetts Governor from 1858 to 1861, before going back to Congress as a Union Republican from 1865 through 1873, and as an Independent from 1875 to 1879, and again from 1889 to 1891.

By 1856, the Whigs were on their last leg as a viable political party. Most Northern Whigs had defected to either the Republicans or North Americans. Most Southern Whigs felt isolated, but continued to fight the Democracy. But those left in the Whig Party soon joined the Southern Know-Nothings and worked for Millard Fillmore, their national lodge leader, to again serve as President. Fillmore, even though he was a New Yorker, had the trust of many Southerners and had proved "fair" to them during his tenure in the White House by signing the 1850 Compromise.

By 1856, the warning signs of national disintegration were clear. The rambunctious and bitter fall campaign included scores of ratification rallies and torchlight parades on all sides. Representative Preston Brooks, of South Carolina, who had beaten Senator Charles Sumner into unconsciousness on the floor of the Senate earlier that year, declared that "Union or Disunion" was the only question of the election. He called on the South to take Washington by force of arms if Fremont were victorious. Fillmore himself said that if Colonel Fremont became President, the South ought to withdraw from the Union. But support for Fillmore dwindled as Southern Whigs saw that the North was not supporting him. Meanwhile, Fremont was called a "traitor" for trying to break up the Union with his plan to purchase the freedom of all slaves using the national treasury. Southern Know-Nothings also charged that Fremont, whose father was a French Catholic, would be manipulated by the Pope and ran a hateful anti-Catholic campaign against him.

On October 14, 1856, in early state elections, Pennsylvania voters decided between the state Democrats and the Union Party, a coalition of Republicans, Whigs, and Know-Nothings. With the help of $500,000 from New York merchants and Wall Street bankers with ties to the Slave Power, Pennsylvania Democrats won the state contest by a mere 3,000 votes, forecasting the results of the national contest in November.

Then, on November 4, 1856, the National Democracy won nineteen states to eleven for Fremont and the Republicans. The Pathfinder lost to Buchanan by only 500,000 votes nationally. New York went for Fremont through the combined Republican and sympathetic North American vote. Only five Northern states, including Buchanan's home Pennsylvania, Illinois, and Indiana cast winning tallies for the Democracy, which lost ten states it had carried four years earlier. But the Electoral College total tallied 174 for Buchanan, 114 for Fremont, and 8 for Fillmore, who carried Maryland and took 21.5 percent of the nation's total popular vote.

The Southern Know-Nothings and Whig total ended up being the difference between victory and defeat for the new Republican Party. In Philadelphia, Fillmore won 36 percent of the vote. However, 1856 was the final curtain call for both the Whigs and the Know-Nothings. Democrat James Buchanan was elected President of the United States, but he was the first minority President since John Quincy Adams, and that meant future problems for the Democrats and for the nation.

In 1860, the Democracy would further fracture into two competing parties with three Presidential Nominating Conventions that produced two competing presidential candidates. On the brink of Civil War, the National Democratic Convention at Charleston became deadlocked by the Two-Thirds Rule required for nomination and adjourned without a candidate. The Northern Democracy reconvened at Baltimore and nominated Stephen A. Douglas, of Illinois. The Southern Democracy then settled on John Cabell Breckenridge, of Kentucky. That split insured the first Republican national victory in the party's second presidential race. But Lincoln would become a minority President, as Buchanan had been in 1856, and the fateful rush to war had already begun. As the Liberty Party of 1840 had hoped, the country was splintering over slavery.

The Tenth National Democratic Presidential Nominating Convention and the Election of 1868

Convention-at-a-Glance

Event: Tenth National Democratic Presidential Nominating Convention
Date: July 4-9, 1868
Location: Tammany Hall, 32 East Fourteenth Street, New York City
New York Governor: Reuben E. Fenton, Union
New York City Mayor: John T. Hoffman, Tammany Democrat
Convention's Permanent President: Former Governor Horatio Seymour, New York
Number of Delegates: 317 from thirty-eight states, two-thirds of whom were required for the nomination, or 211½
Candidates for Nomination: Associate Supreme Court Justice Stephen J. Field, California; former Governor James E. English, Connecticut; Senator Thomas Andrews Hendricks, Indiana; former Governor Joel Parker, New Jersey; Sanford E. Church, New York; Senator Reverdy Johnson, Maryland; Major General Francis Preston Blair, Jr., Missouri; Supreme Court Chief Justice Salmon Portland Chase, Ohio; former Congressman George Hunt Pendleton, Ohio; General Winfield Scott Hancock, Pennsylvania; Judge Asa Packer, Pennsylvania; President Andrew Johnson, Tennessee; Senator James R. Doolittle, Wisconsin
Presidential Nominee: Horatio Seymour, New York
Age of Nominee: 58
Number of Ballots: 22

Vice Presidential Nominee: Francis P. Blair, Jr., Missouri

Platform Positions: Immediate restoration of all the states to their Rights in the Union; amnesty for all past political offenses; regulation of the elective franchise by the states themselves; payment of the public debt in the lawful money of the United States; equal taxation of every species of property including Government bonds and other public securities; economy in the administration of the Government; reduction of the standing army and navy; abolition of the Freedmen's Bureau and "all political instrumentalities designed to secure Negro supremacy;" expulsion of corrupt men from offices; restoration of rightful authority to, and the independence of the Executive and Judicial departments; subordination of the military to civilian power to end the usurpations of Congress; an end to arbitrary seizures and arrests, military trials, and secret star-chamber inquisitions; praise for Chief Justice Chase and President Andrew Johnson.

Campaign Slogans: "Reduce Taxes Before Taxes Reduce Us;" "For Seymour, Blair and Liberty;" "Peace, Union and Constitutional Government;" and "The Union, the Constitution, and the Laws"

Campaign Songs: "The White Man's Banner"; "The Seymour Schottisch"; "Blair's Polka"; and the "Tammany Grand March"

The Tenth National Democratic Presidential Nominating Convention and the Election of 1868

"Gentlemen of the Convention: Your country looks to you to stay this tide of disorganization, violence, and despotism."—August Belmont, National Democratic Chairman

By the time the United Democracy, as the Democratic Party was then called, first met in New York City for its Tenth Presidential Nominating Convention in 1868, the nation's murderous Civil War had been over for three years. The deep political bitterness and hatred it had engendered were not. In Congress, the Republican Party's most vociferous foes of the South took control of Reconstruction in the wake of Lincoln's death. The martyred President's plea for "malice toward none, charity toward all" was thrown aside by the "Radical Republicans" with their harsh Reconstruction laws and imprudent Impeachment of President Andrew Johnson, a War Democrat from Tennessee whom Lincoln enlisted as part of his 1864 Union Party ticket.

The first Reconstruction Act, passed in March 1867, two years after the end of the war, placed the South under authoritarian military control, abolishing state Governments and dividing the South into five military districts. Johnson, seeking to follow Lincoln's admonitions, found the law too strict. He fought back by removing allies of the radical Congress, which in turn, passed the Tenure of Office Act to protect those appointed by Lincoln. Johnson defied that Act by dismissing Lincoln's Secretary of War, Edwin McMasters Stanton. The House of Representatives, under the leadership of Radical Republican Thaddeus Stephens, of Pennsylvania, and Benjamin F. Butler, of Massachusetts, (a different Benjamin Butler than Van Buren's associate) then voted articles of Impeachment against Johnson on February 25, 1868. The Impeachment Trial in the Senate lasted from March 5 to May 28, 1868, with President Johnson's defenders arguing that he had committed neither "high crimes" nor "misdemeanors."

Johnson escaped conviction by a 35 to 19 vote, one short of the two-thirds required to evict him from office. One of the deciding votes to acquit Johnson came from Lincoln's former Illinois colleague, Senator Lyman Trumbull, author of the Thirteenth Amendment to the Constitution that forever abolished slavery. Six other Republican Senators, Fessenden, Fowler, Grimes, Patterson, Ross, Van Winkle, and Henderson sided with twelve Democrats to save the embattled President.

After the sensational Senate trial, Democrats still stood firmly behind Johnson and accused the Radical Republicans of inciting a run-away Congress that only an election could stop. All the Republican dissenters were vilified by their party and its supporters. Republicans still charged Democrats with "treason" and treachery, as they had done before and during the war.

On May 20 and 21, with the trial still under way in Washington, the National Union Republican Convention met at the Crosby Opera House in Chicago. Called "The General's Convention" because of the presence of numerous Union Generals, it nominated the nation's supreme military commander, General Ulysses Simpson Grant, of Illinois, as its candidate. (Grant, 46-years-old, was named Hiram Ulysses by his parents, but when at age 17 he was mistakenly enrolled in West Point as Ulysses Simpson Grant, he retained the new tag even though Simpson was his brother's name.) Grant was, as a result of his war victories, the most popular man in the nation. Speaker of the House, Schuyler Colfax, of Indiana, a leader of the Radical Republicans, was nominated to be his Vice President. Grant supported Republican Reconstruction policies in the South, including the enfranchisement of former slaves, repayment of the national debt with hard currency, and increased immigration. But his campaign appeal was reduced to one phrase that he wrote upon accepting the nomination: "Let us have peace."

Then it was the Democracy's turn to offer a candidate. "All day, Friday July 3, 1868," The *New York Times* reported, "trains continued to empty Democracy upon the city." Early that morning more than 1,200 "Pendleton shriekers," or supporters of the pre-Convention favorite George H. Pendleton, "The Young Eagle of the West," arrived from Ohio, followed by the Keystone Club and the Americus Club of Philadelphia, most of whom were committed to their favorite son, General Winfield Scott Hancock. Other delegates followed from all points west and south. The *Times*, a Republican paper at the time, observed that the mood among the delegates was one of "doubt, perplexity, and general mystification" about the party's future after the war and about whom the Convention would select as its candidate to battle Grant. The paper wryly noted that, "With the Democracy have come, apparently, all the thieves in the country . . . detectives report pickpockets swarm in all parts of the City." Within hours delegates filled the lobbies of hotels across New York City, plotting strategies for the victory of their candidates.

To combat the "treason" charges of the Republicans and the disrepute their party had fallen into with the people for sparking the war and then for urging a premature and defeatist peace, the Democrats wanted to publicly proclaim their patriotism. So on July 4, 1868, Democrats from both Northern and Southern states converged on the newly-constructed headquarters of the Tammany Society at 32 East

Fourteenth Street, next to the Academy of Music. Thousands of people gathered on the sidewalk and the normally busy business street in front of the six-story Victorian brick building festively decorated with American Flags and red, white, and blue bunting. Atop the huge hall stood a larger than life statue of the Society's patron saint, the Delaware Indian Chief Tammanend. Not only was the symbolic date in July important to redefining their party's image with voters, the Fourth of July date was held most sacred to the host organization.

Captain John Cameron of the Eighteenth Precinct and three other officers tried in vain to control the crowd that pushed forward toward the locked doors. Several women fainted before a police "posse" arrived to push back the throng and convince Tammany to open its doors early. But because of close inspection of every ticket and badge, it took over forty minutes for the mass to gain entry. Finally, the spectators and partisans filled the great meeting hall, informally called the "Wigwam."

Tammany held its council meetings and sponsored other cultural events for its constituents inside its Wigwam. The chamber's towering vaulted ceiling was colorfully painted with semi-clad mythological nymphs and ornate patterns, and a giant geometric chandelier hung above the rows of benches reserved for delegates on the main floor. Flag bunting hung from every balcony all around the circular hall where spectators gathered between rows of Corinthian pillars. The heat inside the building on that July day became oppressive.

The Tammany Society had been formed in 1783 in the wake of the American Revolution and named after Tammanend, who became St. Tammany in the Society's lore, meant to replace the British patron St. George. Dedicated to the ideals of Liberty, the organization was initially composed of conservative Federalists, but during the Jeffersonian era it became Republican, and after Jackson, Democratic in its sympathies, especially as it allied itself with the influx of European immigrants who flooded New York City and upon whose loyalty it built its electoral power. By 1868, that dedication to civic virtue was being tested by the blatant thievery of Tammany's current political boss, William "Bill" Marcy Tweed, a man who was known to nine out of ten city residents. As Tammany's Grand Sachem, Tweed was at the center and often behind the scenes of many crucial events of the National Democratic Convention of 1868.

At exactly 12 p.m., on Saturday, July 4, 1868, August Belmont, of New York, Chairman of the National Democratic Committee, pounded his gavel to establish order inside the ornate hall filled with 317 delegates and thousands of spectators. All of them had been screened by Tammany's sergeant-at-arms, H. O. Moore, to insure that New Yorkers had a good share of the space to cheer on cue. As many as 1,000 more tickets than seats had been issued, and the hall was packed far beyond

90

reasonable capacity. Beside the speaker at the rostrum, scores of newspaper reporters from across the land were crammed together, poised at their telegraph equipment on the front desks. Western Union had run extra wires into the hall connecting the Convention with every part of the continent. The galleries were filled with rank and file party leaders from coast to coast who took off their coats, ties, and vests in the heat. Scores of handsomely-dressed women were seated in the wings of the several tiers. Below Belmont on the stage, the delegations were seated beside their state pennons. A pleasant hum, "like a hive of bees," resonated through the hall.

Chairman Belmont was one of New York's most successful bankers, a former U.S. Consul General to Austria and Minister to the Netherlands. He originally had come to the U.S. from Germany as an agent of the Rothchild banking empire, before opening his own bank a year before the Convention. The *New York Times* said, "the financiers of London, Frankfort, and Amsterdam naturally listen to him as a trust-worthy exponent of the condition and prospects of the United States." Belmont's Call-to-Order was greeted with thunderous applause from the enthusiastic crowd.

When the stately banker, carefully groomed and with bushy sideburns, finally established quiet, he began: "It is my privilege today to welcome you to this hall, constructed with so much artistic taste and tendered to you by time-honored Society of Tammany." He was interrupted with loud cheers that demonstrated the special allegiance of many observers in the hall. "I welcome you to this magnificent temple, erected to the Goddess of Liberty by her staunchest defenders and most fervent worshipers." Again the imposing financier was stopped by loud clapping.

"I welcome you to this good city of New York, the bulwark of Democracy, which has rolled back the surging waves of Radicalism through all the storms of the last eight years; and I welcome you, gentlemen, to our Empire State, which last fall redeemed herself from Republican misrule by a majority of nearly 50,000 votes, and which claims the Right to lead the vanguard of victory in the great battle to be fought next November for the preservation of our institutions, our laws, and our liberties." Here again Belmont was halted by the surging wave of crowd support.

He then expressed confidence that their work would lead to victory in November. Belmont noted: "The American people will no longer remain deaf to the teachings of the past. They will remember that it was under successive Democratic administrations, based upon our national principles, the principles of constitutional Liberty that our country rose to a prosperity and greatness unsurpassed in the annals of history. They will remember the days when North and South marched shoulder to shoulder together in the conquest of Mexico, which gave us our golden empire on the Pacific; our California and Oregon, now the strongholds of a triumphant Democracy. They will remember the days when peace and plenty reigned over the whole Union, when we had no national debt to crush the energies of the people, when the Federal tax-gatherer was unknown throughout the vast extent of the land, and when the credit of the United States stood as high in the money marts of the world as that of any other Government." His recollections elicited more applause.

"And they will remember, with a wise sorrow, that with the downfall of the Democratic party, in 1860, came that fearful Civil War which has brought mourning and desolation into every household; has cost the loss of a million of American citizens, and has left us with a national debt the burden of which drains the resources, cripples the industry, and impoverishes the labor of the country."

Belmont continued his assault. "When the victor and the vanquished were equally ready to bury the past and to hold out the hand of brotherhood and good-will across the graves of their fallen comrades, it was again the defeat of the Democratic candidate in 1864 which prevented this consummation . . . Instead of restoring the Southern states to their constitutional Rights . . . the Radicals in Congress, elected in an evil hour, have placed the iron heel of the conqueror upon the South." Loud applause showed the audience was passionate about the issues of Reconstruction.

"Military satraps are invested with dictatorial power, overriding the decisions of the courts, and assuming the factions of civil authority; whole populations are disfranchised or forced to submit to test oaths alike revolting to Justice and civilization; and a debased and ignorant race, just emerged from servitude, is raised unto power to control the destinies of that fair portion of our common country." The delegates agreed with his racist but popular assessment.

"These men, elected to be legislators, and legislators only, trampling the Constitution under their feet, have usurped the functions of the Executive and the Judiciary, and it is impossible to doubt, after the events of the past few months, and the circumstances of the Impeachment Trial, that they will not shrink from an attempt hereafter to subvert the Senate of the United States, which alone stood between them and their victim, and which had virtue enough left not to allow the American name to be utterly disgraced, and Justice to be dragged through the dust." The Convention broke into cheers.

"In order to carry out their nefarious program," Belmont charged, "our army and navy are kept in times of profound peace on a scale which involves a yearly expenditure of from one to two hundred millions [there were still 50,000 troops in uniform]; that prevents the reduction of our national debt, and imposes upon our people a system of the most exorbitant and unequal taxation, with vicious, irredeemable, and depreciated currency. And now this same party, which has brought all these evils upon the country, comes again before the American people, asking for their suffrages.

"And whom has it chosen for its candidate?" Belmont mockingly inquired. "The General commanding the Armies of the United States. Can there be any doubt left as to the designs of the Radicals, if they should be able to keep their hold on the reins of Government? They intend constitutional usurpation of all the branches and functions of the Government, to be enforced by the bayonets of a military despotism," Belmont angrily shouted to the assembly. His pronouncement was answered with a loud ovation.

"It is impossible that a free and intelligent people can longer submit to such a state of things . . . . They will not calmly stand by to see their Liberties subverted, the prosperity and greatness of their country undermined, and the institutions bequeathed to them by the fathers of the Republic wrested from them." The delegates and guests roared. "They must see that the conservative and national principles of a liberal and progressive Democracy are the only safeguards of the Republic."

The wealthy Democrat, who was trying to repair a badly-damaged party concluded, "Gentlemen of the Convention: Your country looks to you to stay this tide of disorganization, violence, and despotism. It will not look in vain, when next November the Roll shall be called, and when state after state shall respond, by rallying around the broad banner of Democracy, on which, in the future, as in the past, will be inscribed our undying motto: 'The Union, the Constitution, and the Laws!' " The acclaim for Chairman Belmont was passionate and long sustained. He had stated in short the entire complaint of his party. Nor was there dissent among the delegates or the spectators. The great banker was a political savant, measuring the national landscape and seeing danger, but also setting an agenda for possible victory for his wounded party.

When the noise again subsided under his gavel, Mr. Belmont introduced the Temporary Chairman of the Convention, the Honorable Henry L. Palmer, of Wisconsin, who wanted to "congratulate our country at large, that, on this bright and beautiful anniversary of our nation's birth, once more a Convention of the Democracy of this country is assembled in which all states are represented." Again the energetic crowd broke loose with cheers. Handkerchiefs fluttered throughout Tammany's lavish Wigwam.

Then a prayer by Reverend Dr. Morgan, Rector of St. Thomas's Church, of New York City, asked for blessings upon "this Convention" and for the "peace, good order, and welfare of the nation." Mr. E. O.

Perrin, of New York, whose voice was loud enough to be heard over the cheers, was made the Convention's Temporary Secretary.

Palmer's duty was to get the program moving by making committee assignments and to conduct affairs until a Convention President was named. But before he had a chance, a dispute arose over the rules. General McCook, of Ohio, led off the first floor debate by making a seemingly simple motion to conduct the Convention according to the rules of the House of Representatives. His motion was seconded.

But Erastus Brooks, of New York, a Tammany ally, rose to complain about those rules. "There are many gentlemen in this Convention who do not recognize the rule of the present House of Representatives," Brooks noted to applause. General McCook replied that Brooks "does me an injustice if he thinks I would move the adoption of the rules of the present House, if I did not know that they had not dared to change one of the time honored rules that were established under Democratic auspices."

Governor Richardson, of Illinois, added, "I do not know whether this Radical Congress have overthrown any of the important rules of the House of Representatives, but they have done so much damage, so much mischief, so much outrage, so much wrong, that they may have violated some of these rules." He suggested the Convention employ the rules that had regulated its 1860 Baltimore Convention. Former Congressman Francis Kernan, of Oneida, New York, suggested the rules of the 1864 National Convention in Chicago would better be adopted, and his amendment won the first vote of the proceedings.

Concealed within this simple exchange was the first contest of the Convention. In making his motion, McCook, a leader of the Ohio Pendleton forces, had hoped to surreptitiously adopt rules that would have allowed the presidential nomination of his candidate with a simple majority vote. The Tammany forces, ever alert to parliamentary maneuvers, blunted Ohio's effort and insured that the "Two-Thirds Rule," used at all previous Democratic Conventions, prevailed for nominating a presidential candidate.

The episode, the *Times* remarked, showed that the Convention, "is to be the scene of rather sharp practices upon the part of the opponents of Pendleton, who will spare nothing of adroitness or trickery to compass his defeat." "Gentleman George" Pendleton was a "soft money" man who favored the use of "Greenbacks" rather than gold to pay back the nation's debt to bond holders. Easterners who held many of those bonds wanted to be paid back in gold which would hold its value, rather than the inflationary greenbacks which were worth but seventy cents on the dollar. Pendleton's "Ohio Plan" meant more Greenbacks and higher prices for the farmer. The *Times* prophetically noted that the parliamentary skirmish "showed too, that the Westerners are no match for their Eastern brethren who are of quicker perceptions, more fertile in resources, and more apt to seize the exact moment when it is possible to achieve a desired end." The remark was prescient.

In the preliminary voting, Mr. Dowdall and several members of the Illinois delegation complained that their votes had been disregarded by their chairman because of the "Unit Rule," a practice at past Democratic Conventions that required each state to vote as the majority of the delegation dictated. The Unit Rule was important since the presidential nominee had to secure two-thirds of the votes of all delegates, the "Two-Thirds Rule." Splintered delegations made that difficult, as had been the case in 1860, when no one was able to win two-thirds of the delegates and the party divided North and South, with two presidential candidates, thus insuring Republican victory. The Illinois delegate agreed that the Unit Rule should apply to the presidential nomination, but not to other matters. His complaint was ignored by the chair and the Unit Rule stood for most delegations.

Finally, several committee assignments were made. General J. A. Green, Jr. represented New York on the Committee on Organization; J. A. Hardenburgh represented New York on the Committee on Credentials. Mr. Emery, of Maine, and C. H. Reeve, of Indiana, then rose to complain that tickets for spectators were not being fairly distributed, evidence that Tammany ruled as far as accommodations went. Although a committee with representatives of each state was assigned that task, the Tammany organization had taken control of the process.

On the day before the meeting, state chairmen themselves had to wait "for tickets like a newspaper boy at a circus ticket window" outside a Tammany meeting room while the Executive Committee made allotments. The *Times* reported that Inspector Leonard and a large contingent of police were on hand with orders that no person without a badge or ticket was to be admitted. Complaints were overruled by Chairman Belmont who noted, "Each delegation had its allotment of tickets to be distributed to as many spectators as the hall will hold. The tickets will be given out in this manner for each day of the Convention."

Rising to refer to the recent acquittal of the President during the Impeachment Trial, Mr. E. Steele, of California, presented a resolution praising the, "stern and unflinching integrity of the President of the United States, Andrew Johnson, and of his faithful Cabinet advisers, excluding always therefrom Edwin M. Stanton," (Stanton, Lincoln's Secretary of War, had been dismissed by Johnson, sparking the Impeachment ordeal) "without whose actions the political control of the country would have been usurped by the congressional majority of the Republican Party and a Dictatorship and Privy Council in perpetuity would have been established in lieu of our free representative Democratic Government." Steele alleged that these actions threatened "the safety of the country, the liberties of the people, and the unity, permanency, and prosperity of the nation . . . ." The delegates and spectators concurred, loudly cheering his assaults on their domestic enemy.

The Convention was set to adjourn until later that Saturday evening, but not without objections from Mr. Brooks, who sought to postpone further business until after the Independence Day celebrations and "the Sabbath." He warned, "Warm as it is in this mid-day weather, when the gas is lighted in this hall the atmosphere here will be still more oppressive." Besides, he noted that the City of New York had made "great preparations" for a Fourth of July celebration, including a large display of fireworks. And he invited everyone to indulge in the festivities planned for them by their host.

But former Congressman Robert McClelland, of Michigan, objected that, "there are many of us who have come from a great distance to attend this Convention . . . because of the great importance of the occasion. We are anxious to complete our labors and return to our homes." His motion did not prevail. In the end, the great body adjourned to join New York's patriotic party, with an agreement to reconvene Monday morning, July Sixth at 10:30 a.m., as suggested by Mr. Brooks.

However, before they vacated the hall, the assembly listened to a reading of the Declaration of Independence. A delegate from the floor wryly inquired whether there was in attendance any military commander who might object. Chairman Belmont wittily responded, "I suppose no such person exists in the Empire State." And so those words of allegiance, which meant one thing to post-war Republicans, and another to Democrats, rang through the hall, ironically beginning: "When in the course of human events, it becomes necessary for one people to dissolve the political bands which have connected them with another . . . ."

Then the over-heated crowd headed out of the hall into an "almost intolerably hot" afternoon for New York City's celebration, including a military parade featuring four brigades of the New York National Guard that marched up Fifth Avenue to Thirty-Eighth Street, over to Madison Avenue and down to Twenty-Third Street and past the Clarendon Hotel at Eighteenth Street and a reviewing stand occupied by Mayor John T. Hoffman, a Tammany man, and other dignitaries. That night, fireworks costing $30,000 blasted away from fourteen sites around the city, including City Hall and the Battery. Police Superintendent Kennedy instructed his men to stringently enforce new regulations against firing guns and cannons on the streets in celebration. As a result, the holiday was, the *Times* reported, "the least disastrous to life and limb within recollection of the city's oldest inhabitants."

Managers for the candidates used the weekend hiatus to seek converts to their cause. An "army of bummers and blowers," as the *Times* called them, worked the hotels, with "unabated zeal" to gain support on platform positions or for their candidate for nomination. The *Times* concluded that there was "apparently no disposition to surrender in any quarter." Meanwhile, members of the Committee on Resolutions worked all weekend trying to hammer out a platform. Progress was slow, as they were inundated with resolutions from various factions. Many other delegates simply rested or went to church to repair themselves for the coming political battle. The corridors of the hotels were "hot as furnaces thrice heated," so others escaped the city altogether over the Sabbath. Those who remained found scattered about the lobbies numerous copies of carefully prepared biographies of Pendleton, former Governor Joel Parker of New Jersey, and others. Also, "there was some carousing going on," the *Times* confirmed and much alcohol was consumed over the course of the Convention week.

On Monday morning, July 6, 1868, Mr. Palmer called the Convention back to order. Reverend William Quinn delivered a prayer to the weary delegates who had been meeting in private all weekend, asking that, "wholesome laws may be enacted, and that they be administered with clemency and mercy, restraining vice, encouraging the practice of good works . . . ."

The first order of business on Monday was committee assignments. Mr. Hiester Clymer, of Pennsylvania, who had run unsuccessfully for Governor in 1866, was named chair of the Committee on Organization. The Honorable Horatio Seymour, of Utica, New York, was appointed Permanent President of the 1868 Convention. Seymour was a former two-term New York Governor and had been presiding officer of the 1864 Democratic Convention in Chicago. He was handsome, tall, slender, charming, and well-read in history and geography. A man of dignity, he projected a magnetism that appealed to the public. One biographer also said he was, "very stealthy, earnest for power, and reckless for fame." He owned some of the best land in the Mohawk Valley and lived a life of aristocratic leisure when not politically engaged. His name elicited cheer after cheer from the home crowd who, although not always his ally in state political disputes, was anxious to advance New York in the affairs of the national party. Seymour also was genuinely popular with out-of-state Democrats who knew New York's leadership was essential to re-establishing their post-war party. Governor Bigler, of Pennsylvania, also wanted the position, but New York relegated that honor to itself.

Not unexpectedly, Grand Sachem William M. Tweed, deputy street commissioner of New York City, as well as a New York state Senator, was designated as a Convention Vice President, one coming from each state. He sat on the large stage where he could watch, and, perhaps, at a decisive moment help control events at the podium. He saw himself as a potentate in the councils of state, so he deserved a seat at the national council in his own Wigwam.

Before Seymour delivered his opening address, a Wisconsin delegate complained that he could hear nor see anything, and the sergeant-at-arms helped clear the floor. Governor Bigler then escorted Seymour to the rostrum. The patrician former Governor was met with wild enthusiasm by the men on the floor and in the galleries, as well as from the women lining the edge of the stage and balconies.

"Gentlemen of the Convention," Seymour began, "I thank you for the honor you have done me in making me your presiding officer." He then delivered a broadside attack on the Republican Party, and the platform and candidates it adopted in Chicago that May. "We are trying to save our country from the dangers which overhang it. We wish to lift off the perplexities and the shackles which in the shape of bad laws and crushing taxation now paralyze the business and labor of our land." His last line stirred shouts of support.

"We are forced to meet the assertions of the resolutions put forth by the late Republican Convention . . . In the first place, they congratulated the perplexed men of business, the burdened tax-payer, the laborer whose hours are lengthened out of the growing cost of the necessaries of life, upon the success of that Reconstruction policy which has brought all these evils upon them by the cost of its military despotism, and the corruption of its bureau agencies." In short, all society was suffering.

Seymour's second complaint was specifically directed against Republican monetary policy and claims to, "renounce all forms of repudiation (of debt) as a national crime." Seymour demanded. "Then why did they put upon the statue books of the nation the laws which invite the citizens who borrow coin to force their creditors to take debased paper, and thus wrong him of a large share of his claim in violation of the most solemn compact?" Seymour also attacked the $500 million taken in taxes used "to uphold a despotic military authority, and to crush out the lives of the Southern states." Instead of paying off the national debt, Republicans were ruining the credit of the nation, Seymour charged. He called the issuing of worthless paper money "covert repudiation." He described how the policy robbed the nation's Civil War veterans, their widows, and children, and how it made a mockery of the nation's declared belief in the eight-hour day.

Seymour also denounced the usurpation of the Judiciary by the military in the South. "If within the limits of ten states of this Union, an American citizen, stung by a sense of his wrongs, should publicly and truthfully denounce the men in power because, in the very language of the Declaration of Independence, ... 'They have erected a multitude of new offices, and set forth swarms of officers to harass our people and eat out their substance,' he would, in all human probability, be dragged to prison . . . From this outrage there can be no appeal to the courts.''

Seymour added incredulously, "They put in nomination a military chieftain who stands at the head of that system of despotism that crushes beneath its feet the greatest principles of the Declaration of Independence . . . In view of these things," Seymour wondered, "can there be one man in this Convention who can let a personal ambition, a passion, a prejudice, turn him aside one hair's breadth in his effort to wipe out the wrongs and outrages which disgrace our country?''

Unknowingly, his question foreshadowed the Convention's outcome. His answer was a burst of cheers. "Can we suffer any prejudices, growing out of our past differences of opinion, to hinder us from uniting now with all who will act to save our country?" Again the roar in the hall halted him. "I thank God that the strife of arms has ceased, and that once more in the great Conventions of our party we can call through the whole Roll of States and find men to answer to each." Here a tremendous and continued cheering swelled forth from the audience.

Seymour concluded, "The passions of hate and malice may linger in meaner breasts, but we find ourselves upheld in our generous purposes by those who showed true courage and manhood on the field of battle. In the spirit, then, of George Washington, and the patriots of the Revolution, let us take the steps to re-inaugurate our Government, to start it once again on its course to greatness and prosperity." Another wave of cheering followed his remarks. Seymour had enhanced his standing with the Convention.

When order was restored, Mr. Brooks, of New York, offered a set of resolutions adopted by the National Labor Union that had met in Tammany's hall two days before the United Democracy assembled. Among other things, the resolutions declared that, "the producing classes, agricultural, mining, mechanical, intellectual and moral, are the most important portion of all communities; and that the distributors, financiers, and statesmen, together with their aides, civil and military, are of secondary consequence, being simply created of the former to disseminate wealth, maintain order, conserve Justice, and keep intact the integrity of the nation.''

Therefore, "the national honor must be preserved by paying its debts in good faith . . . the public interest demands the withdrawal of the circulating notes of the national banks . . . we demand equal taxation on every species of property . . . no more of the public domain should be granted to any corporation, under any pretext whatever . . . we call for enforcing the Eight-Hour Law . . . that the low wages, long hours, and damaging service to which the multitudes of working girls and women are doomed, destroyed health, imperil virtue, and are a standing reproach to civilization; that we would urge them to learn trades, engage in business, join our labor unions . . . . '' And the National Labor Union promised to vote for no candidate who thought otherwise.

No sooner had the Democracy heard an appeal from Labor than Seymour introduced a memorial from the Women's Suffrage Association to assorted cheers and laughter. The treatise was signed by suffragettes Elizabeth Cady Stanton, Mrs. Horace Greeley, Susan B. Anthony, and Abby Hopper Gibbons, although Seymour prudently mentioned only Anthony knowing the husbands of the others were notorious enemies of his party. The women wrote urging the Democracy to take action and to "demand the enfranchisement of the women of America; the only class of citizens wholly unrepresented in the Government; the only class, not guilty of crimes, taxed without representation; tried without a jury of peers; governed without their consent . . . . We are not idiots, lunatics, paupers, criminals, rebels, nor do we . . . bet upon elections. We lack, according to your constitutions, but one qualification–that of sex–which is insurmountable.'' Again, there was considerable laughter on the floor of the Convention.

The women blasted the Republicans upon whom they had depended in the past. "The party in power has not only failed to heed our innumerable petitions, asking the Right of suffrage, poured into Congress and state Legislatures, but they have submitted a proposition to the several states to insert the word 'male' in the Federal Constitution, where it never has been, and thereby put up a new barrier against the enfranchisement of women. This fresh insult to the women of the Republic, who so bravely shared the dangers and sacrifices of the late war, has roused us to more earnest and persistent efforts to secure those Rights . . . .''

The women concluded their argument with an appeal to the march of history. "It needs but little observation to see that the tide of progress in all countries is settling toward the enfranchisement of women, and that this advance step in civilization is destined to be taken in our day. We conjure you, then, to turn from the dead questions of the past to the vital issues of the hour,'' they pleaded. The reading elicited some applause and the petition was quickly referred to the Committee on Resolutions, where it died without action.

The Committee on Credentials then submitted a complete list of official delegates from thirty-eight states and the District of Columbia. The New York delegation included Tweed's associates Congressman John Morrissey, and A. Oakey Hall, known as "The Elegant,'' an actor soon to be Mayor of New York City, as well Peter B. Sweeney. They were all engaged in robbing the city of New York of millions of dollars, and in the years to come would fall under criminal indictment. But in 1868, the Tweed Ring was only beginning its grand escapade of public graft and corruption. Tweed wanted something from this 1868 election; not a President, but his own Governor, who could pass a Home Rule provision for New York City so his activities would escape scrutiny. Tweed believed that whoever nominated the candidate controlled the party.

Among the thirty members of the New York delegation was a future Governor, Samuel Jones Tilden, who would in 1876 become winner of the popular vote in the presidential election before having the Electoral count "stolen" from him. Tilden had become party chairman in 1866. Henry J. Sickles also represented New York. The rest of the Monday morning session was taken up in various delegate resolutions in support of the President and denouncing the Republican oppression, all of which were referred to the Committee on Resolutions, which was working furiously to produce a platform.

On the Convention floor, New York showed an early preference for President, when A. Oakey Hall asserted that "the nation's thanks are due to Chief Justice Chase for his distinguished ability, impartiality, and fidelity to constitutional duty in presiding over the Impeachment trial." There was loud applause at the mention of the first name of the Convention's presidential possibilities. Chase's gifted daughter Kate was in New York overseeing the campaign of the Chief Justice.

Chief Justice Salmon Portland Chase, in his earliest political years a Whig who sometimes voted Democrat, had been a founder of the Liberty, Free Soil, and Republican parties, and had served as a member of Lincoln's war cabinet. He had been elected Ohio Governor on a Free Soil/Democrat ticket. Was it now possible he could return to the Democracy or be welcomed by them? Lincoln had said Chase was "insane on the subject of the presidency." Times and issues were changing fast. This might be his last chance to grab the golden ring. But would Democrats support him at this Convention? Could he possibly run on a platform that advocated repudiation of the nation's debt by allowing payment in paper instead of gold, when as Secretary of the Treasury he had fought against that position? Who were his allies in the hall? Were Ohio or New York ready to turn to him if Pendleton was thwarted? Oakey's resolution was referred to committee.

At the start of the Convention, The *New York Times* calculated that Pendleton, of Ohio, had a clear majority of supporters, but that the friends of Chief Justice Chase were dead set against the former Congressman because of his soft money proclivities. "The bitterness which the Chase managers manifest toward Pendleton will almost certainly insure their defeat," the *Times* predicted. "The vote devoted to Pendleton is sufficiently large to prevent the nomination of any other candidate." It added, "The presumption is that Pendleton himself will fail, but we take it that Pendleton's friends will still in effect control the nomination. The other candidates are impatiently waiting for something to turn up." The Pendleton leaders were worried about how to put together a two-thirds bloc.

The New York delegation pitted itself against those who favored Pendleton. The *Times* said that Pendleton, "had the numbers but lacked discipline and leadership. The New Yorkers, acting with the unity and precision of a closed corporation, showed that they had lost none of the ancient skill by which they were accustomed to control public bodies." It was a skill Tweed, particularly, possessed. Tammany even controlled communication between delegations by cramming delegates on benches on the floor so tightly together they could not move from delegation to delegation to confer or strike deals. But Tammany was everywhere on its home turf.

Tweed had started his tainted career organizing volunteer fire company number six in 1848, using a tiger's head as its symbol. The fire company became the core of his Tammany political organization, and he retained the sign of the tiger as its symbol. Tweed first served from 1852 to 1855 as a member of New York City Common Council and was known as one of the "Forty Thieves." At the same time, from 1853 to 1855, he was a member of Congress, representing the Thirty-Third District. But he knew the real action was back in New York and he returned to run the city that hosted this Convention.

Another resolution was read from the chair urging, "That the amnesty proclamation of Andrew Johnson, President of the United States, be approved by this Convention." This resolution was adopted by the assembly. August Belmont offered another resolution that gave thanks to "the Sachems and members of the Tammany Society for having provided and surrendered their magnificent edifice for the accommodation of the Convention . . . ." Then on the motion of Mr. White, of Maryland, the Convention adjourned until the afternoon.

President Seymour received "three cheers" when he again convened the assembly for the second Monday session. Speaking for the Committee of Conservative Soldiers and Sailors, General Thomas Ewing, Jr., stood before the body and asserted, "We have no sympathy for those purposes that have been falsely and dishonestly substituted by the Republican Party for the avowed objects of war. We care not for their dogmas of Negro suffrage; we abhor their measures of white disenfranchisement." He was applauded. "We cannot, shall not, associate with them longer." A conference of more progressive Soldiers and Sailors had endorsed the Republicans in May. Then, since the Committee on Resolutions was still deliberating, the Convention adjourned for the day.

The Third Day of the Tenth National Democratic Convention, Tuesday, July 7, 1868, began with a prayer by the Reverend Dr. Plummer, who urged the deity to: "Deliver not this nation over to misrule, to despotism, to anarchy, to sensational animosity, nor to internecine strifes.''

Mr. Wright, of Delaware, rose to read a letter from Alexander Hamilton Stephens, former Democratic Congressman from Georgia and former vice president of the Confederacy, who after his release from prison had been elected to the U. S. Senate, but was refused a seat. In coming years, Stephens would return to the House of Representatives and serve as Georgia Governor. Stephens wrote, in part, ''in the future, as in the past, we will adhere with unswerving fidelity to the Union under the Constitution....'' However, ''the perpetuation of the Union in its integrity depends upon the preservation of the states in their political integrity . . . .'' And Stephens denounced Republicans, ''whose revolutionary policy and measures have brought such general discord, strife and war with its attendant ills upon a large portion of the country. . . .'' He insisted that, ''The Right of suffrage, of who shall exercise political power, is a matter that rests, under the Constitution, exclusively with the several states.'' The former Confederate leader's letter was also referred to the Committee on Resolutions. Throughout the Convention, observers noted the silence of the Southern delegates in the hall who were content to let the North and West wrangle over details and plea of their plight. They generally favored President Johnson or General Hancock as their nominee.

Finally, on this Third Day of the Convention, Henry C. Murphy, of New York, took the podium to read the party platform which had been unanimously adopted in committee. He began, ''The Democratic Party in National Convention assembled, reposing its trust in the intelligence, patriotism, and discriminating Justice of the people; standing upon the Constitution as the foundation and limitation of the powers of Government, and the guaranty of liberties of the citizen; and recognizing the questions of slavery and secession as having been settled for all time to come by the war, or the voluntary action of the Southern states in Constitutional Conventions, and never to be renewed or reagitated; does with the return of peace, demand:''

The crowd breathed deeply at the way four years of strife had been acknowledged and overcome. ''First: Immediate restoration of all the states to their Rights in the Union. Second: Amnesty for all past political offenses, and the regulation of the elective franchise in the states, by their citizens.'' It was of course understood that such a resumption of the power of enfranchisement would mean restrictions of the Right to vote for former slaves who now regulated their former masters. ''Third: Payment of the public debt of the United States as rapidly as practicable . . . paid in the lawful money of the United States. [That phase, ''lawful money,'' was vague enough to accommodate both Pendleton who was a ''Greenback man,'' as the *Times* called him, and Seymour and the New Yorkers who were ''hard money'' creditors.] Fourth: Equal taxation of every species of property, according to its real value, including Government bonds and other public securities."

The platform also called for, "economy in the administration of the Government, the reduction of the standing army and navy; the abolition of the Freedmen's Bureau; and all political instrumentalities designed to secure Negro supremacy . . . expulsion of corrupt men from offices [here the Southerners had their most effective influence on the Convention from behind the scenes]; the restoration of rightful authority to, and the independence of the Executive and Judicial departments of the Government; the subordination of the military to civilian power, to end the usurpations of Congress and that the despotism of the sword may cease."

The Democracy's 1868 platform further denounced, "arbitrary seizures and arrests, and military trials and secret star-chamber inquisitions . . ." that had "converted the American capitol into a Bastille . . ." The Democracy then officially saluted "the learned Chief Justice" Chase, who had "been subjected to the most atrocious calumnies, merely because he would not prostitute his office to the support of the false and partisan charges preferred against the President." And finally, the Democracy saluted the President himself, for "resisting the aggressions of Congress upon the constitutional Rights of the states and the people," saying he was "entitled to the gratitude of the whole American people . . . ."

This document of the United Democracy of 1868 called upon, "all who desire to support the Constitution and restore the Union, forgetting all past differences of opinion to unite with us in the present great struggle for the liberties of the people . . . ." When he completed his recitation, Murphy was greeted with "a scene of the wildest enthusiasm." Delegates and spectators threw their hats into the air, waved handkerchiefs, and clapped in sustained applause that lasted several minutes. The assembly overwhelming endorsed the document without a single dissenting vote inside the Tammany Wigwam.

The *New York Times,* which reported the proceedings of the Convention accurately, but injected Republican partisanship in its analysis, called the platform, "a strange mixture of fact and fustian, of courage and duplicity, of propositions that are lucid and propositions that are muddy." On the question of Reconstruction, the *Times,* said, "trickery comes into full play . . . It seems these Copperheads have learned nothing at all. They come along here with all their old airs and assumptions. . . . The people will not tolerate the supremacy of this old Copperhead faction . . . and with that overthrow crush out its existence." (During the war, Northerners with Southern sympathies were called "Copperheads.")

The Washington *Chronicle* called the Democratic platform, "a victory of the Pendleton men and the Southern rebels: Democratic ascendancy means the ascendancy of the very men who first plotted and afterward led the rebellion." Another journal said the platform, with its soft money plank, was "a direct slap in Seymour's face," since he was a financial conservative, although he made no objection when it was presented. The Worcester, Massachusetts, *Spy*, wrote, "The platform would . . . insure the defeat of the Democrats. . . . We hoped for the credit of the country that the party would not prove so insensible to all the promptings of integrity and honor as to base their claims to support upon an open repudiation of the national engagements."

The Convention lumbered forward. After hearing President Seymour clarify that the "Two-Thirds Rule" referred to two-thirds of all delegates and not just two-thirds of those voting, the Convention immediately turned to a Roll Call of the States for the purpose of placing names into nomination for President of the United States. With 317 delegates certified, the Secretary determined it would take 211½ votes to nominate a candidate for the presidency.

President Seymour first admonished the gallery of New Yorkers who had been boisterous throughout the proceedings. "Before the states are called, I wish to say one word to the audience. It has been a source of complaint, and the Chair perhaps has been much at fault, that we have allowed so much latitude to those who have come up to witness our proceedings. There has been so much that went straight to the Democratic heart, that we could not repress such manifestations." He also acknowledged that somehow "a large share of this audience is drawn from the great city in which we meet . . . " and appealed to their honor as hosts to restrain themselves.

Seymour also affirmed, before nominations began, tellingly it would turn out, that any state could nominate any name at any time during the Roll Call of States. All week managers for the potential candidates had been working the delegations at hotels such as the St. Nicholas, the Fifth Avenue, and the St. Cloud without a clear consensus emerging.

Connecticut was the first of the names called by the Convention Secretary to offer a candidate to stand against General Grant in November. Mr. Eaton rose: "It will be remembered that after the passing through a terrible Civil War, which lasted over four long and weary years, the clouds of despotism hung over the land. All was gloom, all was darkness; all was desolation. At last, sir, there arose a star in the East, and my own gallant little commonwealth broke through the gloom and elected a Democratic Governor." The crowd cheered its feat and eventually Eaton named his candidate, a rich New Haven manufacturer and former Governor, James E. English.

Mr. Richardson, of Illinois, when called, said his state would cast its votes for Mr. Pendleton, of Ohio, but would let Ohio make the nomination of its native son, which it did after General Anderson, of Maine, nominated 42-year-old, General Winfield Scott Hancock, who in the last conflict proved his "lion-hearted courage and great magnanimity."

Born in Pennsylvania, Hancock had fought in the Mexican War, the Seminole War, and commanded troops at Antietam and Fredericksburg during the Civil War. He was brilliant at Gettysburg and Spottsylvania, where he captured 4,000 rebels. After the war, he commanded the Central Military District that included Louisiana and Texas. He would win the Democratic nomination in 1880, but lose a close election to another Civil War general, James Garfield, of Ohio. Now a cheer at this Convention went up for him that showed he was in contention in 1868. But the *Times* noted that the Hancock men in the hotels were, "in bad temper and swear freely—a sure sign that they feel hopeless of the results."

A minority representative from Maine arose to second a nomination. Mr. Emory intoned, "in behalf of the laboring masses of Maine, who look to the action of this Convention to relieve them from the burden of debt and taxation under which they are now groaning," and endorsed "the Honorable George H. Pendleton, of Ohio."

Other states passed until New Jersey answered the call with the nomination of its former Governor Joel Parker. "During the late war, he sustained the general Government with all the force at his command, but at no time did he permit the Federal power to make any encroachment upon the Rights of the State," boasted Mr. Little, of New Jersey. "At one time he was the only Democratic Governor in the entire North."

New York followed. State party chairman Samuel J. Tilden rose to announce that his delegation was unanimously behind, "a gentleman who has been repeatedly submitted to the ordeal of a popular vote in the State of New York and has always come from the trial with distinguished success . . ." He proposed Sanford E. Church, New York's Lieutenant Governor from 1851 to 1854 and other offices. The galleries could not restrain themselves in their endorsement of a fellow New Yorker. Tilden's nomination was a courtesy to a favorite son. The New York delegation's early purpose was to encourage as many favorite son nominations from other states as a way to impede the progress of Pendleton, whom they unalterably opposed because of his soft money position. If New York yielded to him for the sake of party unity, Pendleton's nomination was certain.

Next, Ohio's General McCook formally submitted Pendleton's name in a sentence that set off another round of roars. Oregon backed up Pendleton's nomination with a pledge of support. Their candidate, George

Hunt Pendleton was born in 1825 near Cincinnati and educated in private schools in Ohio, before he studied German in Heidelberg. He served in Congress from 1857 to 1865. He had been the Democrat's vice presidential nominee unsuccessfully running for Vice President with General George B. McClellan four years earlier. A year after this Convention, he was defeated in his bid to become Governor of Ohio. Pendleton would serve in the U. S. Senate from 1879 to 1885, before posting as U. S. Envoy Extraordinary and Minister Plenipotentiary to Belgium. The *New York Times* observed that in the Convention, "everywhere were the Pendleton men, blatant and aggressive, prophesizing ruin and disaster if their man" was overlooked and insisting that "no other Democrat can carry Ohio, Indiana, and Illinois" in the general election. They also claimed Pendleton could win the nomination without the votes of the New York delegation.

Judge Woodward, of Pennsylvania, diverted the momentum for Pendleton with a long-winded endorsement of a local favorite, Judge Asa Packer, founder of the Lehigh Valley Railroad, who among other civic goods had personally endowed Lehigh University. After all, he was "one of the largest tax-payers in the country" and "railroads are the greatest achievement of modern civilization," Woodward crooned. Packer had risen from poverty to become a millionaire and a member of the Thirty-Fourth and Thirty-Fifth Congress. The *Times* noted that his nomination had, "mystified, almost horrified" Convention leaders who were trying to settle on a candidate, because it further splintered the vote and encouraged other favorite sons. Some thought he may have been working with New York to stall Pendleton.

When Tennessee was called upon, Thomas A. R. Nelson stood and nominated a man, "who springing from poverty and obscurity has obtained the highest office within the gift of the people, one who has engaged in the mightiest political contest that our nation ever saw," Nelson was halted with cheers, "one who was in favor of the Union during times that tried men's souls . . . who, after his elevation to the presidency, has been maligned, calumniated, traduced, vilified, and persecuted by the Radical party, one who has stood up nobly to the principles of the Constitution . . . one who has battled for the Constitution against the efforts of those who have attempted to destroy it . . . one who deserves the confidence of the whole American people. . . ." At the mention of Andrew Johnson's name the Convention commenced enthusiastic cheering that included those who intended to vote against re-nomination.

The *Times* estimated that the Johnson men were "few in numbers, but confident, in proportion to their weakness, that by some miracle or hocus pocus Johnson will come up from his present interment. These prophecies find but few believers." The paper also speculated that his recent amnesty proclamation for rebels would "gain him some Southern supporters."

Wisconsin closed out the initial round of nominations by presenting two names. Senator James R. Doolittle, said Mr. S. Clark, was "a gentleman whose reputation is so world-wide that no eulogy from myself or any other delegate can add a particle to his laurels . . . a gentleman who has separated himself from the Republican Party when it was in the zenith of its glory and power throughout the country." Then Henry L. Palmer, of Wisconsin, endorsed George H. Pendleton.

After a round of the Roll Call when no more states offered new names, Mr. Miller, of Pennsylvania, moved "that the Convention now proceed to ballot." Alabama cast 8 votes for President Johnson; Arkansas 5 for English; California passed; Connecticut 6 for English; Delaware 3 for Pendleton; Florida 3 for Johnson; Georgia 9 for Johnson; Illinois 16 for Pendleton; Iowa 8 for Pendleton; Kansas 2 for Pendleton, 1 for Frank P. Blair, Jr., ½ for Thomas A. Hendricks; Kentucky 11 for Pendleton; Louisiana 7 for General Hancock; Maine 4½ for Hancock, 1½ for Pendleton, 1 for Johnson; Maryland 4½ for Pendleton, and 2½ for Johnson.

Massachusetts cast 11 for Hancock, 1 Pendleton; Michigan 8 for Senator Reverdy Johnson, of Maryland, who had served as Zachary Taylor's Secretary of State and as defense attorney in *Dred Scott v. Sanford*; Minnesota 4 for Pendleton; Mississippi 9 for Hancock; Missouri 5 for Hancock, 1 for Church, 2½ for Hendricks, 2½ for Hancock, ½ for Johnson; Nebraska 3 for Pendleton; Nevada 3 for Parker; New Hampshire 1 for Doolittle, 2 for Hancock, 2 for Pendleton; New Jersey 7 for its former Governor Parker; New York 33 for favorite son Church; North Carolina 9 for Johnson; Ohio 21 for its statesman Pendleton; Oregon 3 for Pendleton; Pennsylvania 21 for Packer; Rhode Island 4 for Doolittle; South Carolina 6 for Johnson; Tennessee 10 for Johnson; Texas 6 for Johnson; Virginia 10 for Johnson; West Virginia 5 for Pendleton; Wisconsin 8 for Doolittle; and California came in with 3 for Parker, 2 for Pendleton. Clearly, some delegations were ignoring the Unit Rule.

At the end of the First Ballot, George H. Pendleton had stacked up 105 votes; President Johnson trailed with 65; while Church totaled 34; Hancock attracted 33½; Asa Packer 26; English 16; Parker and Doolittle 13 each; Reverdy Johnson 8; Thomas A. Hendricks 2½; and Frank P. Blair, whose letter denouncing Reconstruction had been published the prior day seemed to gain him favor among Southern men, had ½; for a total of 317, with 211½ needed to nominate.

The Second Ballot began immediately. By its end, Pendleton slipped to 104; Johnson trailed off to 52; and Hancock moved up to 40 ½. Frank P. Blair, Jr. edged forward to 10 ½ and Thomas Ewing attracted ½. The Convention moved to its Third Ballot. President

Johnson, with 34½, was suddenly losing support in his effort to vindicate himself with a second term of his own; Pendleton gained to 119 ½; Hancock picked up ground with 45½. States were holding their ground while operatives of each camp circulated among the delegates on the Wigwam's floor trying to drive home a deal that might secure victory. The congestion on the floor made that difficult.

On the Fourth Ballot, North Carolina startled the assembly by casting all 9 of its votes for Convention president Horatio Seymour. Instantly the galleries and many on the floor broke into enthusiastic cheering. Seymour, concerned at the sudden turn of events, took the podium in near panic. "I trust I may be permitted now to make a single remark. Very much to my surprise, my name has been mentioned. I must not be nominated by this Convention. I could not accept its nomination if tendered, which I do not expect. My own inclinations prompted me to decline at the outset; my honor compels me to do so now. I am grateful for any expression of kindness. But I trust it will be distinctly understood that it is impossible, consistent with my position, to allow my name to be mentioned in this Convention against my protest. The Clerk will proceed with the Call."

At the end of the Fourth Ballot, Pendleton led the way with 118½; Hancock followed with 48½; Johnson fell to 32; Hendricks, also a secondary favorite of the New York delegation, gained to 11½. Efforts to adjourn failed. The Fifth Ballot was stalled when the Indiana delegation left the meeting hall for deliberations. In the interim, a National Executive Committee was formed, with one delegate from each state, which New York saw as discriminatory against its teeming population. Tilden said, "It is enough that a state of four million like New York should be neutralized by the small states of the Union. . . . Let's not add the territories having a very small population."

A memorial listing the grievances of the State of Tennessee was read, enumerating the "oppressions, usurpations, and misrule this state has been subjected to by the minions and agents of the party now in possession of the Government of the United States." And it complained of "the disenfranchisement of two-thirds of the white, and the surrender of the ballot to the Negro." (One local response was formation of the Ku Klux Klan.)

Indiana reported back for Pendleton, and at the close of the Fifth Ballot, the President of the United States received no votes for re-nomination; Pendleton crawled forward to 122; Hancock was at 46; Hendricks at 19½; John Quincy Adams received 1 vote from South Carolina. New York tried to adjourn, but Pendleton delegates answered with cries of "No, no." The Sixth Ballot proceeded and only Hendricks edged forward with 30; Johnson reappeared on the tally with 30 votes. The Convention seemed stalemated. Exhausted, delegates finally adjourned until 10 a.m. Wednesday morning. Deal making and consultations continued throughout the night in the hotels, clubs, and lounges where delegates retreated.

On the Convention's Fourth Day, July 8, 1868, the names on the new National Executive Committee were announced. August Belmont represented New York, publisher Wilbur Story, of Chicago, represented Illinois. As the Roll Call was about to resume, Indiana exercised its right to formally nominate Thomas Andrews Hendricks. His name elicited loud applause, although he already had been gaining among the candidates. Mr. Graham V. Fitch, of Indiana, said Hendricks was a man, "of unimpeachable private character and unimpeached public record. He is not, he never was, an office-seeker himself, but whatever position has been bestowed upon him by the partiality of the citizens of his own state has been bestowed unsought and by acclamation. He is second to no man within our borders in ability, in devotion to the Union, in attachment to the principles of Democracy, in integrity of purpose, and in firmness in the discharge of duty."

Hendricks had been born in 1819 in Ohio, but his family moved to Indiana when he was a young child, and there he gained a classical education, graduating from Hanover College. After he was admitted to the bar, Hendricks was elected a state representative in 1848, and served in Congress from 1851 to 1855. He lost re-election in 1854, became a land commissioner, then lost the race for Indiana Governor in 1860 to Oliver P. Morton. Hendricks was sent to the U.S. Senate in 1863 and was still serving there when the New York Convention convened. He would be elected Vice President of the United States with Grover Cleveland in 1884, before dying in office the next year.

Then another Indiana delegate made a speech in favor of Pendleton whom he said the Indiana delegation had endorsed before the Convention. The Seventh Ballot began and Pendleton picked up steam to 137½; Hancock held at 42½; Hendricks advanced to 39½. At the end of the eighth tally, Pendleton's momentum increased with 156½; Hancock fell to 28; Hendricks climbed to 75. By the conclusion of the Ninth Ballot, Pendleton was easing back to 144; Hendricks climbed to 80½, thanks to New York which suddenly switched as a unit from favorite son Church. After the Tenth Ballot, Pendleton stood at 147 ½; Hendricks 82½. The Eleventh Ballot produced little movement. No lasting deals could be sealed.

At the end of the Twelfth and Thirteenth Ballots the stalemate tightened and delegates felt frustrated. Hostility between the camps of the nominees, particularly between Ohio and Indiana, was preventing compromise. Bosses were looking for a way out of the dilemma. Pennsylvania was holding fast to favorite son Packer, Wisconsin to its favorite son Doolittle. At the end of the Fourteenth Ballot, Pennsylvania unified around Hancock. Pendleton, Hancock, and Hendricks were balanced against each other on a tightrope of regionalism.

By the close of the Fifteenth Ballot, the count stood Hancock 79½; Pendleton dropped back to 129½; Joel Parker had 7; Andrew Johnson 5½; James R. Doolittle 12; and Thomas A. Hendricks 82½. The Roll rolled on through the Sixteenth and Seventeenth Ballots, when Hancock garnered 137½; Pendleton suddenly faded to 70½; and Hendricks held at 80. Half a vote for Chief Justice Chase was cast to entice others.

Before the Convention began, the *Times* had reported that, "The Chase men have a well-selected lobby, and openly say they will secure the nomination of their favorite by the use of money. The sums they advanced for this purpose are estimated variously from one to three million dollars. If the Chase men fail in their first preference, their next attempt will be to secure the selection of Hendricks." In this environment, it was not unlikely that Tammany was ready to enter the bidding when the time came, since Chase was one name they admired. Or perhaps they had another favorite upon whom to place their considerable resources looted from the citizens of New York.

An attempt by Samuel Tilden to adjourn was deflected and the Eighteenth Ballot was called, with Hancock charging forward to 144½; Hendricks gained to 87; Pendleton fell to 55½. A debate broke out over whether individual delegates ought to vote as individuals instead of units. But, a motion to adjourn passed at 4:04 p.m. The Pendleton men were in a panic. First, their horse couldn't clear the two-thirds hurdle. Now he was falling behind the new leaders. Who would they support? What would they take now to put someone else over?

The Convention's fifth and final day, Thursday, July 9, 1868, was called to order by President Pro Tem Thomas L. Price, of Missouri. Seymour, although on the stage, said he was feeling slightly ill. Perhaps he had gotten wind of a rumor. Reverend D. Plummer, of South Carolina, offered a prayer that declared, "Our great men have conceived chaff and brought forth stubble. Our land is filled with widows and orphans. Even stout hearts among us have often been ready to fall for looking after those things which were thought to be coming upon us. We have hoped for succor, and behold sadness; for salvation, and behold perplexity. . . . Let us no more pervert our blessings to the nourishing of our personal or national vanity, nor to malevolence, worldliness, or ungodliness."

Before the Roll Call resumed, Mr. Brodhead, of Missouri, rose to address the Convention. "We have reached the Fifth Day of our session without any successful result. I now ask leave to present to the Convention another name for their consideration." He formally nominated former four-term Congressman, Major General Francis Preston Blair, Jr., of Minssouri, because he was, "eminently possessed of those

111

qualities most needed at this time, firmness of purpose, moral courage, and indomitable will.''

After the applause halted, Mr. Miller, of Pennsylvania, complained about manipulation of the proceedings. "I notice, sir, by the report of the proceedings of this Convention yesterday, that it is rather made a matter of congratulation by a portion of the press, that by the superior shrewdness or 'sharpness,' for I believe that is the word used, of certain politicians, the rules of this Convention can be utterly ignored. Now, sir, I allude to the announcement of the change in the vote of the delegation from New York . . . it should content itself with simply voting." His objection was met with cries of "Order." The President Pro Tem evaded the issue by resumption of the Roll Call.

Mr. Rose, of California, placed into the deliberation the name of its favorite son, Associate U. S. Supreme Court Justice Stephen J. Field. Rose said Field was standing "up like a wall of fire against the encroachments of Radical domination," and would "stand as the guardian of the Constitution of his country against the Radical party at Washington." Field's name set off a tumultuous demonstration.

Then the pivotal event of the Convention took place. Clement Laird Vallandigham, of Ohio, asked to read a communiqué. Vallandigham was former editor of the *Western Empire* and served as a Congressman from Dayton from 1858 to 1863. A leading anti-war "Copperhead," he had been arrested and convicted of treasonous speech during the Civil War. President Lincoln had ordered his release and banishment to the Confederate States. Vallandigham ran for Governor from his Canadian exile in 1863, and lost. His exploits made him both a hero to some and pariah to others.

As Vallandigham approached the stand, applause of anticipation rolled through the great hall. The letter he read was addressed from the Fifth Avenue Hotel, in New York City: "My Dear Sir," the epistle began. "You know better than any one the feelings and principles which have guided my conduct since the suggestion of my name for the presidential nomination. You know that while I covet the good opinion of my countrymen, and would feel an honest pride in so distinguished a mark of their confidence, I do not desire it at the expense of one single Electoral vote. . . ." His words sparked great applause. ". . . or of the least disturbance of the harmony of our party. I consider the success of the Democratic Party in the next election of far greater importance than the gratification of any personal ambition, however pure and lofty it might be." Again, the Convention erupted with loud cheers.

"If therefore, at any time, a name shall be suggested, which, in the opinion of yourself and those friends who have shared our confidence, shall be stronger before the country, or which can more thoroughly unite our own party, I beg that you will instantly withdraw my name, and pledge to the Convention my hearty and zealous and active support for its nominee." It was signed, Vallandigham said, by none other than the early favorite of the Convention, George H. Pendleton, who was greatly cheered for his magnanimity, especially by his shocked backers. Vallandigham secretly opposed Pendelton, and was working behind the scenes to find his replacement for the nomination.

Vallandigham shouted so all could hear that the letter was "a higher eulogy in behalf of this distinguished gentleman than any words I could utter." His assessment was reinforced by long and continued applause and cheers for Pendleton, "the young Eagle of the West," who had made a good run. But something was afoot, for why was he yielding now? Had he simply peaked? Had a deal been struck? Who was the other name to whom he had referred? His ardent admirers were puzzled.

The chair called for the Nineteenth Ballot, and Ohio cast its 21 votes for Judge Packer, of neighboring Pennsylvania. But Pennsylvania stood pat with 26 for General Hancock, who now looked to have a path to the nomination to match General against General in the general election, if Hancock could overcome Hendricks. For a moment, it was Pennsylvania against Indiana. The vote stood Hancock 135 ½; 12 for Doolittle; 107½ for Hendricks; 6 for English; 13½ for Blair; 15 for Field; ½ for Chase; 22 for Packer; and 4 for Seymour.

On the Twentieth Ballot, Hancock edged forward again with 142½; so did Hendricks with 121. It was a two horse race. But, on the Twenty-First Ballot, the stalemate seemed to reemerge, neither side wanting the other to win or their man to lose. How many ballots would it go? the weary delegates wondered. Ohio was the key.

Mr. Hunter, of Missouri, offered a resolution to adjourn to St. Louis in "September next." President Seymour, back at the rostrum, banged his gavel and ruled the resolution out of order. The Secretary began the Twenty-Second Ballot: Alabama cast 8 for Hancock; Arkansas 5 for Hendricks; California 5 for Hendricks; Connecticut 6 for English; Delaware 3 for Hancock; Florida 3 for Hendricks; Georgia cast 9 for the Northern General Hancock, and received applause; Illinois was applauded as well when it cast 16 for its Indiana neighbor, Hendricks.

Indiana cast 13 for Hendricks; Iowa 8 for Hendricks; Kansas 2 for Hendricks, and 1 for Hancock; Kentucky passed; Louisiana cast 8 for Hancock; Maine 4½ for Hancock, 2½ for Hendricks; Maryland 6 for Hancock, 1 for Hendricks; Massachusetts passed; Michigan called out 8 for its southern neighbor, Hendricks; Minnesota 4 for Hendricks; Mississippi 7 for Hancock; Missouri 2 for Hancock, 8 for Hendricks, 1 for English; Nebraska 3 for Hendricks; Nevada 3 for Hendricks; New Hampshire ½ for Hendricks, 4½ for Hancock; New Jersey 7 for Hendricks; New York declared its 33 votes belonged to Hendricks; North Carolina added 9 for Hendricks. The deadlock tightened like a noose.

Then Ohio was called upon by the Secretary. General McCook, its Chairman spoke in his stentorian voice used to addressing large crowds of comrades-in-arms. "Mr. Chairman," McCook bellowed, "I arise at the unanimous request and demand of the delegation from Ohio, with the consent and approval of every public man in the state, including the Honorable George H. Pendleton, to again place in nomination, against his inclination, but no longer against his honor, the name of Horatio Seymour, of New York."

Amid the roar that answered his call, Seymour, erect at the stand, turned ashen and felt a wave of dizzy apprehension. McCook was continuing. "Let us vote, Mr. Chairman of the Convention, for a man whom the Presidency has sought, but who has not sought the Presidency." Applause thundered back.

"I believe in my heart that it is the solution of the problem which has been engaging the minds of the Democrats and conservative men of the nation for the last six months," pronounced McCook, to the response of "Good! Good!" The Ohio chairman exhorted, "I believe it is the solution which will drive from power the Vandals who now possess the Capitol of the nation." Again applause beat against him. "I believe it will receive the unanimous assent and approval of the great belt of states, from the Atlantic . . . to the Pacific Ocean. . . ." Then he concluded, "I had almost forgotten to cast the 21 votes of Ohio for Horatio Seymour." Ohio worried that if it didn't act quickly, Hendricks would win the nomination. And it was rumored that Pendleton wanted to block Chase, who the New Yorkers had been prepared to push to end the deadlock. But what was the price?

Seymour was now at the rostrum and as soon as the waves of cheers subsided, he addressed the body that in the heat of the moment seemed to be about to take up his name against his will. Never in American Convention history had a candidate been nominated against his desires. "Gentlemen of the Convention," Seymour loudly responded amidst cheers. The handsome political leader of the Empire State looked dashing against the chaos of the scene that engulfed him. Immaculately clad, aristocratically groomed, he looked all the part of a President, but he was possessed by a kind of fear that everything he loved in his style of life was about to vanish, and yet such an honor had been within his ambition.

"The motion just made by the gentleman from Ohio excites in my mind the most mingled emotions," he began. Again, applause circled through the brand new Tammany Wigwam seething with anticipation and excitement. "I have no terms in which to express my gratitude . . . ," Seymour was interrupted with more expressive cheers, "for the magnanimity of his state, and for the generosity of this Convention." The delegates were now exuberant. "I have no terms in which to tell of my

114

regret that my name has been brought before the Convention. God knows that my life and all that I value most in life I would give for the good of my country, which I believe to be identified with the Democratic Party."

Several from the crowd shouted. "Take the nomination then."

Seymour continued undaunted. "I do not stand here as a man proud of his opinions, or obstinate in his purposes; but upon a question of duty and of honor I must stand upon my own convictions against the world." Another in the crowd called out, "God bless you, Horatio Seymour."

"Gentlemen, when I said here at an early day that honor forbade my accepting a nomination by this Convention, I meant it," Seymour lectured the feverish multitude. "When in the course of my intercourse with those of my own delegation and my friends, I said to them that I could not be a candidate, I meant it. And now permit me here to say that I know, after all that has taken place, I could not receive the nomination without placing, not only myself, but the great Democratic Party, in a false position." No one could ever know what fear he harbored, whether a personal revelation or something else left unsaid. He later commented that he thought the nomination would send him to his grave within the year.

He sought his exit. "But gentlemen of the Convention, more than that, we have had today an exhibition, from the distinguished citizen of Ohio that has touched my heart, as it has touched yours. I thank God and I congratulate this country, that there is in the great State of Ohio, whose magnificent position gives it so great a control over the action of our country, a young man, rising fast into fame [Pendleton was just 43 years old], whose future is all glorious, who has told the world that he could tread beneath his feet every other consideration than that of duty; and when he expressed to his delegation, and expressed in more direct terms, that he was willing that I should be nominated, who had stood in such a position of marked opposition to his own nomination, I should feel a dishonored man if I could not tread, in the far distance, and in a feeble way, the same honorable pathway which he has marked out."

Gallantry could not conceal the fact New York had won. Pendleton, whom they had battled all Convention, had bowed out. Perhaps in a gesture of ironic revenge they had cast the nomination upon the leader of their opponents, despite the fact that he had stood aloof as Convention President. Now the Convention threw its acclaim on Ohio.

"Gentlemen," Seymour concluded, "I thank you and may God bless you for your kindness to me; but your candidate I cannot be." The Convention responded with three rousing cheers for Horatio Seymour. "Bewildered and embarrassed," the Convention President hastily left the Wigwam's stage and fled the Convention with his associates, escaping to the house of his friend Colonel John Dash Van Buren on Ninth Street, hoping that some other workable solution would be found to the Convention's stalemate. (Tradition dictated that nominees did not attend Nominating Conventions because it tarnished them with overt ambition.) Thomas L. Price, of Missouri, assumed his position as Chair of the Convention.

Clement Vallandigham took the floor again. "Mr. President: In times of great public exigency, and especially in times of great public calamity, every personal consideration must be yielded to the public good." The Convention agreed. "The safety of the people is the supreme law, and the safety of the American Republic demands the nomination of Horatio Seymour, of New York." Wild cheers echoed his demand. "Ohio cannot, Ohio will not accept his declination and her 21 votes shall stand recorded in his name." More cheers followed and cries of "Good, good!"

"And now I call upon the delegations from all the states represented on this floor; upon all the states of this Union, from the Atlantic to the Pacific," Vallandigham dramatically gestured, "from the great lakes to the gulf, disregarding those minor considerations which justly it may be, properly I know, tend to sway them in casting their ballots, to make this nomination unanimous; and before God, I believe that in November the judgment of this Convention will be confirmed and ratified by the people of all the United States." A thundering applause, immense and sustained, rolled through the tumultuous Wigwam. Ohio had unleashed a stampede.

"Mr. President," called out Mr. Kernan. "Belonging to the delegation from the State of New York, and coming from the district where the President of this Convention lives, I cannot, as an individual delegate, refrain from asking the indulgence of this Convention in making one or two observations. And in order that we may relieve everybody, in order to relieve our Chairman from every bit of sensitiveness on the question of honor, I desire to say, on behalf of the delegation from the State of New York, that they have had neither lot nor part in the motion, which in our hearts we yet rejoice to hear from the State of Ohio.

"We heard but recently that some such movement was thought, by wise and good men, necessary for the safety of our country, but our hearts were coerced out of deference to the sensitiveness of the gentleman who presides over this Convention, and we told them that we could have neither lot nor part in it, unless others overcame that which we had never been able to do."

Later, some Democrats complained that somehow the New York delegation was indeed behind the sudden turn of events. Although Kernan presumed to speak for the New York delegation, he did not speak for Boss Tweed who may well have been more than suggestive on the surprise outcome. No one spoke of what became of the three million dollars the *Times* had reported that Chase people, meaning some in New York, were ready to use to try to influence the nomination with delegates ready to make a deal. Had the money helped Ohio decide when it became apparent their man could not win?

Kernan seemed to believe otherwise. He reviewed the days of Convention voting which had come short of the goal of a nominee. He continued, "New York has steadily voted her judgment, with kind feelings to other candidates. We have pronounced as our second choice for a distinguished citizen from Indiana. But it seems to me that, after this long struggle, and in this crisis of our affairs . . . in reference to our distinguished chairman, that his honor is entirely safe. No one can doubt that he has steadily and in good faith declined; but now that his honor is safe, his duty is to his country. . . ." Thus, New York gave its public blessing to its former Governor.

A great ovation followed his remarks. Seymour had exhibited grace in conduct of the Convention. He was a man of integrity and great political skill. The Roll Call of the States continued with Oregon, which cast 3 votes for Hendricks. Pennsylvania cast 26 for Hancock; Rhode Island 4 for Doolittle; South Carolina 6 for Hancock; Tennessee gave 4 for President Johnson, 1½ for Hendricks, 3½ for Hancock, and 1 for Seymour; Texas cast 6 for Hancock; Vermont 5 for Hendricks; Virginia 10 for Hancock; West Virginia 5 for Hancock. Meanwhile, the commotion among the delegates on the floor became animated as delegations debated the development.

Mr. H. L. Palmer, who subsequently had assumed the Chair, called upon Wisconsin, whose Chairman shouted: "The delegation from Wisconsin has steadily supported a distinguished citizen of that state for the position of President of the United States. But I am now instructed by the delegation to change that vote, and in making this change I am instructed to second the State of Ohio and cast their 8 votes for Horatio Seymour."

His announcement set off tremendous cheering on the floor and in the galleries.

Kentucky followed by shifting its 11 votes to Seymour, and the rush to nomination was on. State after state altered its original vote and jumped on the Seymour bandwagon. Hats and handkerchiefs were waved as Massachusetts, North Carolina, Mississippi, switched as well, and the giant brick building shook with uproarious applause and all the delegates jumped to their feet cheering. The Roll Call was completed. State banners swayed back and forth. Suddenly, outside of the Convention hall a cannon was set off, despite the new law against firing weapons, the traditional sign that a nominee for President had been selected by the Convention, and the cheering inside intensified to an even higher pitch.

117

Each cannon blast was answered by thunderous cheers of the Convention as states continued to shift their votes.

Mr. Stuart, of Michigan, yelled at the top of his lungs. "When so much wisdom as is here today, with a voice so united as this, speaks for the distinguished son of New York, the greatest statesman, in my judgment, now living, Michigan cannot consent to withhold her voice in this general expression, not only in confidence of him, but, sir, this expression of patriotic determination to rescue this country from the grasp of the most desperate rebels that ever seized upon the reins of the Government." Stuart was answered with louder cheers. "It is a question of Constitution; it is a question of country; it is a question of whether this blessed Union, and the freedom of these millions is to live, or whether it is to be buried deep down in everlasting oblivion and infamy. Sir, under these circumstances, it is with infinite pleasure that Michigan casts her vote for Horatio Seymour, of New York."

After more states joined the rush to Seymour, Samuel Tilden, of New York, spoke in favor of his political ally. "It is fitting that on this occasion New York should wait for the voice of all her sister states. Last evening I should not have believed, did not believe, the event which has just happened to be possible. . . . There was but one obstacle, and that was in the repugnance, which I take upon myself the whole responsibility of declaring to have been earnest, sincere, deep-felt, on the part of Horatio Seymour to accept this nomination. I did not believe that any circumstances would make it possible, except Ohio, with whom we have been unfortunately dividing our votes, should herself demand it, and to that I thought New York ought to yield."

He then cemented the nomination with New York's approval. The passion of his incredulity makes it unlikely a reformer like Tilden, despite his position as a Tammany Sachem since 1856, had orchestrated such a change in events. But Tilden was known as a cold and strategic political operative who wasted little time on human emotions, albeit committed to reform. He is unlikely to have had anything to do with a possible Tweed deal, although he also benefited in New York's sudden victory.

Mr. Clark, of Wisconsin, commented, "I see around me, on the floor and in the galleries, ladies and gentlemen who desire also to be heard . . . I therefore move that they ratify it by giving three cheers for Horatio Seymour," which they did.

The Secretary of the Convention then spoke. "The following is the result of the Twenty-Second Ballot: All the states having voted, and the vote of the full Electoral College having been given, the Roll stands for Horatio Seymour, 317 votes." For the next five minutes, the Tammany Wigwam writhed and wiggled with wild cheering and hoopla traditional to party celebrations. The United Democracy had its nominee to face General Grant. Tweed on stage joined in the merriment of the moment. Could anyone have orchestrated the passion of the crowd before him?

A tremendous chorus of nine cheers followed the final toll and wild excitement swept through the magnificent hall that Tammany built. Here also was a nomination that Tammany's influential political leader greatly favored for reasons of his own and whose hidden influence seemed to be at work. Tammany's "Honest John" Kelly had dined privately with Tilden and Seymour at Delmonico's at Fifth Avenue and Twenty-Sixth Street near Madison Square the evening prior. What was said? It was reported that Seymour had made a passionate plea for Chase to the New York delegation the prior evening. Now this sudden resolution gave him the nomination against his publicly stated will. Tilden later entertained the Ohio delegation at Delmonico's where perhaps the plan was launched. Other meetings took place at the Manhattan Club. Tammany's reach was wide. The three million dollars which the *Times* had mentioned remained unaccounted for.

"There had been something done during the previous evening," the *Times* reported the next day. "There had been a meeting of prominent gentlemen at the Manhattan Club, which was generally believed to have arranged matters; but how, nobody knew. Hence there was an eager expectancy everywhere throughout the hall . . . The bitter antagonism between East and West was still apparent. . . ."

The *Times* also noted that, "the conviction had grown stronger since the previous night that the prospects of the party were being frittered away in the fruitless balloting. . . ." Hence the Convention was in a condition that a bold, adroit move in any direction was almost certain of success." The Convention had a psychology of its own, but it had a brain as well that directed its deliberations. However it had happened, the first post-Civil War Democracy had a new national leader to take its case to the people. To this day, no other person has been nominated for the Presidency by a major political party against his will.

Horatio Seymour, the 1868 Democratic nominee for President of the United States, had a distinguished pedigree. Born in Pompey Hill near Utica in 1810, he was admitted to the New York bar in 1832. His early political training came as a secretary to Governor William Learned Marcy from 1833 to 1839. He launched his own political career as Utica's mayor in 1842, the same year he was first elected to the New York Assembly. Seymour was re-elected in 1844 and became its Speaker in 1845, proving indispensable in the fight to pass legislation authorizing the Erie Canal. In the famous split of the New York Democracy, Seymour, a conservative, was associated with the Hunkers against the Barnburners. Always an able statesman, he served as a unifier when the party came back together after the election of 1848.

Philosophically, Seymour was a Jeffersonian Democrat who opposed the tariff and centralization of the Federal Government. He also stood against nativism, mandatory abstinence from liquor, and Abolition. Seymour ran for New York Governor six times, first in 1850, losing to the Whigs. Two years later, he was victorious and used his term to reform schools and prisons. But he lost re-election in 1854 in the backlash against the Kansas-Nebraska Act. He also attracted the ire of temperance voters when he vetoed a prohibition measure, even though he was a teetotaler.

Seymour returned to the Governor's mansion from 1862 to 1864, supporting the Union during the war, although he was highly critical of Lincoln's suspension of constitutional Rights, such as habeas corpus, and he disputed the constitutionality of Lincoln's Emancipation Proclamation. During the New York City draft riots of 1863, Seymour personally quelled some of the disturbance with his bold speeches on the steps of City Hall and at Wall Street. But since he had been a vocal opponent of the draft, Horace Greeley charged that Seymour was part of the Copperhead conspiracy that plotted the riots and he was portrayed as the ring leader in opposition political cartoons.

Seymour also drew the wrath of New York voters by calling for a negotiated peace between North and South in 1864 and was defeated in his reelection bid. But his personal integrity and reputation for sagacity made him a compelling choice for a party seeking to overcome its darkest hour. Ultimately, the division between Democrats of the East and West, between conservatives and radicals, contributed to Seymour's surprise nomination. Few outside the Convention, consumed with its own magical hysteria, thought he had much of a chance against the victorious General Grant. Seymour said, "I did not seek the nomination, nor did I desire it. I was forced, compelled by the very peculiar circumstances in which I was placed to accept it." Years later, he added, "The failure to insist on my declination of the nomination then was the mistake of my life."

After an hour recess inside the Tammany temple, nominations for Vice President commenced. Illinois nominated favorite son General John A. McClernand, who immediately stood and withdrew his name. Iowa nominated Asa C. Dodge, former Congressman, Senator, and American Minister to the Court of Spain. Kansas nominated native son General Thomas Ewing, Jr. Former Confederate General Preston, of Kentucky, nominated General Francis (Frank) Preston Blair, Jr., of Missouri.

Confederate General Wade Hampton, of South Carolina, weighed in, "Our state wishes me to say the soldiers of the South cordially, heartily, and cheerfully accept the right hand of friendship which is extended to them. . ." and then he seconded the Blair nomination. After the names of Ewing and Dodge were withdrawn, the Roll was taken and Francis P. Blair was unanimously nominated to run with Seymour.

Frank Blair, Jr. had been born in Missouri but raised in Washington by his famous father, a Jacksonian Democrat who became a founder of the Republican Party. He was educated at North Carolina and Princeton, and entered the legal profession at St. Louis in 1843. He was a private in the Mexican War and Attorney General for the Territory of New Mexico after that war. He had served in the Missouri House of Representatives from 1852 through 1856, before he was elected as a Republican to Congress, serving on and off from 1857 to 1864, with time away to fight in the Civil War. After the war, he engaged in bitter fights with the Radical Republicans, and left that party for the Democracy. Blair, it was rumored, was a heavy drinker. In years to come, he would serve as a U.S. Senator from Missouri, from 1871 to 1873.

Its business done, the Tenth National Democratic Convention adjourned "sine die" at 3:50 p.m., Thursday, July 9, 1868, with Horatio Seymour the first candidate in Convention history to personally turn away from the presidential nomination and still be nominated. Seymour was formally notified of his nomination that night at the Manhattan Club by a delegation consisting of one delegate from each state.

"How was it done?" the *Times* speculated. ". . . 'Walk into my parlor,' said the New York Spider to the Democratic flies; and the flies accepted the invitation. And a pretty parlor Tammany was found to be. The spider was there in all his glory, and the poor flies, after being rendered helpless in his meshes, were slaughtered without mercy. The delegates, we doubt not, came to New York in full reliance on the good faith and decency of their host. Their idea was, that they were about to attend a deliberative body. A brief experience taught them the emptiness of their expectations. New York, instead of acting the host, insisted on playing the master. . . . Greatly to its disgust, Tammany insisted on carrying their platform, but when the balloting was reached, their firmness gave way. The game of Tammany was from the beginning one of intrigue."

Boss Tweed, who had sat on stage with the other Convention vice presidents, had much to gain in Seymour's victory, not that he cared much for Seymour. (Within a few years, Seymour would join Tilden to dethrone the king of graft.) But Tweed's candidate for New York Governor, New York City Mayor John T. Hoffman, who had lost a previous gubernatorial race, would have an easier time winning with Seymour sweeping New York. Hoffman's election was essential to passing home rule provisions for New York City and removing the state supervision that hampered the Tweed Ring's wholesale looting of the city treasury.

To the charges of a deal with New York and Tweed's Ring, Clement Vallandigham responded that Seymour was, "an eloquent orator, an able and experienced statesman, an accomplished gentleman, sober and righteous . . . a man of the strictest integrity; the candidate of no "ring" or faction, and one who will not himself steal, nor permit theft in others . . . who was nominated against his will, and without a pledge or promise to any one on any subject." Judge Allen G. Thurman, of Ohio, a future U.S. Senator, called Seymour a "high-minded, honorable man . . . one of the greatest and purest of the public men of our times."

Seymour appeared in public on July 10, the evening following the end of the Convention, to give a speech inside the Tammany Hall, accepting the nomination and endorsing the party platform. The Tammany Wigwam was packed and illuminated with calcium lights. Fireworks were fired outside at intervals.

Former Governor Seymour was greeted with loud cheers. He told the wild throng that he would stand upon the party's platform and "take an active part . . . in the great struggle." He added, "I congratulate you, and all conservative men, who seek to restore order, peace, prosperity and good Government to our land." Blair followed with a rousing call to fight for "the restoration of our race." Some Southern Democrats, not in attendance, found Seymour's public appearance repugnant, since presidential candidates were expected to stay above the political contest. They felt he should taste defeat as a result. Seymour himself felt he had been dropped into "a sea of trouble."

The *New York Times* called the results of the Democratic Convention a "revolutionary ticket" and it editorialized: "We cannot forget that the Horatio Seymour who is to wrestle with Grant for the presidency did what he could to weaken the Union soldier on the battlefield. The alliance of Seymour, who plotted against the Union, with F. P. Blair, who gallantly fought to save it, would be most incongruous, but for the epistle with which the latter sought to commend himself to the good graces of the Convention. Nothing more revolutionary than his proposition has appeared. It threatens the overthrow of Reconstruction."

Blair had written a public letter that announced his intentions: "There is but one way to restore the Government and the Constitution, and that is for the President-elect to declare these [Reconstruction] acts null and void; compel the army to undo its usurpations of the South, disperse the carpet-bag state Governments, allow the white people to reorganize their own Governments. . . ."

The *Times* also tried to rebuff claims that Seymour was, "a great statesman," saying "Grant displayed more statesmanship in his negotiations with Lee, in the advice he gave to the President, in the measures he urged upon Congress, in the policy he sought to secure in the South, in the execution of his duties, civil and military, than Seymour ever dreamed of."

The puzzle over how Seymour had won the nomination continued to baffle observers for weeks afterwards. The *Times* said the question was, "more intricate and less liable to be solved than the most famous production of Chinese ingenuity . . . the longer it was considered, the less men knew about it." The paper conceded that even if there were a conspiracy of New Yorkers, Seymour may not have been a party to it. "Seymour's appearance and manner when the crisis came upon him" was evidence in his favor. "The man is either a consummate actor or he suddenly encountered a most unexpected event when Ohio put him in nomination. For a moment he was thrown off his balance and stood unpoised, irresolute before the vast assemblage." Whether he had been sincere in previous rejections of the nomination, whether he intended to obtain it by other means, are different questions. He made an earnest speech for Chase on the night before his own selection." Seymour told a reporter from the *New York Sun*, "Had I been as cool as I am now, I should have declined."

None-the-less, August Belmont and New York State party Chairman Samuel Tilden ran the Unified Democracy's 1868 campaign and handled the finances. Tilden traveled from state to state urging organization. Seymour was in constant contact by letter from Utica. Each member of the Democratic executive committee contributed $10,000 to the electoral effort. Other funds were raised from sympathetic big donors, such as patent medicine king H. T. Hembold, who contributed $40,000. William Corcoran, of Washington, D. C. added a substantial sum. The party sold a book of Seymour's speeches for party orators. Seymour's friend Cyrus Hall McCormick, of Illinois, donated $12,000 and sat on the campaign finance committee raising funds from others.

Nearly a month passed before Horatio Seymour submitted his official letter of acceptance from Utica. On August 4, 1868, he responded, noting that the nomination was "unsought and unexpected." He recalled that, "It was my ambition to take an active part, from which I am now excluded, in the great struggle going on for the restoration of good Government, and of peace and prosperity to our country. But I have been caught up by the whelming tide which is bearing us on to a great political change, and I find myself unable to resist its pressure." He confirmed that the platform resolutions passed by the Convention were "in accord with my views. . . ."

Seymour explained his slow response. "I have delayed the mere formal act of communication to you in writing what I thus publicly said . . . for the purpose of seeing what light the action of Congress would throw upon the interest of the country. Its acts, since the adjournment of the Convention, show an alarm lest a change of political power will give to the people what they ought to have, a clear statement of what has been done with the money drawn from them during the past eight years. . . ."

Seymour charged, "The congressional party has not only allied itself with military power, which is to be brought directly to bear upon the elections in many states, but which also holds itself in perpetual session, with the avowed purpose of making such laws as it shall see fit, in view of the elections which will take place within a few weeks." Never before in the history of our county has Congress thus taken a menacing attitude towards its electors," Seymour wrote. "Under its influence, some of the states organized by its agents are proposing to deprive the people of the Right to vote for Presidential Electors, and the first steps are taken to destroy the Rights of suffrage. . . . There is a dread of some exposure that drives them on to acts so desperate and impolitic."

Seymour also set out the qualifications for the office he sought. "No man can rightfully enter upon the duties of the presidential office, unless he is not only willing to carry out the wishes of the people, expressed in a constitutional way, but is also prepared to stand up for the Rights of minorities. He must be ready to uphold the free exercise of religion. He must denounce measures which would wrong personal or home Rights, or the religious conscience of the humblest citizen of the land. He must maintain, without distinction of creed or nationality, all the privileges of American citizenship."

These duties Seymour said he was ready to fulfill, that he was, "strengthened by the cooperation of the great body of those who served in the Union army and navy during the war. Having given nearly 16,000 commissions to the officers of that army, I know their views and wishes. They demand the Union for which they fought. . . . They called upon the Government to stop in its policy of hate, discord, and disunion, and, in terms of fervid eloquence, they demanded the restoration of the Rights and liberties of the American people. When there is such accord between those who proved themselves brave and self-sacrificing in war, and those who are thoughtful and patriotic in council, I cannot doubt we shall gain a political triumph which will restore our Union, bring back peace and prosperity to our land, and will give us once more the blessings of a wise, economical, and honest Government," Seymour concluded.

Upon official notification of his nomination, the incendiary Blair wrote that: "The issues upon which the contest turns are clear, and cannot be obscured or distorted by the sophistries of our adversaries. They all resolve themselves into the old and ever-recurring struggle of a few men to absorb the political power of the nation. This effort, under every conceivable name and disguise, has always characterized the opponents of the Democratic Party, but at no time has the attempt assumed a shape so open and daring as in this contest.

"The adversaries of free and constitutional Government, in defiance of the express language of the Constitution, have erected a military despotism in ten of the states of the Union, have taken from the President the power vested in him by the supreme law, and have deprived

124

the Supreme Court of its jurisdiction," Blair charged. "Whole states and communities of people of our race have been attained, convicted, condemned, and deprived of their Rights as citizens, without presentment, or trial, or witnesses, but by congressional enactment of ex post facto laws. . . ."

Blair bitterly made his racist complaint: "The same usurping authority has substituted as electors in place of the men of our race, thus illegally attainted and disfranchised, a host of ignorant Negroes who are supported in idleness with the public money, and are combined together to strip the white race of their birthright through the management of freedmen's bureaus and emissaries of conspirators in other states. And, to complete the oppression, the military power of the nation has been placed at their disposal, in order to make this barbarism supreme."

Blair chided Grant: "The military leader, under whose prestige this usurping Congress has taken refuge in the condemnation of their schemes by the free people of the North, in the elections of the last year, and whom they have selected as their candidate, to shield themselves from the result of their own wickedness and crime, has announced his acceptance of the nomination, and his willingness to maintain their usurpations over eight millions of white people at the South, fixed to earth with his bayonets.

"He exclaims, 'Let us have peace!' " Blair countered, " 'The empire is peace,' exclaimed Bonaparte, when freedom and its defenders expired under the sharp edge of his sword. The peace to which Grant invites us is the peace of despotism and death. . . Negro suffrage (which the popular vote of New York, New Jersey, Pennsylvania, Ohio, Michigan, Connecticut, and other states had condemned as expressly against the letter of the Constitution) must stand, because their Senators and Representatives have willed it. . . . Although declared unconstitutional by the Supreme Court, and although the President is sworn to sustain and support the Constitution, the will of a fraction of a Congress . . . must stand against the will of the people," Blair blasted.

"It is 'revolutionary' to execute the will of the people! It is 'revolutionary' to execute the judgment of the Supreme Court!" Blair sarcastically continued, "It is 'revolutionary' in the President to keep inviolate his oath to sustain the Constitution! This false construction of the vital principle of our Government is the last resort of those who would have their arbitrary Reconstruction sway and supercede our time-honored institutions'. The appeal to the peaceful ballot to attain this end is not war, is not 'revolution'. "This is the only road to peace. It will come with the election of the Democratic candidate, and not with the election of that mailed warrior, whose bayonets are now at the throats of eight millions of people in the South, to compel them to support him as a candidate for the presidency, and to submit to the domination of an alien race of semi-barbarous men. No perversion of Truth, or audacity of misrepresentation, can exceed that which hails this candidate in arms as an angel of peace," Blair concluded. In the election, the Republicans would make those in the country who didn't already fear Blair, tremble at the prospect of his ascension to the presidency.

Throughout the campaign, Republicans called Democrats the party of treason and secession, something for which voters seemed intent on punishing them. They called Seymour a "Copperhead" who had undercut the war effort and incited the draft riots. They said Blair's election meant "revolution." Republicans attracted plenty of help from the nation's financiers who had made millions from the Civil War and who supported the party's "hard money" policy of repaying the national debt with gold rather than paper currency.

The *New York Times* editorialized that: "What Grant did for the Union, every man and woman, every boy and girl, every Northerner and Southerner, every foreigner and Americans knows." But it asked, "What was Horatio Seymour doing for his country? Was he exerting his powers of mind and position in their behalf? Or was he acting in such a way as to encourage the enemy, to discourage our army and people, and to throw the weight of the Empire State on the side of the disunionists? He was an effective ally of the Copperheads, and exerted his energies to array the state against the Republic. He sowed the seeds of sectional quarrels. . . . It was a shameful and fearful history throughout; and yet it is a reward for his conduct at that time that he has been nominated as the Democratic candidate for the presidency."

Nor were Republicans above personally attacking Seymour. William Cullen Bryant, editor of the *New York Evening Post*, charged that insanity ran deeply in Seymour's family. In fact, both his father and brother had committed suicide and his mother died in an insane asylum. Seymour half expected the same fate himself. Bryant asked for legislation to protect the country in the event the President went mad. The theme was taken up with a vengeance by Republican stump speakers. Meanwhile, the Astors, Vanderbilts, and Jay Cooke all donated large sums to the Republican assault.

Democrats countered that the Republican Congress was driving the economy into prolonged crisis with its corruption and military expenditures. Seymour waged a letter-writing campaign to party leaders across the nation trying to rally support. The popular General George McClellan endorsed Seymour in a widely-publicized October Third letter. Seymour thought that the nation's soldiers, North and South, would vote against Grant, "since he slaughtered them too ruthlessly." Tammany Hall pitched in $327,000 to help the Seymour ticket in New York.

By October, August Belmont, the national chairman, felt discouraged about the outcome. Hendricks and Indiana Democrats were upset by the Convention's outcome and the inside dealing by the New Yorkers, but by election time would come around to supporting the national party. Supreme Court Justice Chase supported neither Seymour nor Grant. After the four "October States" voted Republican in state elections, the *New York World* posted sensational headlines calling for a new Democratic ticket to replace Seymour and Blair with Chase to save the November election. Out West, McCormick also called for a replacement. President Johnson still held out a glimmer of hope that he would be put back on the ticket to defeat Grant. Seymour wrote that he would not "shrink from defeat."

But Tilden and Belmont prevented any candidate changes. President Johnson then telegraphed the nominee in Buffalo, urging him to take to the stump with "inspired tongue." The campaign had become bitter, in part because of Frank Blair's blistering rhetoric against Reconstruction. To soften Blair's impact, Horatio Seymour entered the campaign himself. Flouting lingering tradition, Seymour took to the campaign trail, speaking in Chicago on October 24, and then in Detroit, Indianapolis, Columbus, Pittsburgh, and Philadelphia, and at railroad stops in between, preaching "the gospel of peace," and even calling for improvement in the condition of the Negro. Unlike Blair, Seymour's speeches were restrained and rational. But he was spitting in the wind against the prestige and popularity of General Grant, who himself made few political speeches during his trip out West to inspect the condition of the Indians, for whom he had great sympathy.

On November 3, 1868, voters rendered their decision. Blacks were only allowed to vote in seven states. Of the 5,716,072 votes cast, Seymour won 2,703,249, while Grant attracted 3,012,823, or 53 percent. Yet, Grant was victorious by a mere 309,583 votes, hardly an overwhelming victory and one that showed the nation still wearily divided and uneasy about the post-war reconciliation. However, in the Electoral College, Grant was dominant, winning 214 to 80. Grant took twenty-six states, including Indiana, to eight for Seymour, including Delaware, Kentucky, Maryland, New Jersey, Oregon, and New York, which he won by more than 10,000 votes to the chagrin of Republicans.

The Southern states of Mississippi, Texas, and Virginia were prohibited from participating in the election since they had not yet been readmitted to the Union. Elsewhere in the South, Seymour and the Democrats won only Louisiana and Georgia. Seymour was hindered by the fact that Republicans controlled the franchise in the Southern states. And he lost several close contests in the North, in part due to the new black vote. Grant won Massachusetts by just 77,000 votes and California by just 514 votes. Seymour fought a valiant battle, but could not overcome the odds. (He retired from politics and refused the 1876 gubernatorial nomination, before dying that year.)

The *New York Times'* November 4, 1868, headline proclaimed a single word: "Victory!" Below that it exulted, "Magnificent and Overwhelming Republican Triumph." However, elsewhere it noted, "We regret to add that the probabilities seem against the success of Mr. John A. Griswold for Governor. . . " Hoffman pulled in many more votes for New York Governor, than Seymour did for President. "The [New York] Democrats cared comparatively little for the presidency," the *Times* reported. "They are abundantly consoled for the defeat of Seymour by the success of Hoffman . . . the Democracy of this state. [meaning thereby Tammany], will have the ascendancy and control of its councils. The Erie Railroad is a tool in the hands of the Ring already, and its money and direction are used remorselessly to augment its political power and swell the personal fortunes of its individual members. The patronage and general influence of the executive branch of the state Government will be in the same hands, and used for the same ends".

"Tammany has played its game with adroitness and success," the *Times* continued. "By dictating the platform and the candidates it destroyed all chances of national success; and by bending all its efforts to elect Hoffman, it secured all the advantage of such success as the party might achieve, to itself. Its rejoicings over the result confirm the charges of treachery to the party which have been so lavishly heaped on the Ring by the leading organs of the Democracy outside the State. . . This election, unless we are mistaken, will put an end to the Democratic Party as at present organized." The paper's prediction proved true. Four years later, in July, 1872, a defeated Democracy simply endorsed the candidate of the protest Liberal Republican Party, their former enemy, Horace Greeley, in a six-hour Convention in Baltimore.

The *Times* also noted that while the election was quiet in the city, "Many who attempted to vote illegally were arrested, and a great many more succeeded in depositing fraudulent votes. The army of special deputies appointed by the Sheriff swarmed at the various polling places, and did much to obstruct the voting of the Republicans. . . The returns from this City show the startling fact that in more than twenty districts, the polled vote exceeded the registered vote all the way from five to fifty. It is by such infamous frauds together with the illegal naturalization, that the State of New York is made to give a Democratic majority." Mayor Hoffman resigned in December 1868 to be sworn in as New York's new Governor. A. Oakey Hall, Tweed's partner in crime, won a special election to replace Hoffman as Mayor.

After the election, Horace Greeley called for a congressional probe into Tammany vote fraud during the election of 1868. The 900-page congressional report, filed in February of 1869, found the election to be the most tainted in city history with "organized corruption" in Manhattan and Brooklyn. In advance of the election, Tammany Judges had conducted wholesale naturalizations of 33,318 aliens and Tammany had padded the voter rolls with hundreds of illegal "round robin" voters who moved from precinct to precinct voting repeatedly before they received their reward of cash or drink. Tweed had followed upstate returns by telegraph and adjusted the city's vote as necessary to keep a winning margin.

New York City's Democratic totals were up by as much as 50 percent in 1868. Showing Tammany's real interest, gubernatorial candidate Hoffman out-polled Seymour's totals in New York City by 4,000 votes. The Republican-controlled Congressional commission charged that without fraud in New York City, Grant would have won New York State by 17,000 votes. The Commission did not examine whether Republicans would have allowed Democrats to win more Southern states.

Three years after the election, Tilden and Seymour led a coalition of seventy reformers who brought Tweed down from his golden throne. Two years after the 1868 Convention, James Watson, New York City Auditor, was killed in a Central Park carriage accident. Before Tammany could replace him with its own man, the state appointed an honest accountant who exposed millions of dollars in Tweed Ring graft and corruption. Finally in 1871, the *New York Times* received documents that proved Tweed's illegal schemes. The corruption of his "Ring" was well known, but always without the critical proof. Subsequent investigations showed that six out of eight New York newspapermen were on Tweed's payroll.

When evidence finally surfaced, the *Times* owner George O. Jones, turned down a $5 million bribe not to print evidence he uncovered. "I made up my mind not long ago to put some of those fellows behind bars, and I'm going to keep them there," he announced. "Only be careful that you don't first put yourself in a coffin," Tweed supporters warned. This time the honest press prevailed and the Tweed Ring was broken. Horace Greeley wrote that the Tweed Ring, "was the most corrupt gang of political adventurers that ever ruled and robbed a helpless city."

From 1861 to 1870, Tweed had run the city as a deputy street commissioner. With Peter B. Sweeny, who was a delegate to the 1868 Convention, and Richard B. Connolly, Tweed, also a member of the Board of Supervisors, created the "Ring" that looted the city of up to $200 million. As Commissioner of Public Works, he controlled all city contracts. The marble and stone quarry he owned supplied stone for major public works like the Brooklyn Bridge. Tweed's New York Printing Company had a contract for all official city printing. He was also a member of the New York State Senate from 1867 to 1871. Tweed became the director of banks, gas and insurance companies, and railroads.

He owned five mansions worth millions of dollars and was familiar at the exclusive clubs in New York and Connecticut, riding in a trim carriage, flashing his diamond rings.

The investigation showed that Tweed controlled the police department and every job seeker in the city paid him a stipend for his position and other favors. With the help of Governor Hoffman, he had won his new Home Rule Charter for New York City, known as the "Tweed Charter" that removed state supervision and opened the city's resources to unchecked graft. After Tweed's exposure, the reformers won a city election and took back the city treasury.

Tweed was convicted of massive fraud, and sentenced to twelve years in prison, plus a $12,750 fine. In 1873, his sentence was reduced mysteriously to one year, a $250 fine, and he was released. But he was jailed again on civil charges. Bribing his jailers, Tweed escaped to Spain, before being caught and returned to New York, where he died in the Ludlow Street Jail in 1876, the same year the presidential election was "stolen" from another Democrat, New Yorker Governor Samuel J. Tilden. The resolution of that electoral struggle led to Northern withdrawal of military supervisors from the South and an end of Grant's efforts to suppress the Ku Klux Klan, leaving generations of freed blacks to the brutal reaction of Jim Crow segregation.

As it turned out, Grant's administration was almost as corrupt as Tweed's. The nation's business was essentially turned over to the special interests of industry and finance. The party of liberation, as the Republicans had been in the beginning, now became seen by many as the party of protected wealth, graft, and corruption, a protector of the tariff and the million-dollar "Trusts."

New York Presidential Politics

Vice President George Clinton

Vice President Aaron Burr

Governor DeWitt Clinton

Vice President Daniel D. Tompkins

President Stephen Grover Cleveland

President Chester Alan Arthur

Vice President Levi Parsons Morton · Alton Brooks Parker

Gerrit Smith

Henry Lloyd Garrison

Lewis Tappan

Elizur Wright

James G. Birney

President Andrew Jackson

President William Henry Harrison

Tecumseh

1844

William Jay

President James Knox Polk

Senator Henry Clay

Senator John Caldwell Calhoun

Liberty 1847

Senator William Henry Seward

Thurlow Weed

Frederick Douglass

John Brown

Free Soil 1848

President Martin Van Buren

President John Quincy Adams

Senator Lewis Cass

Charles Francis Adams

President Millard Fillmore

Senator John Adams Dix

Benjamin Franklin Butler

Dred Scott

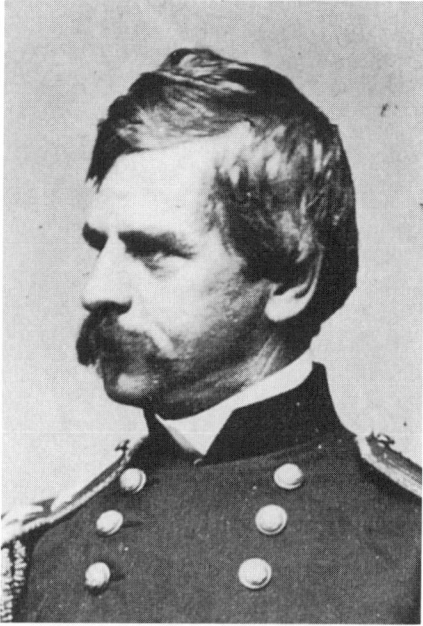

Nathaniel Prentiss Banks

President James Buchanan

John Charles Fremont

Horace Greeley

Governor Horatio Seymour

William Marcy Tweed

Samuel Jones Tilden

George Hunt Pendleton

President Andrew Johnson

Clement Laird Vallandigham

Senator Thomas Andrews Hendricks

James Preston Blair, Jr.

President Woodrow Wilson

President Warren Gamaliel Harding

Senator Oscar Wilder Underwood

William Jennings Bryan

Eleanor Roosevelt

Senator James Duval Phelan

Senator Robert Marion LaFollette

Senator Henry Cabot Lodge

At left, John William Davis

Below left, William Gibbs McAdoo

Below right, Governor Alfred Emanuel Smith

The Twenty-Fourth Democratic National Presidential Nominating Convention and the Election of 1924

Convention-at-a-Glance

Event: The Twenty-Fourth Democratic National Presidential Nominating Convention
Date: June 24–July 9, 1924
Location: Madison Square Garden, Madison Avenue and Twenty-Sixth Street, New York City
New York Governor: Alfred Emanuel Smith, Tammany Democrat
New York City Mayor: John F. Hylan, Tammany Democrat
Temporary Chairman: Pat Harrison, Mississippi
Permanent Chairman: Senator Thomas J. Walsh, Montana
Number of Delegates: 1,446 delegates with a total of 1,098 votes; two-thirds or 732 needed for nomination
Largest Crowd: 18,000
Candidates for Nomination: Senator Oscar Wilder Underwood, Alabama; Senator Joseph T. Robinson, Arkansas; William Gibbs McAdoo, California; Former Senator Willard Saulsbury, Delaware; Senator Samuel M. Ralston, Indiana; Governor Jonathan M. Davis, Kansas; Governor Albert Cabell Ritchie, Maryland; Senator Woodbridge N. Ferris, Michigan; Governor Charles W. Bryan, Nebraska; Governor Fred H. Brown, New Hampshire; Governor George S. Silzer, New Jersey; David Franklin Houston, New York; Governor Alfred Emanuel Smith, New York; Former Governor James Middleton Cox, Ohio; Senator Carter Glass, Virginia; Ambassador John William Davis, West Virginia
Presidential Nominee: John William Davis
Age of Nominee: 51
Number of Ballots: 103
Vice Presidential Nominee: Governor Charles W. Bryan, Nebraska

Platform Positions: Honest government; tariff revision; a graduated tax upon incomes; no nuisance taxes, sales taxes, nor any other form of taxation that place burdens on consumers; relief for distressed farmers and opening of foreign markets to their products; support of the cooperative marketing movement and an export marketing corporation; cut rates on railroads and creation of new waterways to relieve exploitation of farmers; reversal of deflation policy which "bankrupted hundreds of thousands of farmers and stock growers in America, and resulted in wide-spread industrial depression and unemployment"; recovery of the navy's oil reserves "fraudulently or illegally leased" to private interests; retention of water power; public control and conservation of natural resources such as coal, iron, oil, and timber; a national reforestation policy, new roads, deep waterways, and flood control; support for the mining industry; legislation ending "gradual financial strangling of innocent investors, workers, and consumers caused by the indiscriminate promotion, refinancing, and reorganizing of corporations on an inflated and over-capitalized basis, resulting already in the undermining and collapse of many railroads, public service and industrial corporations, manifesting itself in unemployment, irreparable loss and waste"; support of public education which is the "responsibility of the states"; decent living conditions for postal employees; support for collective bargaining; laws regulating hours of labor and conditions; public works for the unemployed; limits on campaign contributions; enforcement of the prohibition laws; attack on "the spreading of heroin addiction among the youth"; "exclusion of Asiatic immigration"; improvements of the national parks, harbors and breakwaters, and the Federal roads, and of the Territory of Hawaii; condemnation of the betrayal of "Armenia for the Chester Oil Concession"; rejection of war as "a relic of barbarism" which is justifiable only as a measure of defense; sweeping reduction of armaments by land and sea; a joint agreement with all nations for world disarmament; a national referendum on the League of Nations; and support for Freedom of Religion, Freedom of Speech, and Freedom of Press.
Campaign Slogans: "A vote for Coolidge is a vote for Chaos!" "Equal Rights for All, Special Privileges for None"

The Twenty-Fourth Democratic National Presidential Nominating Convention and the Election of 1924

"Show this administration an oil well and it will show you a foreign policy."—Senator Pat Harrison

After its experience with Tammany Hall in 1868, over half a century passed before the National Democracy dared to return to New York. A world war had come and gone and America had become an international power facing critical issues at home and abroad. To debate these momentous questions and to select a candidate to stand for election in November against President Coolidge, the Twenty-Fourth Democratic National Presidential Nominating Convention opened its deliberations on Tuesday, June 24, 1924. It would become the longest Convention in political party history.

The nation's oldest political party gathered within the cavernous interior of the old tower-trimmed Madison Square Garden at Twenty-Sixth Street and Madison Avenue, some twelve blocks north of Tammany's headquarters. The 1,446 delegates and equal number of alternates, along with 13,000 spectators jammed into the city's premiere arena decorated with 13,500 American flags that covered every open space in the hall. Another 3,500 large flag banners hung from the three tiers of balconies along with banners of Democratic Presidents Jefferson, Jackson, Cleveland, and Wilson. As the opening gavel banged, another 10,000 smaller flags fluttered down from the ceiling making the festive opening memorable for its pageantry.

A detail of 1,200 New York City policemen was assigned to protect and control the Convention, with a sub-headquarters set up underneath the speakers' platform and a relay system of phone booths scattered about the hall. Crowd control outside the Convention was essential as the number of spectators climbed. Scores of city detectives were already rounding up pickpockets, confidence men, and others with criminal intent with orders to remove them on charges of vagrancy. Police were also warning the public to be alert to price gouging of tickets. Their efforts proved effective. At Convention's end, no one had been robbed or assaulted.

An additional one hundred Federal agents had been dispatched from Washington to New York to clamp down on the smuggling and production of illegal beverages that flowed into the city in anticipation of the Convention in violation of the Eighteenth Amendment, also known as Prohibition. The Feds conceded that New York City would never be completely "Dry," but said they could try to keep it "arid" during Convention week. There was, however, no controlling the hotel room drinking among the "Wet" delegations or the constant efforts by the New York delegation to allure out-of-town delegates and alternates with the secret location of nearby speakeasies. They were warned by their leaders to resist the liquid entertainments and other vices offered them by those seeking to promote New York aims at the Convention.

Delegates wandering down Broadway to Madison Square Garden were likely to encounter emblematic donkeys on the marquees of the theaters along the "White Light" district. No doubt they also noticed cabarets that had been padlocked by Federal agents. The "White Way" hadn't been this Dry since Prohibition began. Delegates also were anxious to take in shows such as the Ziegfeld Follies, or "I'll Say She Is!" starring the Marx Brothers at the Casino at Broadway and Thirty-Ninth Street, or Douglas Fairbanks in "The Thief of Bagdad" at the Liberty Theatre at Broadway and Forty-Second Street. They also found that all the shops along Fifth Avenue were decorated with flags and bunting, and many of the political visitors stopped at Altman's, Gimbel's, Saks, and Lord & Taylor's not far from the Garden.

State delegations were assigned to blocks of seats on the floor. States planning to make nominations were given honored places along the center aisle. California was next to New York, which was followed by Ohio. The balconies towered straight above the delegates on all sides, no different than at one of the prize fights staged in the Garden. The main platform was at the north end of the arena with a speakers' stand at its front end extended into the delegations like a large oratorical tongue, symbolic of the thousands of words that would issue forth from it in the days that followed.

The speakers' stand at the end of the walkway was equipped with two microphones connected to twenty-four amplifying horns in a double circle of twelve speakers each. For most of Convention history, delegates had come to the national party conclaves only to hear nothing of the speeches in gigantic halls. Now every delegate, it was falsely hoped, could hear every word. No one had predicted the decibel level of the delegates themselves could drown out the new electric speakers.

The same two microphones on the speakers' stand were connected to a new radio broadcasting system that sent the Convention's proceedings into homes across the nation for the first Convention year ever, courting potential voters. (The Republican Convention in Cleveland a few weeks earlier was the first covered by radio.) At the White House, President John Calvin Coolidge, of Massachusetts, and his vice presidential running mate, Charles Gates Dawes, of Illinois, would listen to their opponent's deliberations. The vacuum tube was fast replacing the crystal radio sets, and the nation supported 591 radio stations reaching as many as an estimated six million listeners.

Graham McNamee, of New York radio station WEAF, was in charge of the broadcasting duties from the Convention press table. But twenty stations including less-than-a-month-old WGN, WLS which had gone on the air in April of 1924, along with WMAQ, out of Chicago, were picking up his reports and re-broadcasting them as far South and west as possible. The *New York Times,* which sold for two cents in Greater New York, noted "Radio will do much to advertise a candidate. When he makes a speech before a visible audience the gathering will be much larger if he has been a broadcaster." The paper added, "Radio will let the women voters hear the candidates, whereas in other years women have not attended the great mass meetings because of the crowds and lack of seating capacity in halls and auditoriums." Women were voting in their second presidential election.

The largest Convention telegraph room ever run by Western Union Telegraph Company was located in the basement of the Garden. Many outposts around the nation still relied on telegraph to get first news reports. More than 125 newspaper men and women were covering this Convention, and were stationed at press tables on the large platform to watch the proceedings. Many mingled in the crowd.

All the previous week delegations had been arriving by train and deluging the city's hotels and lobbies with their political gossip. The party faithful were both optimistic that the Democracy could over-turn a scandal-ridden Republican administration, and apprehensive about regional and party divisions that were beginning to show their ugly face. The Democratic Party had always been a loose coalition of diverse regional alliances which, as in the case of the Civil War, had not always held together. Some feared fatal divisions in this Convention between rural and urban, religious and secular, Protestant and Catholic factions that could wreck their election chances.

Most of the talk was about the titanic contest shaping up between the forces backing early delegate leader and victor in the handful of state primaries, William Gibbs McAdoo, of California, and those of New York Governor Alfred Emanuel Smith. McAdoo had been U.S. Secretary of the Treasury during the Great War and was the Progressive son-in-law of former President Woodrow Wilson. As much as McAdoo tried to run against a corrupt Republican administration in Washington, at this Convention, he uncomfortably stood against another Progressive, the popular Governor of the Empire State, Al Smith. Smith had a long and impressive record passing Progressive legislation in the New York legislature, and he was a tremendous vote getter. Most of all, he was popular in his home town where he had risen from the tenements near the Brooklyn Bridge to the highest office "which was in the gift" of his

135

state party. Both pre-Convention favorites were in New York City directing their forces and both seemed confident of victory.

From his headquarters in the Prudence Building at Forty-Third Street and Madison Avenue, the ever-likeable Al Smith had predicted victory to the newspaper hounds, because, as he said, delegates "wanted a winner." He confidently told the *New York Times*, "You can write the headline now, boys, 'Smith wins the nomination.'." Franklin D. Roosevelt, who was managing his mentor's campaign, added, "There's not a shadow of doubt about it."

Asked to define a Progressive Democrat, Smith replied, "If you want to see an example of Progressive principles, read my annual message to the legislature." As to his progress corralling delegates so he could win the nomination, Smith told newsmen in the days before the Convention that he had been swimming at Coney Island and hadn't had time to talk to many delegates. Smith was cocky and bluff and his managers were busily working the delegations to get promises to make Smith their second choice when their favorite sons began to fade. It would be "suicidal to nominate anyone except Al Smith," argued delegate T. H. Cowles, of California, who would be locked in for McAdoo under the Unit Rule.

McAdoo, whose followers the *Times* said, exhibited "almost religious fervor," came to New York attacking Wall Street and soon had added the editors of the New York papers to his list. "All I ask for is fairness," McAdoo pleaded. "We don't want anything else, but I do feel that the men and women coming here from other states are entitled to receive fair information from the newspapers. It makes no difference to me personally." After Tammany failed at negotiations to bring about a peace treaty between Governor Smith and publisher William Randolph Hearst, his *New York American* came out against the "Booze and Boodle" candidate Smith and endorsed McAdoo. Most of the other New York papers, however, gave McAdoo a hard time and favored Smith. Throughout the week before the Convention convened, the city's papers reported possible defections from the McAdoo campaign. Since its strategy was to build momentum until there was a stampede to nomination, any talk about defections was a serious problem for McAdoo, and the editors knew it.

"The fight in this Convention," explained Morrison Shafroth, a McAdoo floor leader, "is not between McAdoo and Smith, but between McAdoo and the bosses. The same reactionary gangsters who wield a certain amount of power in every Convention are out for the sole purpose of defeating McAdoo because he is Progressive," he charged. "William Jennings Bryan made the issue clear at the Baltimore Convention in 1912, the issue of the New York bosses against the people. . . . It is becoming clear that the same situation will arise in this Convention."

As for New York, McAdoo told reporters he loved the city where he had lived for over two decades before moving to Washington and then retiring two years before the Convention to California. But he added, "This city is also the citadel of privilege. Here is that seat of that invisible power represented by the allied forces of finance and industry, which, reaching out into the remotest corners of the land, touches the lives of the people everywhere through its control of the Republican Party and of Government itself, when that party is in power.

"This 'Invisible Government' is reactionary, sinister, unscrupulous, mercenary and sordid," McAdoo charged. "It is wanting in national ideals and devoid of conscience. It is rooted in corruption and directed by greed and determined by selfishness. Its fruits have been graft and debauchery which threaten the foundations of democracy and menace the liberties of the people."

Although most observers were predicting a long and spirited Convention, few could have anticipated how long or how contentious this one would be. The previous record for length was set in Charleston in 1860, when the Democratic national meeting broke up after fifty-seven ballots and no nominee under the Two-Thirds Rule. Two new Conventions sprang up in its place to nominate Southern and Northern Democratic tickets. In Baltimore in 1852, it took Democrats forty-nine ballots to nominate Franklin Pierce. In 1912, Woodrow Wilson required forty-six ballots to win the Democratic nomination. And the 1920 Democratic National Convention in San Francisco went forty-four ballots before confirming James M. Cox, the former Governor of Ohio.

"This Convention will not nominate on the Fifth Ballot, nor will it nominate on the Tenth Ballot," Cook County Illinois political boss, George M. Brennan, a Smith floor leader, told the *Times*. Thomas B. Love, National Committeeman from Texas, disputed that: "Mr. McAdoo will be nominated before ten ballots have been taken. . . . It is possible that we may attain the peak of our strength long before that, say on the Fifth Ballot. One thing I will safely predict—the balloting will be marked by a crescendo of acclaim from the McAdoo supporters from the moment his name is placed before the Convention until he is declared the nominee. We will lay down a barrage of enthusiasm every time the result of a ballot is announced. . . ." But a *New York Times* headline before the national meeting even began announced that a "Survey Shows Convention Deadlock Is Virtually Certain."

McAdoo came into town triumphantly. He had won primaries in North and South Dakota in March; beat Smith 68 to 7 percent in Wisconsin in early April; won Illinois, Nebraska, Pennsylvania in April, while losing New Jersey and Ohio; and he was victorious in California and Oregon and Montana in May. Overall, McAdoo won about 60 percent of all Democratic primary votes in 1924. Cox was his closest competitor with about 10 percent.

But almost as soon as he arrived in New York, he was on the defensive. The anti-McAdoo forces were doing whatever they could to derail his momentum built up through nationwide primary wins. One tactic was to complain that McAdoo had taken money as a consultant from the Doheny oil interests. The anti-McAdoo forces played on the fear that such an accusation might rob the party of the corruption issue in the campaign. California's former U.S. Senator James Duval Phelan admitted McAdoo once had worked for the oil magnate, but retorted that a man had the right to capitalize on his reputation.

"I do not see anything in this that affects Mr. McAdoo's honor or character in the least degree," McAdoo's friend noted. "When he left public office the only thing he took with him was his reputation for integrity, honor, and capability. Naturally, clients floated to him. He left the office to make a competence for his family. As a great statesman in the West has said, 'A man must eat.' He is entitled to capitalize on his reputation and experience."

Judge David Ladd Rockwell, McAdoo's campaign manager, observed, "It has been confidently believed by the stand-pat Republican leaders that Mr. McAdoo would lose the first primaries and thus be eliminated. The effort failed. In such widely separated states as South Dakota and Georgia, he won overwhelming victories. Mr. McAdoo's march toward victory had began." Rockwell confidently told the *Times*, "No Wet, reactionary clique can defeat him." He referred to New York's Tammany Hall and its alliance with the machine in Cook County, Illinois, Boston and elsewhere that was backing Smith.

Prohibition was a slowly building issue. The Eighteenth Amendment had brought resentment and outright disobedience. It was as unpopular with the majority as it was passionately supported by the minority. Republicans had avoided taking it up at their Cleveland Convention weeks earlier. But Prohibition split Democrats, regionally, morally, and religiously. Lobbying delegates in New York, members of the Association Against the Prohibition Amendment, argued that, "Neither Mr. McAdoo nor any other Dry can be nominated in this Convention. We have sufficient votes to prevent it."

Meanwhile, L. H. Musgrove, chairman of the Anti-Saloon League, charged that the Smith forces were raising questions about religious freedom as a "smokescreen" to hide him as a "Wet candidate." Smith, a devout Catholic, finished every day in the Governor's Mansion with a private drink, often shared with other legislative leaders. Smith had said he was committed to enforcing the Prohibition law, but favored local revision of the law to allow beer. As the Convention neared, he refused to restate his position, coyly saying, "Everybody knows where I stand on the issue."

At exactly noon, June 24, 1924, Cordell Hull, of Tennessee, chairman of the Democratic National Committee, banged his gavel to call the Convocation to order. Patrick Cardinal Hayes, of New York, delivered the first invocation, much to the distaste of some Southern and Western delegates who saw the Catholic prelate as part of a New York conspiracy to control the Convention, dictate its platform, and command its candidate. Cardinal Hayes thanked the "Father of might, wisdom, and justice" for blessing "our mighty and glorious Republic of more than one hundred millions of freemen, dedicated to political, social, and religious Liberty. . . ."

"Religious Liberty" would become a central debate in this Convention as the days wore on. The Cardinal concluded his prayer with the traditional Catholic "Our Father." "And lead us not into temptation, but deliver us from evil. Amen." Thereafter, many of the Convention's invocations would feature a covert struggle between Catholic and Protestant last lines of "The Lord's Prayer," as if each were making a larger political case against the other.

Charles A. Greathouse, of Indiana, Secretary of the Democratic National Committee, who was serving as Convention Secretary, announced that the Convention's Temporary Chairman, Senator Pat Harrison, of Mississippi, would deliver the keynote address to set the Democracy's themes for the forthcoming campaign. Harrison had a mighty task ahead of him and would become sick from exhaustion before the Convention closed. He began the First Session by recalling events surrounding the 1876 campaign in which New York's reform Democratic Governor, Samuel J. Tilden, battled to overturn two terms of corruption that characterized the Grant years.

"There was corruption then," Harrison blasted, "there is a Saturnalia of corruption now. There were disgraced public officials then, repudiated by their party and under arrest," he charged, laying down the opening salvo. "But today Fall goes unmolested on his ranch in New Mexico." (Harrison referred to Albert B. Fall, President Harding's Secretary of the Interior, who had just resigned because of his role in the "Teapot Dome Scandal" in which naval oil reserve lands at Teapot Dome, Wyoming, and Elk Hill, California, were leased to Harry F. Sinclair's Marathon Oil Company and other oil concerns in exchange for private loans and perhaps bribes. Seven years after the 1924 Convention, Fall was convicted of fraud and served two years in prison.)

Harrison continued, "Daugherty's attorney was chairman of the committee created to oil the steam roller of the worst boss-ridden Convention in a generation." (Harrison alluded to Harry Micajah Daugherty, the Ohio lawyer who had managed President Harding's political climb to the White House and who was rewarded with the post of U. S. Attorney General, only to be forced to resign in disgrace after

Harding's death. He would be twice tried and exonerated by a hung jury for conspiring to defraud the Government in Teapot Dome. The Convention that Harrison condemned was the June 1924 Republican assembly at Cleveland that nominated Calvin Coolidge, the "accidental President," who assumed office when President Harding died from heart failure on August 2, 1923.)

Harrison's attack stimulated unified applause from the delegates and the thousands of spectators packing the Garden's galleries. Millions of Americans followed on their home radio sets. "The first step in reform must be the people's choice of honest men from another party, lest the disease . . . infect the body politic . . . ," the Mississippi Senator insisted above the din of talking delegates. After all, Harrison maintained, "The Democratic Party is the friend of business, big and small, it delights to see the reflected glory from burning furnaces and prosperous farm homes. . . ."

Harrison asserted that "The corner stone of the Republican Party is special privilege, and today its grip is more firmly tightened and its place more secure than at any time in its long history. It needs no cards to gain admittance to the White House, no password to the congressional committee rooms . . . . Crooked business needs only to gesture or special privilege to wink to make this administration understand and do." Then using images of the great world war still fresh in the minds of his listeners, he promised, "They may direct their poisonous gases at us, but no camouflage can be contrived that will give cover and protection to the Pharisee."

Harrison next took on the Harding/Coolidge record, beginning with the tax cut that the Republican Secretary of the Treasury, Andrew William Mellon, former president of the Mellon National Bank, had sought to pass. "Under its benign provisions, an income of $5,000,000 was to receive a reduction of $1,331,832, while an income of $3,000 would have received only $8.75." The Convention laughed at the irony. "It would have opened an avenue of escape to every tax-dodging capitalist in America," Harrison complained. "The champions of the proposal believe that prosperity should come from the crumbs that fall from the tables of the rich; that if you legislate solely to make the well-to-do prosperous, their prosperity will seep through upon those below. The Republican Party is the ancient enemy of the income tax," he roared.

"The administration said that if we would increase taxes on 3,580,585 income taxpayers and reduce the taxes on 5,400 it would release money for productive enterprises . . . ." But Democrats refused. The Mellon Plan, as it was called, had been blunted by congressional Democrats in cooperation with Progressive Republicans. Instead, "every taxpayer in America will get a 25 per cent reduction this year," the Mississippi Senator boasted to applause. Next, Harrison took on the

Republican Fordney-McCumber Tariff, which he called "the most flagrant repudiation of campaign pledges in all the history of political parties . . . . Every line of it added to the living costs of the American consumer . . . . The so-called representatives of the people surrendered completely to the representatives of the predatory interests . . . and the replenishment of the Republican exchequer." He noted that it had added $4 billion in "additional burden upon the American masses, but revealed the nation's hypocrisy toward war-torn Europe . . . The doctrine of Equal Rights to none and special favors to some" was firmly embedded in the Republican tariff.

The Convention's Temporary Chairman pointed out to the huge and unsettled throng, which was listening half-heartedly, that when the Republicans came to power they had investigated the war expenses and contracts given by Democrats and were unable to find any evidence of corruption. He drew his contrast, noting the "first official act of Calvin Coolidge was the appointment of a private secretary who had traded and trafficked in public patronage." And he recalled how the Republican Senate was forced "to convict its own Republican National Committee for 'framing' " a Democratic Senator [Senator Walsh, of Montana] who had uncovered Teapot Dome. "But in this dark drama," Harrison scolded, "the American people know and prefer the highly patriotic and cleansing work of Thomas J. Walsh to the foul infamy and thievery of Albert B. Fall." His indictment elicited more applause. "The mask is off," he taunted. .

"With an administration honeycombed with graft and corroded with corruption, it is refreshing to reflect upon the innumerable Republican investigations into expenditures of the preceding Democratic administration. Following that period, the most momentous in our country's history, which called for the mobilization of our strongest and best, a period that necessitated the expenditure of over $40 billion to prosecute and win the war . . . fifty-one separate committees appointed, controlled by fifty-one separate Republican majorities . . . . What were the results? Where is the tainted dollar spent? Where was the defrauded soldier? Name the Democratic Cabinet officer disgraced," Harrison challenged. They "did not point to a single act that reflected discredit upon any Democratic official." His patriotic exoneration set off sustained applause from the 1924 Democracy.

The Coolidge administration, consumed by its "carnival of corruption," had ignored the distress cries of the nation's farmers, Harrison charged. He worried about "the diminishing purchasing power of the farmer's dollar. Starving herds, rotting grain, and rusting spindles have not stirred the sleeping spirit or warmed the chilly coolness of the President." The Mississippi Senator cited other issues, the "development of Muscle Shoals, of soldiers' pensions," of the 1,357 bank failures during the four-year Harding-Coolidge term.

In contrast, the Democratic Party of Woodrow Wilson kept alive the "idealism" of its recently fallen leader. While entry into the League of Nations had been blocked by Republican Senators, other questions of world cooperation and assistance for the prevention of war and the promotion of international cooperation loomed large before the Convention. "Henry Cabot Lodge, who made Coolidge at Chicago," Harrison jeered, "and unmade him at Washington . . . attempts to weave new webs of intrigue, and again ensnare and mislead the American people."

(Harrison was referring to the events in the "smoke-filled backrooms" 408-410 of the Blackstone Hotel in Chicago where during the 1920 Republican National Convention a "Senate Cabal" including Lodge had broken a deadlock by selecting their Senate colleague and poker pal, Warren G. Harding. Lodge's Massachusetts Governor, Calvin Coolidge, was added later to the ticket. Lodge was leader of the "Irreconcilables" who sank Wilson's League of Nations Treaty. Democrat James M. Cox also had raised the League issue during his 1920 campaign, before losing by seven million votes.) "Too long has this cultured gentleman and his intriguing cohorts denied peace to a suffering world," Harrison bitterly said of Lodge, who would die days after the November election. "Give Lodge hell!" yelled delegates.

"They are not willing to employ their power and talents against our country joining the present World Court, but they seek to chloroform the existing plan, to dismantle it, to destroy it. Thus, this unholy conspiracy against the peace of the world is carried forward . . . . And yet the President through it all did not raise his voice . . . . What America needs now is not a Sphinx, but a Paul Revere to awaken it and call it back to duty and high resolve. Oh, for one in the White House with . . . . the fine fighting qualities of a Woodrow Wilson."

With those words, the Convention broke into spontaneous rolling applause and led by the Idaho banner, delegates marched about the all-purpose hall for twenty minutes. Their demonstration ended with Anna Case's rendition of "The Battle Hymn of the Republic" with which delegates gleefully sang along. Then, Harrison, who sat during the parade, again stepped to the rostrum and resumed, "It is the spirit of him who twice led us to victory, and whose soul has taken its flight and whose remains now lie in yon crypt at St. Albans, the late Commander-in-Chief of the World's greatest fighting forces in its greatest crisis. . . ." (Wilson had died on February 1, 1924, and was buried in Washington, D. C.) "How different were the foreign policies of our Government under Woodrow Wilson and under the Harding-Coolidge administration. It is the difference between a keynote and a keyhole policy of statesmanship . . . .

"Oil has become the Open Sesame of power." The delegates laughed. "Truly the administration might have boasted of two 'Secretaries of Oil.' " Again laughter rocked the hall. What were the consequences? Harrison cited the administration's indifference to the slaughter of "the Armenian followers of Christ, driven like cattle into exile, dying of starvation and exposure in the highways; when Christian churches and Christian homes were being given to the flames and ministers of the gospel importuned the administration for a note of protest, it was refused; but the moment the oil magnates of the land sought a concession in the oil fields of Mosul," the administration was quick to sign the Lausanne Treaty. "Show this administration an oil well and it will show you a foreign policy," Harrison growled. Laughter and applause followed.

"Never before in all its history has America turned a deaf ear to the appeal of humanity or the call of civilization," Harrison chided. "When Woodrow Wilson's plan for world adjustment was wrecked by the selfish and jealous hands of reactionary Republican leadership, world hope for peace was shattered and European rehabilitation indefinitely deferred....This administration cannot escape its responsibility for the feverish condition of the world." The campaign that would follow determined how important this appeal to Justice and internationalism in foreign affairs had on the American people of the 1920s Jazz Age.

Harrison turned to the campaign at hand. "We will drive every rascal from high position . . . we will eliminate governmental favoritism . . . we will lay bare campaign bribery and punish election frauds. We will go to the relief of distressed agriculture . . . . Recognizing our obligations as a great humane power, we will assume in manly fashion our responsibilities to the world. . . . Neither the cries of radicalism nor the threats of conservatism will swerve us from our fixed purpose," he cried.

"Ladies and gentlemen of the Convention, may I say in closing that this is a Democratic year? Victory is within our grasp if we reach out for it." Then Harrison prophetically cautioned, "Let us remember that too much is at stake for the hideous form of friction to frown upon this Convention....Nothing must happen here to divide our councils or dampen our ardor," he warned. "The fires of Democracy must not flicker. There must be no sulking; there can be no mutiny," he preached. "Winning is not wicked. Strategy is no sin . . . . No matter who may be the choice of this Convention, we will rally around our leader, clad in the armor of a righteous cause . . . keep the faith, keep the faith," he shouted.

The Temporary Chairman stepped back from the microphones and 'the Convention rose to its feet in powerful simultaneous approval, loud and prolonged. Then the delegations of the 1924 Democracy marched in unison about the old Madison Square Garden in joyful and grand demonstrations.

When things died down, the delegates were warmly welcomed by New York City's Mayor John F. Hylan, a Tammany man who was usually at odds with Governor Smith. But on the night before the Convention, Hylan had hosted a dinner for 3,500 delegates and political leaders in the grand ballroom of the Hotel Commodore, the headquarters for the New York delegation. Governor Al Smith sat one seat away from the Mayor and received his praise. But the *New York Times* observed that "the greatest of all the attractions" at the elaborate affair was the party's three-time presidential candidate, William Jennings Bryan, of Florida, who was pledged to McAdoo. Meanwhile, the orchestra played songs boosting Smith, such as "East Side, West Side" and "We'll All Go Voting for Al."

U. S. Senator Royal S. Copeland, of New York, just back from Boston, told reporters, "New England has gone wild over New York's favorite son." But Bryan snapped at the newspapers: "Al Smith won't be nominated. He hasn't got a chance. You people here in New York may want him, but you New Yorkers are always forgetting that there is quite a bit of country beyond this state. The Middle West and the West don't know him. And the South won't have him at all."

Now within the Convention hall, Hylan began his welcoming address: "I heartily and cordially welcome you to the City of New York." He outlined a series of events promised to entertain the delegates in their spare hours. He noted he was, "the first Mayor in over half a century to welcome a Democratic National Convention to this city." He inaccurately, it turned out, hoped that "new ties of friendship," meant an end to "suspicions, distrust, and misunderstanding" between the sections of the country.

Then he bragged about New York City's six million inhabitants, the city's "present preeminence in wealth and power and civic renown," its "genuine Americanism" and "aggressive and unselfish devotion to American institutions," and "spirit of tolerance among the city's varied interests, and a racial and religious concord." He declared that, "It is here that the Englishman and the Irishman, the Scot and the Welshman, the Huguenot and the Hollander, the Frenchman and the German, the Italian and the Swede, the Jew and the Gentile, the Protestant and the Catholic, recognizing that over and above everything else they are American citizens, enjoying the fullest religious and civil liberties, all strive with a common hope and common purpose. . . ." Hylan sought to settle down the early antagonisms among delegates that were rumored to be overflowing, and his remarks elicited applause from many of the delegates.

Mayor Hylan ended with his commitment to the party's common

mission. "The American Flag, not the dollar sign of predatory groups, must fly atop the Capitol at Washington." And he too warned, "The Democratic Party cannot afford to have it said that Wall Street dictated the nominees emerging from this Convention . . . . Wall Street is not merely a world-famed business section, with a river on one end and a graveyard on the other . . . . Wall Street is a hotbed of political and financial schemes and plots for the control of everything from the food you eat to the clothes you wear." (Just days earlier, the *New York Times* had reported that New York was "gradually stepping into London's position as the money capital of the world.")

The Secretary then announced Convention committee assignments. Mrs. Katherine S. Pfohl, of New York, was assigned to the Committee on Credentials; Senator Royal S. Copeland, of New York, to the Committee on Permanent Organization; John J. Fitzgerald, of New York, the Committee on Rules and Order of Business. (In an early clash in the Committee on Rules, McAdoo advocates attempted to change the Two-Thirds Rule required to nominate a candidate into a mere majority. They were blocked in their efforts by Smith delegates.) Joseph A. Kellogg, of New York, was assigned to the Committee on Platform and Resolutions that would see so much controversy; Norman E. Mack, of Buffalo, and Elisabeth Marbury, of New York City, were slated as National Committeeman and Comitteewoman.

Meeting sites were announced. The Committee on Credentials was assigned to the Madison Square Hotel, 40 East Twenty-Sixth Street; the Committee on Resolutions went to the East Room on the first floor of the Waldorf-Astoria, which was sitting not far from the Garden on Thirty-Fourth Street on the future site of the Empire State Building that Al Smith would manage. An official reception for female delegates was called at the Commodore Hotel. Other delegates were offered motor transportation to "Greystone," the Yonkers country residence of Mr. Samuel Untermeyer. The estate was once lived in by the party's 1876 presidential nominee Samuel J. Tilden. (As it turned out, a violent thunderstorm wrecked the party and flooded the city's subway.) A reception for service men and women was scheduled at the Imperial Hotel at Thirty-Second Street and Broadway, to discuss the plight of disabled vets and related matters.

The Convention's First Day concluded with a resolution stating that the body, "profoundly laments the death of that incomparable American, Woodrow Wilson, whose leadership and achievements constitute an epoch in the world's history." Then at 3:30 in the afternoon, the Convention adjourned and delegates spilled into the city to have a good time.

The Second Day of the Convention, Wednesday, June 25, 1924, started with a brisk northwest wind cooling the city. But as the week progressed, the heat returned and made the Garden feel like a baking oven. The day was dedicated to more oratory while the Committee on Resolutions fought over platform planks upon which Progressives and Conservatives, Northern urbanites or Southern Church goers, Prohibitionists or anti-prohibitionists could agree. Indeed, this Convention was divided between rural and urban values and candidates, and the factions struggled throughout the event for power. (The 1920 Census was the first to show that U. S. cities had overtaken the farms in population.)

The Right Reverend Thomas F. Gailor, Bishop of Tennessee, asked that the divinity, "defend our liberties. Preserve our unity. Save us from discord and confusion and from every evil way." Reciting "The Lord's Prayer," he ended with, "For Thine is the kingdom, and the power, and the glory, forever and forever. Amen."

To great applause, the Committee on Permanent Organization recommended that Senator Thomas J. Walsh, of Montana, the man who had broken open the Teapot Dome scandal and withstood White House attacks, be appointed Permanent Chairman of the Convention. A Miss Kennedy, of the Bronx, was made Vice Chairman. Walsh was escorted to the rostrum by Senator Ferris, of Michigan, and Mrs. Alice Campbell Good, of New York, former Governor Jard Y. Sanders, of Louisiana, and Governor Trapp, of Oklahoma.

The Permanent Chairman then began his slashing address by insisting that: "The nation expects, yea, demands of us, a leader who exemplifies the principles of Government associated with the name of Thomas Jefferson, a leader whose heart is attuned to the pulsations of those who labor on the farm and in the field, in the mills and work-shops, at the forge and in the mines, at the desk and in the household; who heeds the cry of all the people for a larger life, rather than the plea of the few, the favorites of fortune, who are eager to exploit their fellows. . . ."

Walsh derided their Republican opponent's slogan "Back to Normalcy," saying it really meant, "back to the methods and practices of a day that was dead, of a generation ago, when [Mark] Hanna ruled and [Nelson Wilmarth] Aldrich legislated, when the Senate was a millionaire's club, doing the bidding of the 'Invisible Government.' " Walsh mockingly asked, "What clarion voice has been raised from any high official quarter against Forbes, the despoiler of the disabled veteran, or Fall, who bartered away an all-important element of the national defense under circumstances he dare not tell lest he confess criminality?" His indictment was met with solid applause amid general disorder of the delegates.

"I cannot believe," the Permanent Chairman exhorted, "that more than a negligible number regard with unconcern either the ignominy uncovered or the palpable falsehood of the Republican platform . . . . The President of the United States himself has not hesitated to endeavor to shield the delinquents from the public odium to which their derelictions have subjected them by joining in the hue and cry against the investigations that have been conducted under the authority of the Senate and against that body for authorizing them. His message on the subject had for its plain purpose the suppression of an inquiry into the official conduct of a member of his Cabinet . . . . I cannot admit the accusation that the people of America are indifferent to the corroding influence of corruption in office, high or low. But we shall see. They are on trial,'' he admonished.

Walsh turned to the domestic agenda. Amid the roaring prosperity of the 1920s were distressing signals of what was to come within half a decade. ''According to the Secretary of Agriculture, 40 percent of all farmers in South Dakota are virtually bankrupt; 42 percent in Colorado; 50 percent in North Dakota; 51 percent in Wyoming; 62 percent in Montana; and approximately 25 percent in the hitherto prosperous states of Iowa and Minnesota . . . . We are officially informed that the net change of population from farm to town during 1923 was over 1,200,000, accelerating a movement in progress in recent decades that had already excited general alarm . . . . In the face of an impending national calamity the Republican Party is impotent,'' he forecasted.

As for the Democracy, its record, ''is signalized by the enactment of more legislation for the common good than is recorded in our annals for any other equal number of years,'' Walsh said of the Wilson tenure during which the Democracy had assumed its new Progressive demeanor. ''The exigencies arising from the sudden outbreak of the war in 1914, and the collapse of the world's system of exchange, were met in a fashion that defied criticism. When the nation eventually became involved in the sanguinary conflict, its resources in men and material were marshaled in a way that astonished our Allies and brought consternation to the ranks of our enemies. The financing of the great enterprise reflected the highest credit upon the party that undertook its direction. True, the towering genius, the rival in intellect of Jefferson, who held the helm in that period of stress and storm, is no more . . . . But his high ideals, his lofty purposes, his trust in the judgment of the plain people, remain our heritage,'' Walsh extolled the party's recently fallen hero.

The Permanent Chairman ended his stirring oration by contrasting Wilson's legacy again with that of his opponents. ''I know how eager the managers of the campaign for the re-election of President Coolidge are to switch the issues from honest government, the repeal of the new tariff of abominations, relief for agriculture . . . to the League of Nations. It is not so necessary that we immediately join the League,'' he conceded to political reality, ''as it is that we abandon foolish antagonism to any world movement, however commendable in itself, merely because it is in some way associated with the League . . . . In honor to our country, the prosperity of our people demands that we return to the ideals of Woodrow Wilson, that we resume the place he won for us—the moral leadership of the world,'' Walsh concluded as the Convention erupted with loud and prolonged cheers and applause and a small demonstration of marching delegates.

After a number of procedural announcements, the Convention turned to the ceremony of nominating the Democracy's 1924 candidates for President of the United States. Nominating speeches, unlike the early Conventions, were elaborate and rhetorical. At this Convention they were limited to one-half hour, with seconding speeches limited to ten minutes.

The Secretary began the Roll Call of the States with Alabama. The Honorable Forney Johnson came to the rostrum to nominate his state's U.S. Senator, Oscar Wilder Underwood. The Senator had arrived in town on Monday and set up his headquarters on ''candidates row'' on the ground floor of the Waldorf Astoria, next to the West Virginia suite opened to boost the chances of John William Davis, former Ambassador to Great Britain, and like Senator Underwood, a ''Dark Horse'' waiting to see how the McAdoo/Smith horse race would run. ''The Davis sentiment appeared to have taken on form and substance,'' the *Times* noted before the first gavel banged, he was ''coming to the front strongly as a candidate.'' But when asked who he saw as a Dark Horse, Al Smith had replied, ''If there is a Dark Horse, he's too dark for me to see.''

''The Alabama delegation understands that the main issue in the approaching campaign is the fight to preserve the integrity of popular Government . . . ,'' Johnson bellowed. ''The Republican Party's organization misunderstood the victory of 1920, which was nothing more than the inevitable reaction of our people against the administration immediately and unavoidably responsible for war taxes and for the exercise of other abnormal Federal powers incident to the war. . . .

''The Republican officials came into power in 1921 exultant, over-confident, and in a state of suspended morals as a result of the election: and their party organization promptly lost its conscience and its capacity to analyze men and motives . . . . The Cleveland platform has revealed the completeness of the breakdown of Republican morale. The character of General Grant did not prevent the repudiation of his party after the disclosures of 1876, nor will the personal integrity of Coolidge and of Dawes stay a like result today,'' Johnson predicted. (He referred to the President and his vice presidential nominee Charles Gates Dawes, whose ''Dawes Plan'' for German payment of reparations for the Great War was receiving front-page coverage by the New York press as the Convention convened.)

''The first requisite is that your nominee must not only be irreproachable in fact, but he must be known and reputed to be irreproachable. We offer you that man,'' Johnson explained. ''We do not believe that it is possible to find in the history of American politics a man of more constant chastity in thought, in speech, and in conduct than he . . . he is the easiest man to elect in the Democratic Party . . . . He has been the leader of his party in both House [1895-1915] and Senate [1915-1927] . . . . Under his leadership, the Democratic majority in the House of Representatives set a new standard for efficient legislation of the highest type . . . . When he became leader of the Senate minority he again set a standard in declining to lead that column away from the principles of our party for temporary partisan advantage," Johnson said.

"We believe him to be the chief living defender of the sanctity of the Constitution and of Government by law; and he is the master of the tariff . . . . No man before this Convention will have a clearer conception of the economic basis and effect of our international relations, the necessity for assuring a foreign market for our exportable surplus, and the injury of a protective tariff to the agricultural classes which pay and do not receive protection.

"The people of this country know that the Underwood Tariff Bill [Underwood-Simmons Tariff Act of 1913] did not destroy the fair relationship between the price of the products of agriculture and the price of the products of industry, which is the basis of agricultural distress today" Johnson explained. "The Democrat we place before you was a tower of strength in war, one of the many legislators of his party who rendered exceptional service in that crisis; but the school of constructive peace and of limitations of Federal extravagance and function is the school in which he has grown in greatness. . . ."

Then Johnson took up the platform theme that would most trouble and divide this Convention. Underwood now stood courageously against a menace which was infiltrating Southern and Northern communities alike, and he had brought his name to this Convention, if not to win the presidency, then to take forceful action on this definitive issue. "When in 1856 a conspiracy became national in scope against the spirit of fair play declared by the Bill of Rights, the party of your fathers and mine met it squarely. The Democratic platform of 1856 joined battle with the so-called Know-Nothing Party of that date, a quasi-secret order based on the same objective and affording precedent for a similar movement which has intruded into the two main parties today; but a precedent only in party, for the Know-Nothings had the courage to unmask and to stand out as a party." Johnson was interrupted by applause by many of the Northern delegations.

"Whereas, a movement confronting this nation today looks to the establishment within the two parties of a secret super-Government, intimidating Democrats and Republicans alike, exacting pledges of candidates and voters not tested by public discussion and proscribing citizens who pay taxes and bear arms. Above all does the candidate we

149

present condemn the mass action of secret political orders in furtherance of any objective which is plainly contrary to the spirit of the Constitution . . . . The question before this party is whether secret organizations shall be given powers not subject to the Bill of Rights. . . ."

Johnson then named his target by introducing to the Convention a resolution at Alabama Senator Underwood's request denouncing as "un-American and un-Democratic . . . the organization known as the Ku Klux Klan. . . ." Many in the Convention broke into spontaneous applause. Half the delegates leaped to their feet with whoops before marching in the aisles behind their state banners in the biggest parade of the Convention so far. The New York State standard was raised by fashionable James J. Walker, future Mayor of New York City. James J. Hoey, one of Governor Smith's closest advisors, stood on his chair cheering. All ninety of New York's delegates joined with Ohio and Illinois in leading the anti-Klan demonstration. The parade was also a tactical anti-McAdoo show of strength. A serious fight broke out around the Colorado State standard. It quickly was broken up by New York City police. No one tried to seize the Texas standard, home of the Imperial Wizard of the Invisible Empire.

Johnson blew flames into a smoldering issue. Some delegates yelled out, "Soak it to them, boy . . . the harder you hit it, the better we like it." Others remained silent. The Klan was rumored to dominate some of the Southern and Western delegations and its top officers were in town working over individual delegates with hateful anti-Catholic persuasion against Smith and personal intimidation to get the votes they wanted. Smith workers were finding, the *Times* reported, that "many delegates had come to New York prejudiced against the Governor, while others were simply not interested."

Throughout the Convention, many fearful delegates tried to avoid the Klan issue by abstaining from key votes. A Southern Senator of Underwood's statue raising this issue so prominently at the beginning of the Convention showed there were two Southern visions for the future, and that there were brave men who lived by constitutional principles rather than violence and fear in Democratic Dixie. "The fact that he does not come here with the solid backing of delegates from Southern states will not be regarded as a disability when the reason is weighed and understood," Underwood's campaign manager C. C. Carlin told the *New York Times* before the Convention convened.

Johnson concluded his nominating speech: "The history of Liberty discloses no record of greater fidelity in principle than the career of our nominee, no finer courage, no wiser public counselor, no loftier character, no more serene influence in times of crisis . . . . I have the honor to place in nomination for President of the United States the name of Oscar W. Underwood."

The hall exploded with great applause for the courageous Alabaman, and delegates with colorful badges and carrying small American flags marched about the hot and sticky hall. McAdoo delegations remained in their seats, including most of those from Georgia, where on Stone Mountain the modern Klan had been resurrected in 1915. The delegations from North and South Carolina, Florida, Oregon, Washington, Nevada, Idaho, Wyoming, California, Kentucky, Texas, Oklahoma remained tight-lipped.

The Roll Call of the States moved on to Arkansas, and Governor Charles H. Brough rose to nominate its senior Senator from "Arkansas, the gateway to the great Progressive Southwest." His candidate, Joseph T. Robinson, had been, "a youth of adversity, a man of virtue and honesty," who "by force of ability, dint of energy and dynamic personality, reached one of the highest places within the gift of our party.

"Elected to Congress at the early age of thirty, serving with distinction and ability for five consecutive terms in that great representative body, elected by an unprecedented majority as Governor of his commonwealth, and for the past twelve years a potent factor in the epochal deliberations of the United States Senate," Robinson was, as Senator Roscoe Conkling had eulogized his fallen brother-in-law President Grant, "Great in the arduous greatness of things done." Governor Brough added, "He wears no man's collar," and lived a "blameless private and public life." Brough concluded, "a proven leader who can unite all factions of our party, heal all party wounds, a twentieth century crusader for the immortal principles of Democracy and Americanism, Senator Joseph T. Robinson." An enthusiastic wave of applause answered his speech. (Robinson would become the party's vice presidential nominee in 1928, and Franklin Roosevelt's Senate Majority Leader. Brough failed to throw in that Robinson was also the best amateur golfer in Washington.)

The proceedings had dragged on in the heat and McAdoo's managers tried to get a recess before nominating their man, but the Smith forces blocked them. So, former Senator James D. Phelan, of California, addressed the body, nominating the early favorite. Most Southern and Western delegates were wearing badges reading "Mc'll Do." His many devoted female delegates wore bright yellow campaign scarves.

McAdoo had ridden in a special train car across the nation from Los Angeles to New York's Pennsylvania Station, making Progressive speeches along the way, warning of the "Invisible Government" run by wealth, and conferring with party officials to keep the momentum of his campaign rolling. In New York, he was greeted with a band and 3,000 supporters, only a couple of hundred of whom were allowed near the train track where McAdoo descended, with his wife, the former Eleanor Randolph Wilson, who was still dressed in black, mourning her deceased father, President Wilson.

McAdoo hoisted one of his two young daughters on his shoulders to see the crowd. "Three cheers for our next President," someone had shouted. McAdoo assured the crowd, "While we now live in California, we have never lost our love for our old home." He had lived in New York City for twenty years before Wilson called him to Washington. After a short speech, the entire procession marched across Thirty-Second Street to Fifth Avenue, up to Thirty-Fourth Street, then east two blocks to the Vanderbilt Hotel where McAdoo had set up his campaign headquarters and begun personal meetings with state delegation leaders from across the nation.

Senator Phelan began his nominating speech by extolling President Wilson, McAdoo's father-in-law. "What a record of achievement both in war and peace!" he recalled. "During those days there stood by the side of our great Democratic President a man actuated by the same high motives of patriotism, of humanity, and of service. Called to the Treasury of the United States, the very citadel of Government, he cleansed it of the foul growth of favoritism and repelled the insidious attacks of the powerful. He made the Treasury the repository of the people's hopes, the instrumentality of sound finance, the safeguard of honest business and industrial prosperity . . . .

"I shall abbreviate," Phelan confided, "for there is a long story that cannot be told within our limited time. When he decided to retire from his office, which he did voluntarily in November, 1918, his work accomplished, the President . . . wrote, 'In my judgment this Country has never had an abler, more resourceful and yet prudent, a more uniformly efficient Secretary of the Treasury.' " What had McAdoo done to merit such praise? "You have guided the Treasury through all the perplexities and problems of transitional financial conditions, and of the financing of a war which has been without precedent alike in kind and scope. I thank you with a sense of gratitude that comes from the very bottom of my heart," President Wilson had written.

The New York audience in the rafters remained mostly silent in the face of their enemy's fine record. But the floor was alive with pride and applause for its presumptive leader. The Californian continued his argument for McAdoo. "Modern war is fought with money . . . . He had to provide the money. You will remember the Reserve Banks and Victory Loans, when his four campaigns yielded upwards to $18 billion. Against the advice of certain bankers he fixed the rates of interest so that the Country saved . . . $4 billion."

McAdoo was also responsible for setting up the Federal Reserve System. That was one reason why the West and South were so devoted to McAdoo throughout the 1924 Convention. As Phelan declaimed, the Federal Reserve System, "makes the wealth of the Country available for all classes, as reflected by credit. It decentralizes the vast accumulations which, under other regimes, gravitated to centers where money was crowned king by spoilsmen and profiteers, tariff-fed and ferocious, and against whom small business and handicapped industry were to contend . . . . The Federal Reserve System was the revolt of Spartacus!'' Phelan proclaimed.

"Again my friends, he understands our farmers' problems . . . . You might not hear of it in Wall Street, but there are farmers in the West . . . pleading for the bare necessities--an interesting idea for a Convention sitting in the money capital of the nation,'' Phelan bitterly accused, almost contradicting himself about the money now residing in the Federal Reserve. (He was arousing old party passions in the Garden and reawakening an old agrarian split that had culminated in the nomination of William Jennings Bryan at the 1896 Chicago Convention. Bryan had stood against the Wall Street men of gold who were ''crucifying'' the nation's farmers.)

Phelan spoke of the extravagant interest rates charged to the desperate farmers. "In 1918, by a bold and courageous stroke, he ended once and for all this evil. He deposited the people's money in the banks throughout the agricultural sections, thus lowered interest rates and saving the farmers millions in money. He served agriculture notably again in 1914 when the cotton farmers of the South and West faced ruin because they could not export their surplus abroad. Because of the war, American shipping was held up by prohibitive insurance rates. . . . After Congressional approval, he organized the War Risk Insurance Bureau to insure American ships and cargo . . . . He is also responsible for the creation of the $100 million cotton loan fund to provide temporary . . . relief to the people.'' McAdoo had performed other financial miracles that saved ordinary people from ruin as well, and Phelan spoke of these.

McAdoo's other war responsibilities were outlined by Phelan. "From January 1, 1918, to the Armistice on November 11, 1918, there were transported over the governmentally-controlled railroads more than six million living men, soldier and sailors, and a total of 193,000 cars were used for this movement,'' he defensively bragged. ''The railroads were taken over to win the war. . . .''

The Permanent Chairman broke in to quell a sudden uproar in the Garden's upper decks that were stacked with thousands of Tammany men and other New Yorkers who were committed to McAdoo's chief rival at this Convention, their beloved Governor Alfred Emanuel Smith. "We shall not proceed until the Convention is in order,'' Walsh shouted and ordered the Sergeant-at-Arms to clear the aisles on the floor which were clogged with delegates and alternates and others who had been let in by the Tammany ushers at the doors.

Phelan continued by addressing the rising disorder. ''We have

153

received much kindness from New York," he quipped, "but we also ask for a share of its intellectual hospitality." He was supported by a surge of applause on the floor and from sections of the gallery among the non-New Yorkers. He went on to enumerate the many statistics that showed Secretary McAdoo's intimate attention to his nation's needs.

He also praised McAdoo's fair dealings with railroad workers through the Labor Board. Again he taunted, that it would "be of interest to Wall Street, that some of the earnings, fluttered into the pockets of the men who run the railroads down at Pine and Broad and Wall and surrounding streets, from Curb to Curb and from Exchange to Exchange. That is our opinion. When we consider the workers of the land . . . they have long suffered injustice, their poverty in this year has made an appeal to the calloused hearts. . . . "The railway unions were supporting McAdoo, although the American Federation of Labor had declared neutrality. Later, it would endorse the Progressive Party.

Senator Phelan made a slight plea to New York in outlining McAdoo's biography. "Long before he ever thought of entering politics, when he was operating the Hudson Tunnels in New York, he gave equal pay to women for equal work." (In 1902, McAdoo had organized the Hudson and Manhattan Railroad Company, and by 1910 had completed four tunnels under the river.)

Phelan was rewarded with applause. "Born in Georgia," there were loud cheers from the Georgians on the floor, "Bred in Tennessee," again cheers reverberated from the floor, "of Cavalier and Pioneer stock—Revolutionary American, he has handed down his ancestral virtues, and in this war gave three sons to the naval service of his Country." The patriotic Convention approved. "He himself was one of eight children. He has known privation and has practiced self-denial. He understands the problems of the poor. He has the fiber of fortitude. He never quits."

Then Phelan gave McAdoo's position on the issue that had begun to divide the Convention. "He opposes any discrimination on account of religious belief." The hate Catholics, hate Smith currency was alive and well among those in and out of the Convention who had association with the Ku Klux Klan, whose largest kiva was in New York City, as was the case with the Know-Nothings of 1856. At this Convention, the Klan's influence was apparent throughout.

"We want to be able to cooperate with all our fellow citizens without suspicion. It is monstrous to think that, just having come out of the war, one would question the faith of the solider who has fought by his side." Shouts of "Right," pierced the smoky atmosphere. "There is no test in the mind of our candidate but sincerity and loyalty and devotion to the Stars and Stripes. . . . My dear friends, America was the protest of the freemen of the world against the religious bigotry and persecution of the past. . . ."

154

Senator Phelan offered one example. "We know that in our candidate's career when the Jews were cruelly persecuted in Russia, American Jews, protected by our Treaty, were denied their Rights." McAdoo led the counter-offensive to get Congress to act. Then Phelan cited McAdoo's own words, delivered in June 1923, at the graduation ceremonies of the University of Southern California. "In our Country since the war, bigotry and intolerance have attempted to impair the great Constitutional guarantees. In some states, legislation has been attempted to suppress Freedom of Speech and of the Press, and a disposition has been manifest to revive racial and religious prejudices and to destroy that spirit of national unity and cooperation," McAdoo had scolded. "We must resist these tendencies, and hold fast to these great guarantees of human Liberty. Without them, free institutions will disappear." Much applause swelled on the Convention floor and was echoed in the galleries.

"This year demands the return of triumphant Democracy," Phelan finished. "The Progressives of the nation look to the Democratic Party for their leader. There is room in America for only one reactionary party, and the Republicans have preempted that field. . . . Today there has come another man from the West, another Old Hickory, with the same sympathy for the Common Man, the same heritage of American ideals...William Gibbs McAdoo, of California."

Phelan had spoken for fifty-one minutes and his followers were ready to celebrate. Women waved their yellow scarves with the inscription: "Bill McAdoo." A California woman carried a banner, "Wilson in 1916, McAdoo in 1924." Four bands struck up "Over There." The parade stopped before the box of Mrs. McAdoo to salute her. The balconies were unsympathetic. They yelled back, "Give us 'East Side, West Side.' " The McAdoo demonstration that began at 3:10 in the afternoon did not end for one hour and seventeen minutes, finally sputtering in the heat wave that was building inside the Garden. The Smith supporters were unimpressed.

At last Chicagoan George E. Brennan, who was now commander of all the anti-McAdoo forces, was recognized by the chair. "The Convention has been in session for six hours in a torrid atmosphere, and we are all tired," he confessed. "I move, sir, that this Convention take recess until tomorrow morning at 10:30 o'clock." The group then disbanded and the furious hunt for delegates continued among managers of the various candidates for nomination.

Delegates woke up on Thursday, June 26, to newspaper headlines that the Coolidge administration had sued fifty oil companies for conspiracy to violate the Sherman Anti-Trust Act by monopolizing gasoline and fixing prices. Clearly, they were on the counter-offensive. Delegates also commented that this was a slow Convention; already the Third Day and still no platform or vote on a nominee, and plenty of

155

nominations still to come. Even the session starting times were ignored. It wasn't until 11:25 in the morning that Permanent Chairman Thomas J. Walsh called the meeting to order. William A. Porter, of Boston, asked the delegates and guests to participate in silent prayer, followed by the Lord's Prayer. "For Thine is the Kingdom, the power, and the glory forever," he concluded.

Delegates were invited to a reception at Tammany Hall on East Fourteenth Street later that evening, hosted by Thomas Foley, Tammany's new chieftain. That April, Charles Francis Murphy, Tammany's wily leader and mentor to Governor Smith, had died, depriving Smith of a critical strategic resource. Then the round of nominations and seconding speeches continued with Governor William E. Sweet, of Colorado, seconding McAdoo. While he was extolling the former Treasury Secretary for "passage of the Federal Reserve Act, which took money out of Wall Street and distributed it throughout the Country," the gallery packed with New Yorkers interrupted. The Permanent Chairman tried to quell them. "The Convention cannot proceed with its work unless everyone has an opportunity to say what he cares to say . . . ," the Chairman instructed.

Sweet then made a point that ultimately impacted the November election. "Mr. McAdoo's nomination by this Convention will absolutely preclude the organization of a third party on July Fourth at Cleveland. If we are wise we will take this fact into consideration." The Progressives following Wisconsin Senator Robert Marion LaFollette threatened to run a campaign if the Democrats failed to nominate a Progressive candidate and adopt a Progressive platform.

Chairman Walsh next called to the podium a sentimental favorite of New York State and the 1920 Democracy's candidate for Vice President, Franklin Delano Roosevelt. The Chair of the New York delegation was Mrs. Caroline O'Day, of Westchester, but Roosevelt was Smith's campaign manager and had been selected by the Smith crowd to nominate the Governor, as he had in 1920 at the San Francisco Convention. Though stricken by infantile paralysis in 1921, F.D.R. had worked hard to prepare for this his first political appearance since his illness.

The *Times* reported, "Mr. Roosevelt, who had been crippled since an attack of illness three years ago, had been brought to the platform in a wheeled chair. He walked forward on crutches, attended by James A. Lynch, of Poughkeepsie, placed both hands on the speakers' desk and stood with head erect, a vigorous and healthful figure, except for his lameness . . . , his appearance prompted an explosion of cheers as if a charge of dynamite had been touched off."

Roosevelt began by appealing to the noise makers in the gallery. "Let me say on behalf of the New York delegation that we expect that all the guests of the Convention will render the same fair play to all candidates and their friends as we would expect to receive in any other city." Applause on the floor supported his wishes.

"To meet again so many friends whom I have not seen since the last Democratic National gathering gives me a thrill of pleasure," he began with full voice. "At that Convention, where I myself received one of the highest honors of the party, I had the privilege of working and speaking on behalf of the Governor of the State of New York." He was again speaking on behalf of his mentor, Governor Alfred Emanuel Smith, whom Roosevelt said was "greatly loved by his own state." Roosevelt quickly addressed the fears of many delegates. "It has been suggested that we would attempt to sweep him through to victory at this Convention on a wave of emotional appeal. Let me assure you at the beginning that I shall make no such appeal . . . ." The crowd was much more attentive to Roosevelt than it had been to former Senator Phelan when he nominated McAdoo.

"There is no need for me to portray the profound love which goes out to him from every class and every section of the community," Roosevelt affirmed. Then he challenged the delegates, "When you leave this session ask the woman who serves you in the shop, the banker who cashes your check, the man who runs your elevator, the clerk in your hotel . . . and you will be told with a convincing unanimity that first in the affections of the people of the state, far above all others. . . " was their twice-elected Governor. The handsome Roosevelt labeled Smith a "Happy Warrior," and then broadened his appeal. "You equally who come from the great cities of the East and from the plains and hills of the West, from the slopes of the Pacific and from the homes and fields of the Southland . . . keep first in your hearts and minds the words of Abraham Lincoln: 'With malice toward none, with charity to all.' " His request was resoundingly affirmed by applause, and subsequently ignored by feuding delegates.

"The depths to which our Federal Government has fallen have been well portrayed to you," Roosevelt noted, but "for over twenty years in public office the white light of publicity has piteously beaten, and revealed only spotless integrity," he said of Smith. "Under the complete lack of leadership in a Republican White House and a Republican Capitol we have had all of the checks but none of the balances." The Convention laughed at Roosevelt's easy humor. "Therefore we must give to the Country a President capable of restoring teamwork . . . . This man's record is history."

Roosevelt outlined how Smith had worked with a hostile state legislature without abandoning principle. "He was a pioneer for the budget system. He was a pioneer in the reorganization and the simplification of Government departments . . . and appointed to office men and women preeminently qualified for their tasks. Because of his ideals and methods of governing, he has won not only the undivided support of his own party but the public endorsement of the great civic, non-partisan bodies throughout the State of New York . . . He will make the dry bones rattle in Washington," he said. "And that spells the true Progressive." The delegates applauded. The galleries wildly shouted their support.

Roosevelt explained that Smith had also, "obtained laws prohibiting night work for women and the employment of small children. He secured state pensions for widowed mothers and state aid for the promotion of the health of rural communities. That is Progressive! He has sponsored a practical Workmen's Compensation Law. He has established labor boards to mediate disputes between employer and employee. He was responsible for the best factory laws ever passed in any state. That is Progressive." Roosevelt's litany elicited strong applause.

"Under his leadership," Roosevelt continued, "cooperative marketing, the extension of state highways, built for miles not for votes, the diversification of crops, the reforestation of denuded lands have marched hand in hand. That is Progressive! In his first term as Governor every penny of additional appropriations went to the extension of the educational system of the state . . . that is Progressive!" Smith also had reduced, "the income tax of this state by 25 percent, and the direct tax on land values throughout the state by another 25 percent . . . . That is Progressive too."

A delegate's voice rose above the applause, "This is wonderful!" Roosevelt's aristocratic charm was having its full affect on the attentive delegates. Then almost anticipating his own words eight years later, Roosevelt observed, "The most pronounced dangers from which the Country suffers today is a lack of confidence in Government." This time, however, Roosevelt attributed the lack of confidence to a different source. "The loss of faith arises chiefly from the reprehensible acts, the low conception of duty, and the complete lack of leadership of those now in power."

Then Roosevelt explained how Smith could win. "This Governor of ours is the most dangerous adversary that the Republican Party ever had to fear." There was loud agreement, especially from the galleries. "He has been elected to office seventeen times. Chosen Governor of this state first in 1918, he suffered the only defeat of his long career in 1920. But it was a defeat more glorious than victory. When our national ticket in the State of New York went down to defeat under a plurality of 1,100,000 votes, he lost this state by only 74,000. He got one million more votes than I did," Roosevelt laughed. "And I take off my hat to him!" The Convention cheered Roosevelt's gallantry and Smith's vote-getting prowess. "This is an overwhelming demonstration of ability to command the confidence of the great electorate."

Roosevelt outlined the reasons for Smith's popularity. "All the world loves a man who carves his own career." Born of American-born parents, he took upon his shoulders while still a boy the responsibility for the support of his family. A wage-earner toiling with his hands, this man in the space of twenty years, without fortune, without fortuitous aid, with nothing to rely upon except his own indomitable courage, has risen to be a commanding and outstanding figure in the life of the nation. . . . Our Governor not only represents the common people but he embodies in his very being the aspirations of the average man, so that when he speaks, he speaks with the voice of America—he burns with the fire of a divine humanity—the fire that has produced the greatest of leaders of the democracies of the world."

When Roosevelt finished his carefully enunciated, thirty-four minute defense of Al Smith, demonstrations broke out on the floor and lasted for one hour and fifteen minutes, before starting up again. The *Times* wrote, "It provoked the loudest demonstration ever heard at a National Convention." But the paper also noted that the demonstration "lacked the spirit of 1920," referring to the spontaneous outburst of affection for Smith four years earlier at the San Francisco Convention.

The state standards of New York, the District of Columbia, Illinois, New Jersey, Wisconsin, Alaska, Connecticut, Minnesota, Rhode Island, Vermont, Pennsylvania, Massachusetts, Iowa, and Nevada were prominent in the Smith parade and the galleries were demonstrative in their support. Absent from the procession were the states of the South and West that favored McAdoo, and more ominously, were pledged to repudiate Smith. Hundreds of Tammany Hall workers rushed through the south gate of the Garden to fuel the fire for their hometown boy, carrying huge banners with Smith's portrait. The sudden influx solved a mystery of 2,000 missing tickets that Smith people had accused the McAdoo forces of pilfering.

Madison Square Garden was supposed to hold only a maximum of 14,000 people, but with the new crush of demonstrators the crowd swelled to 17,000. Three brass bands and a battery of fire engine sirens blared for Smith. His supporters sang along with "East Side, West Side" and "Tammany." Thousands of rattles, whistles, and buzzers added to the bedlam. The parade halted in front of Mrs. Smith's box near the speakers' platform. Meanwhile, the galleries went wild for Smith.

The *Times* commented, "Yet, it produced no visible effect, except to make delegates who were not already on Smith's side look sourer and sourer as they pressed their fingers in their ears to keep out the waves of sound." Finally, Roosevelt lifted his hands to halt the demonstration. James Hoey aided him by standing on his seat signaling with both hands and the noise came to an end. The *Times* speculated that both McAdoo and Smith "damaged their cause by the protracted and artificial demonstrations of their supporters."

The Roll Call of the States continued and the Honorable Thomas F. Bayard, of Delaware, nominated Willard Saulsbury for President. The favorite son had been a member of the U.S. Senate from 1913 to 1919, and served as President Pro Tem during the World War. Next, Charles M. Hay, of Missouri, seconded McAdoo, referring to Prohibition, "Lawlessness runs riot in the land. Individuals and corporations evade, gangs and groups defy the law." McAdoo was the Dry candidate.

Lewis G. Stevenson, of Illinois, son of the former Vice President under Grover Cleveland, of New York, said his state was "not boss ruled" and he was doing something "unique in the history of political Conventions," nominating someone to consider if, "because of conflicting views and desires," the Convention became deadlocked, and who they could turn to as a solution. Hence, he was not urging their votes for David Franklin Houston, of New York, "the foremost economist of his time" on the early ballots.

Houston had served as Wilson's first Secretary of Agriculture and later as his third Secretary of Treasury. Houston had been endorsed earlier in the week by Harvard University President Emeritus, Dr. Charles W. Eliot. Despite her husband's nomination of Smith, the next morning Mrs. Franklin D. Roosevelt attended a breakfast for Houston hosted by Mrs. Arthur Osgood Choate at the Colony Club.

The Honorable Michael L. Igoe, an Illinois state representative who later would serve in Congress and as the U.S. Attorney for the Northern District of Illinois, seconded Al Smith's nomination on behalf of two-thirds of his state's delegation. But James A. Meeks, from Danville, Illinois, who would serve in Congress during the 1930s, countered with a seconding speech for McAdoo, because, "of the 181,000 Democrats of Illinois who expressed their preference for him in the primary election . . . ."

Frederick Van Nuys, of Indiana, entered the name of its favorite son, Samuel M. Ralston, who had been elected Governor in 1912, and then sent to the U.S. Senate. "He votes right, he thinks right, he is right." He failed to point out that the last time Ralston ran for office with Klan support. Miss Anna Case led the Convention in singing "On the Banks of the Wabash." (The song's lyrics had been co-written with his brother by Theodore Dreiser, of Indiana, who got his break as a news man at the 1892 National Democratic Convention in Chicago.)

Meanwhile, Indiana's Democratic boss, former Senator Thomas Taggart, who owned racing horses back in Indiana, was telling the press about his horse "Senator" who laid back for seven-eighths of a mile, but always crossed the wire first, no matter his early position. Taggart, who had been born in Ireland and been Mayor of Indianapolis, predicted old

Sam Ralston, who had been Indiana's Governor from 1913 to 1917 before going to the Senate in 1923, would do the same.

The Honorable M. F. Healy, of Iowa, spoke on behalf of Smith. He chastised those around the hall who had been demeaning his man with anti-Catholic slurs. "Until I arrived in New York for this Convention, I thought everybody knew the language and the meaning of the First Amendment to the Constitution of the United States." He read it to them. "The men who framed that guarantee knew the long sad story of the past," he added. "They knew how in the early days Christians went down into the catacombs and lived and died there in defense of their Right to worship God according to the dictates of their consciences . . . . They knew the wretched story of the quarrel of the centuries between the Christians and the Moslem; they knew the sad, sad story of the religious wars between people calling themselves Christians. . . . All these tragedies found answer in the First Amendment . . . no one has the Right under the American Flag to discriminate because of race or creed," Healy scolded Smith's opponents.

W. A. Ayes, of Kansas, next nominated its favorite son, the "Farmer Governor of the Sunflower State," Jonathan M. Davis, who was "a real dirt farmer" and who had "demonstrated his ability, honesty, and courage." The Governor's headquarters consisted of a parlor and bedroom at the McAplin Hotel.

Mrs. Alexander Thompson, of Oregon, also seconded McAdoo, saying, "I speak for the women of the Democracy of the United States when I assert that we will accept no candidate for the presidency who does not represent the spirit of Progressivism. . . ." The Honorable William R. Pattangal, of Maine, then seconded Senator Underwood. "They have said he is reactionary. If he is reactionary, the Constitution of the United States is reactionary, for he is today its ablest expounder and its most fearless defender."

The Roll Call continued and the Secretary summoned the Honorable Howard Bruce, of Maryland, to the rostrum, who submitted the name of 48-year-old, Albert Cabell Ritchie. "This Marylander, who is of Virginia blood . . . was a distinguished lawyer before entering public service, has been People's Counsel to the State Public Service Commission, Attorney General of his state, Chief Counsel to the War Industries Board in Washington, and was in 1919, the year of Republican landslide, elected Governor of the State of Maryland by a bare majority of 165 votes. In 1923 . . . his state broke a precedent of nearly one hundred years by re-electing him Governor, giving him the greatest majority ever. . . ."

General Charles H. Cole, of Massachusetts, seconded Governor Smith. "The romantic rise of this boy of the tenements is the most appealing story since the story of Lincoln and the log cabin." A demonstration began but was short-lived, with cries of "Sit down," from hostile delegates on the floor who were impatient with the longevity of events. The Permanent Chair sternly suggested, "If this Convention cannot come back to its business in this city, the Chair will entertain a motion to go somewhere else." His rebuff was met with loud cheers. The Smith supporters settled down.

The Honorable A. M. Cummins, of Michigan, rose to nominate favorite son Senator Woodbridge N. Ferris, who was "a man with a personality so dynamic, a manner of speech so convincing, a manner of living so faith inspiring . . . he has been able to be repeatedly elected to the highest office in the gift of the state." Ferris had started out as a teacher, built an institute, "through whose portals there pass every year 2,000." Senator Ferris also had been Michigan Governor from 1913 through 1916. The exhausted delegates then debated for half an hour whether or not to adjourn, finally voting in the affirmative.

The Fourth Day of the 1924 Democratic Convention, Friday, June 27, began with morning rain. A prayer by the Reverend W. W. Wylie, of New York, who decided to skip the "Lord's Prayer" mini-debate, started the affair. And the Roll Call of the States resumed with William J. Quinn, of Minnesota, who spoke on behalf of Al Smith, "a candidate who will not foreclose himself by merely pointing a finger at the First Amendment to the Constitution . . . or who merely satisfies the whim of a cowardly minority. . . ." He alluded to the fact that many of those supporting McAdoo were practicing anti-religious bigotry.

Newton Diehl Baker, former Mayor of Cleveland and Wilson's Secretary of War, nominated James M. Cox, of Ohio. Cox had been the Democracy's 1920 presidential nominee and had finished second in the 1924 primaries. "No permanently prosperous America is conceivable in a world of recurring wars," Baker asserted, "and no permanently peaceful world is conceivable which does not rest in part upon our cooperation. In any case, it must rest upon principles of Justice, tolerance, and generosity which are traditionally American." Cox had campaigned for entry into Wilson's League of Nations, and had been trounced by Harding, who was an ambivalent internationalist.

"Years of reaction and despair have followed the years of war and destruction," Baker observed. "The Four Horseman of the Apocalypse ride. . . . The people of the world have found it hard to make a fresh start amid the ruins of their material civilization. They have found it hard to stifle the sobs in their throats for their millions of dead. They have found it hard to believe again in any institutions. . . . Larger armies have grown up. More deadly arms have been devised. Nationalistic aspirations have been nursed as promising possible relief from intolerable hardship. . . . The League at Geneva," he was interrupted with loud applause, "has gathered to it the great liberals of the Old World. . . . It

162

has fought disease and vice, lifted Austria and Hungary back to the possibility of orderly national life, repatriated the war prisoners, established a World Court, prevented four wars and stopped one, set on foot the only promising plan of disarmament yet devised, and never moved a single soldier.''

Baker then turned to his nominee. "For three terms as her Governor this son of Ohio demonstrated his capacity as an executive. . . . He was our War Governor. The Constitution of the state was remodeled under his leadership, engrafting modern and liberal principles. . . . A great body of wholesome legislation was enacted by his cooperation with legislatures not always of his own political faith. . . . Without hesitation or wavering he fought the long 1920 campaign, debating with doubt, appealing to our higher emotions, battling back the tide of ills. . . .'' A seventeen-minute demonstration followed Baker's endorsement of Cox.

William M. Maloney, of Montana, next rushed the rostrum to second Smith's nomination. Samuel V. Stewart, of Montana, stood up for McAdoo. Then Eugene D. O'Sullivan, of Nebraska, nominated its Governor, Charles W. Bryan, brother of the party's original Progressive, William Jennings Bryan. O'Sullivan began by offering his condolences for the recent death of New York's Charles F. Murphy, "that great political leader,'' who had served for years as head of Tammany Hall, and who had been one of Al Smith's early strategists. "Nebraska has rejoiced with you that the Democratic National Convention differs from the present National Administration in that it is a place of prayer rather than the subject of prayer,'' he joked. "No living man has more earnestly or efficiently striven for Government by the people than has this candidate.''

Suddenly the Nebraskan was interrupted by noise and disorder on the floor and in the galleries. The Chair banged his gavel relentlessly. O'Sullivan resumed: "No living man has more earnestly striven to put the crown of sovereignty on the brow of the citizen and the badge of service on the public official than Nebraska's project. The tendency toward centralization of power in the Federal Government was never more menacing than now, and never has it been more speciously pleaded than by our accidental President when he said, 'If the states fail to keep step with national legislation and administration, they must give way to national oversight.' This is the reincarnation of the divine Right of kings. . . .''

O'Sullivan outlined Governor Bryan's career as business manager and associate editor of the national newspaper, the *Commoner*. As "mayor of a great Republican city (Lincoln,) he led the municipal ownership forces and secured through municipal ownership cheaper power, light, gas, and ice, and saved the citizens from the exploitation of the coal combine." As Governor, Bryan had cut Nebraska's taxation 13 percent, and cut by 50 percent the number of employees under his jurisdiction, and brought about fifteen-cent gas. Again, O'Sullivan was interrupted by the galleries before quickly concluding amid the disorder, "He believes that the time is ripe, and rotten ripe, for a change." A demonstration in Bryan's favor lasted twenty minutes.

The call of states rolled on. Honorable F. Clyde Keefe, of New Hampshire, nominated the Granite State's favorite son, Fred H. Brown, the first name offered to a Presidential Convention from that state since President Franklin Pierce. "Young Hickory," as Keefe called him (the same moniker used for Pierce,) had served as a Mayor, District Attorney, and the first Democratic Governor elected in sixty years. Brown had lifted his state out of debt and reduced taxes.

The Honorable John E. Matthews, of New Jersey, nominated its favorite son Governor George S. Silzer, elected a year earlier, whom he called another Wilson, because he had fought bribery and corruption in state Government. A half-hour demonstration followed. Elmer H. Geran, of New Jersey, seconded Silzer. A weary delegate shouted, "Make it short." He did. Those at the Silzer campaign headquarters on the third floor of the Waldorf had been pushing the Governor as a Dark Horse if the Convention became deadlocked.

The Honorable J. F. T. O'Connor, of North Dakota, seconded McAdoo. He spoke of the ominous on-going debate raging in the Resolutions Committee held in the Rose room of the Waldorf Astoria and on the Convention floor. "Another issue has come into this Convention," he confided. "We shall meet it like Democracy meets all issues. I want to give you the position of the man whose nomination I wish to second . . . on St. Patrick's Day." Applause roared through the galleries. O'Connor quoted McAdoo who on that occasion said, "I stand four-square with respect to this and every other order under the immutable guarantee of Liberty contained in the First Amendment . . . for the freedom of religious worship," the former Treasury Secretary had said. Applause rippled through the Garden, "Freedom of Speech, Freedom of the Press and the Right of peaceable assembly. That has been the Democratic doctrine ever since the immortal Thomas Jefferson wrote it first as a constitutional provision," McAdoo had proclaimed. (Actually, James Madison drafted the Bill of Rights. Jefferson was Minister to France at the time.)

"I say ladies and gentlemen," O'Connor boomed, "I am opposed in the name of the soldiers and sailors who sleep in deathless silence . . . in the name of the millions of people of my faith, that I honor and respect, the faith that I learned at a mother's knee, in the name of the intelligent Protestants of my state who by legislative act unmasked its members, I say to you as an American citizen, I condemn the order known as the Ku Klux Klan." Great applause engulfed the floor and galleries, and the standards of New Jersey, Pennsylvania, and Rhode Island led a Convention floor parade. The delegations of Georgia, Texas, Kansas, Michigan, and Missouri silently glared at them.

Alben Barkley, of Kentucky, who would become Vice President of the United States under Harry Truman, took the gavel as Acting Permanent Chairman. He ordered the tedious Roll Call to continue with Pennsylvania. Mrs. Carroll Miller seconded Smith. Miller, an "English Quaker and Scotch Protestant" also spoke on behalf of Liberty, mentioning the friends of various religions she knew. "During the World War we were neither Jew nor Gentile, Catholic nor Protestant, we were all Americans." She then painted an appealing domestic picture of Smith: "Because of his tenderness to his mother, of his devotion to his wife and children, of the consecration of his public life to the welfare of his fellow man," applause stopped her, "of his untarnished honesty and courage, I know this man to be one who has completely builded his life upon the Ten Commandments and the teachings of our Lord and Master." Concluding, she called Smith a "true American."

The floor was in an uproar over her remarks with arguments going on between delegates for Smith and McAdoo, each making accusations and denials. Barkley called on Samuel E. Shull, of Pennsylvania, to calm the dispute by seconding Underwood. "We must have a man who neither advocates nor countenances preference or oppression of any section or any class." A voice from the floor shouted: "Amen."

Mrs. Clarence Renshaw, of Pennsylvania, seconded Ritchie, who some were calling the "conciliatory candidate." She asked, "Are Pennsylvania breaking the Tenth Commandment if we covet our neighbor's Governor?" Mrs. Mary E. Herbert, of Pennsylvania, seconded McAdoo. Then Barkley called upon The Honorable Daniel F. Guinan, of Pennsylvania, amid a mixed chorus of cheers and boos. Even as he began his discourse, voices shouted out, "Name the man. Who is he? Name the man. Throw your shot. Name him." Exhausted and impatient, the galleries balked at the tradition of leaving the candidate's name to the last line of a speech.

"I am putting no new name in nomination," Guinan retorted. "Come on, name the man. Say something," the voices demanded. "I have a man in mind, a man who can poll more than 266 Electoral votes." The voices continued: "Is it a secret? Name him. Name the man," they shouted. "Order," Barkley insisted. Finally, Guinan uttered McAdoo's name to scattered applause and boos.

The Roll Call fell upon South Carolina, and Mrs. Leroy Springs, who also seconded McAdoo, saying he "appeals to the imagination of all classes of fair-minded people. . . ."

Mrs. Springs would become the first Democratic woman to receive votes for Vice President. Mrs. George Fort Milton, of Tennessee, seconded McAdoo. Samuel A. King, of Utah, said, "The Democracy of Utah as expressed in a recent state Convention, when, by a vote of 445 to 116, declared for William Gibbs McAdoo." Cries from the floor chanted, "Oil, oil, oil." Smith leaders tried to quiet them.

The chant continued and referred to McAdoo's retainer to serve as a lawyer for oil magnate Edward L. Doheny after resigning from the Wilson administration. The *Evening Post* was charging that Doheny was financing McAdoo's campaign, something both denied. In fact, Doheny issued a press release charging that McAdoo had deserted him when his legal troubles brewed. "I am leaving the privilege of contributing to Mr. McAdoo's campaign fund to those who believe in the efforts of a lawyer who deserts his client when he is under attack after having received substantial retainers for legal services. Those who believe that such a course is ethical no doubt believe that Mr. McAdoo would make a good President of the United States."

More confusion and jeers followed. Roland D. Sawyer, of Massachusetts, was recognized, saying he would be brief. "Good," the crowd retorted. "For three days you have been sitting here, 1,500 delegates, 1,500 alternates, 15,000 guests, and the spectacle of your restraint and harmony have been splendid," he asserted. He seconded Governor Brown, of New Hampshire.

Finally, the Roll Call of the States reached Virginia and Senator Claude A. Swanson approached the podium to nominate Carter Glass of the "Old Dominion." Glass, who was seen as a "Constructive Progressive," was listening to the speech from his suite at the Waldorf. "Mr. Chairman, when I came to this Convention and heard many mutterings of discord and indications of dissention," it made him think of an old legend, Swanson said. "Tradition tells us that the Indians of Virginia were accustomed to meet once each year in a great conclave of tribes, and when they assembled they extinguished all the fire used during the past year and from flint and rock obtained new fire which could only be used during the coming year. This was done as a symbol that with the quenching of the old fire all past grudges and grievances and differences, both tribal and personal, were forgiven and forgotten, and that with the new fire there came new love, new union, and new harmony." His tale elicited sympathetic applause. "May this beautiful legend in spirit pervade this great assemblage. . . ."

Senator Swanson argued that Glass had been, "Handicapped in early youth by privation and poverty, and attained success by courage, by industry, by manliness. . . . For more than twenty years he served in the House of Representatives, recognized as one of its ablest and most distinguished members." He had helped shepherd the Federal Reserve

Act through that body. After McAdoo retired, President Wilson had appointed Glass as his second Secretary of the Treasury. He had resigned to become a U. S. Senator, where he served as chairman of the Joint Committee of the House and Senate that had, "secured the passage of the great Federal Loan Act, which has brought immeasurable relief to the farmer." He also was, "an eloquent and able speaker. Virginia offers you his intelligence, his patriotism, his character, his courage, his cleanness, his honesty, for the service of the nation. . . ."

After a twenty-minute demonstration on behalf of the Virginian, the band played "Carry me back to Old Virginny." Glass was then seconded by Governor E. Lee Trinkle, who called Glass, "The Little Giant of Virginia." Mrs. Kate Waller Barrett, agreed on Glass, adding, "I have been inspired by what New York has shown us. I want to tell you that I do not like you men abusing Wall Street, either . . . . I live on Main Street in old Virginia. But Main Street is made safe by Wall Street, and don't you forget it," she lectured the assembly.

At last the Roll Call reached West Virginia, and Judge John H. Holt nominated John William Davis, of West Virginia, the last name entered into the contest. "As Solicitor General of the United States" under Wilson, Davis "became the trusted and victorious lawyer of the people in many of their controversies before the court of last resort in the nation, and finally was selected as the representative of his Country to the greatest court of Europe [Ambassador to Great Britain], where he illustrated the power and dignity of democratic simplicity. . . . Thirty-six percent of the delegates before me belong to a profession that know that what I say in his behalf is a verity." (Davis was president of the American Bar Association.)

Before the Convention convened, Davis had said, "I have taken, however, in good faith, the position that I am not a candidate for the nomination and that any decision to the contrary must come from the party and not from myself . . . . Elections turn or should turn upon the question of confidence or want of confidence in those who have been entrusted with the administration of the Government." The *New York Times* had reported that, "the talk about the corridors and lobbies at the Waldorf is . . . that Davis is generally looked upon as a man who could become the Democratic standard bearer with credit to himself and the party." But Davis had at least one enemy, William Jennings Bryan, who was insisting that the Convention might as well nominate J. P. Morgan and the Standard Oil interests for whom Davis worked as legal counsel.

Mrs. Izetta Jewel Brown, of West Virginia, added that Davis "was born and reared among these mountains, and his family before him. He has the strength and virility of the mountains in his body, in his brain, and in his character." Four years earlier at the San Francisco Convention, delegates had said Davis was too unknown. "The same people now say he is too well known . . . . They say now that he is a lawyer of Wall Street. Wall Street cannot taint John W. Davis! . . . He has made himself an intellectual power in this, the greatest city of our nation. His clients come from all classes.''

Mrs. Brown added, "I submit to you, Mr. Davis is good looking. He looks every inch the President . . . .'' She noted that the 51-year-old Davis ''holds rather a unique position, in that, although he served in public life for more than a decade, he has never asked for public office, and neither does he today. Three times our great President, Woodrow Wilson, drafted him to important positions. His friends today are suggesting that you draft him again for political service.''

The nominations had come to an end. All together, sixteen men, among them five United States Senators and six Governors had been nominated and seconded over the past two days. McAdoo attracted eleven seconding speeches; Smith seven; Underwood two. Elmer Davis wrote in the *Times* that, ''about 40,000 or 50,000 words were spoken, but anybody who had to sit through it all would be willing to swear that there were at least 40,000,000 . . . . All in all, it was a terrible day.'' Wilted by the heat and exhausted by the cavalcade of rhetoric, the Convention adjourned until Saturday morning. Meanwhile the managers of the candidates were feverishly hunting for support. The Massachusetts delegates marched up Fifth Avenue to Smith headquarters at the Waldorf, shouting his name.

The Fifth Day, and Fifth Session of the Convention, Saturday June 28, 1924, was called to order at 10:35 on a cool and rainy morning. The papers warned of a major platform fight brewing at the Garden. ''Storm over Klan Menacing,'' ''Serious Schism Feared'' the headlines cautioned. Meanwhile, the bookmakers on Wall Street had increased the odds against McAdoo to 5½ to 1; against Smith they remained 2½ to 1.'' One *New York Times* headline that week also declared, ''Smith As Negro's Hope.'' (President Coolidge and his guests on the Mayflower in Chesapeake Bay that day were listening to the proceedings on a ''new high-power radio receiving set.'')

Reverend John Roach Straton, of Calvary Baptist Church, asked that the Convention be sent, ''the spirit of unity and of understanding, and do Thou, oh God, enable us so to act and so to think as that we shall not compromise with evil, or with error, but that we shall stand four-square for old-fashion Americanism, guided by the power of God and doing, as we believe, the will of God.'' Time was taken to appoint a new National Committee.

One observer at the Convention that day was Republican Senator James E. Watson, of Indiana, who sized up the dilemma facing the Democracy. ''Look at it. They can't nominate McAdoo, and they won't nominate Smith. . . . I don't see how they can do anything but nominate

Ralston . . . a fine old fellow and as honest as they make them," he said of his fellow Hoosier.

Would they ever get to the voting? The Chairman of the Committee on Resolutions, Connecticut's Homer S. Cummings, who was a close friend of William McAdoo and would become Franklin Roosevelt's Attorney General, optimistically reported on the delay in producing a platform. "Let me say, my friends, that I have never seen a sub-committee that worked together in greater or more perfect harmony. . . ." He was exaggerating and had no more than six hours sleep since Tuesday evening. "When we come to submit this platform to you it will be a report on every plank unanimously made, except in two instances," he warned them. "I regret to say that great differences of opinion arose." The divisions surfaced over how to present the League of Nations issue, and with the questions of religious freedom and the Ku Klux Klan. A great debate would be staged on the floor of the Convention between the Majority and Minority platform reports.

Cummings asked for a recess until the final document could be completed and told the crowd that, "In all my experience in the service of the Democratic Party, in all the years that I have known political affairs and political events, I have never before witnessed such a scene as took place this morning in the committee room at six o'clock. When we had completed our deliberations and had begun to feel once more welling up into our hearts the spirit of fraternity and were about to dispense, one of the members arose and recited the Lord's Prayer," there was applause, "and we all united in it, and then at the close Mr. Bryan lifted up his voice," then great applause swept the hall for the party's old leader, "in an invocation. . . I do not know that I ought to say these things. . . ." A voice shouted, "You should." And the session was recessed until 3 p.m. so the platform combatants could get some sleep before their great debate.

Before the late afternoon debate began, Franklin Roosevelt slowly made his way down the center aisle to the New York delegation leaning heavily on crutches. At 4 p.m., Chairman Walsh banged his gavel and the Convention settled in to listen to the Democracy's 1924 platform, read by Cummings, Senator Key Pittman, of Nevada, and the Reading Secretary, P. J. Haltigan. It began with a tribute to Wilson and a statement of Democratic Principles, including "Equal Rights to all and special privileges to none."

The 1924 Democratic platform charged that the, "Republican Party is concerned chiefly with material things; the Democratic Party is concerned chiefly with Human Rights." And it reviewed the Progressive achievements of the Wilson years: tariff taxes reduced, creation of a Federal Trade Commission, a Federal Farm Loan system, child labor laws, a good roads bill, Eight Hour Laws, a Corrupt Practices Act, establishment of a Secretary of Labor, and a Federal Reserve System. It contrasted that record with the corruption of the present Republican administration. "A vote for Coolidge is a vote for chaos!"

What did the 1924 Democracy promise in its platform? Honest Government, first of all. Tariff revision, next, and a, "graduated tax upon incomes. . . . The Income Tax was intended as a tax upon wealth. It was not intended to take from the poor any part of the necessities of life." The party also opposed, "the so-called nuisance taxes, sales taxes, and all other forms of taxation that unfairly shift to the consumer the burdens of taxation."

On agriculture, the 1924 Democracy promised relief to distressed farmers and an opening of foreign markets to their products. The party also pledged "to stimulate . . . the cooperative marketing movement and the establishment of an export marketing corporation." Democrats pledged as well to cut rates on railroads and to create new waterways to relieve the exploitation of farmers. The Democracy denounced, "The recent cruel and unjust contraction of legitimate and necessary credit and currency which was directly due to the so-called deflation policy of the Republican Party" to the tune of five billion dollars, which "bankrupted hundreds of thousands of farmers and stock growers in America, and resulted in wide-spread industrial depression and unemployment."

The 1924 platform pledged, "recovery of the navy's oil reserves, and all other parts of the public domain which have been fraudulently or illegally leased or otherwise wrongfully transferred to the control of private interests. We believe that the nation should retain title to its water power. . . . We favor strict public control and conservation of all the nation's natural resources, such as coal, iron, oil, and timber." The 1924 Democracy called for a national reforestation policy, new roads, deep waterways, and flood control. It called mining, "one of the basic industries of this Country" and noted, "We produce more coal, iron, copper, and silver than any other Country. Mining has suffered like agriculture and from the same causes."

Anticipating the great market crash four years later, the 1924 Democratic Platform insisted on, "the immediate passage of such legislation" related to "the gradual financial strangling of innocent investors, workers, and consumers, caused by the indiscriminate promotion, refinancing, and reorganizing of corporations on an inflated and over-capitalized bases, resulting already in the undermining and collapse of many railroads, public service and industrial corporations, manifesting itself in unemployment, irreparable loss and waste. . . ." The Democracy also declared "that a private monopoly is indefensible and intolerable."

The platform committee produced a paragraph of platitudes about Jefferson and public education, asserting "ignorance is the enemy of freedom," and affirming that education was the responsibility of the states. It declared for, "adequate salaries to provide decent living conditions for postal employees." It asserted that, "Labor is not a commodity. It is human." And the party came out for collective bargaining, and laws regulating hours of labor and conditions. Popular history may remember this era as the "Roaring 20s," but "Militant Democracy" declared, "In order to mitigate unemployment attending business depression, we urge the enactment of legislation authorizing that construction and repair of public works be initiated," the position Franklin Roosevelt adopted less than a decade later during the Great Depression. Indeed, this 1924 document contained more than a few ideas that would shape Roosevelt's New Deal.

The Democratic platform took special aim at campaign contributions. "The nation now knows that the predatory interests have, by supplying Republican campaign funds, systematically purchased legislative favors and administrative immunity. The practice must stop." The Democracy called for "national elections kept free from the poison of excessive private contributions. To this end, we favor reasonable means of publicity, at public expense. . . ." And it favored, "the prohibition of individual contributions, direct and indirect, to the campaign funds of Congressmen, Senators, or presidential candidates, beyond a reasonable sum to be fixed in law. . . ."

One debate had raged wherever the delegates gathered, and that was over the future of Prohibition. Miss Helen L. Baughan, of the National Liberal Alliance, was among those lobbying for "modification" of the law, speaking for "over ten million voters who have recorded their ballots in a nation-wide referendum conducted in twenty states . . . for modification. . . ." The Anti-Saloon League was lobbying just as hard to stop Smith, who it considered to be the ultimate Wet. In the end, the 1924 Democrats sidestepped the issue by reaffirming their faith in the "Rights of the states" and condemned "the efforts of the Republican administration to nationalize the functions and duties of the states." They also attacked the Republican administration for its failure "to enforce the Prohibition Law," while accusing it of "trafficking in liquor permits." That was a backhanded slap at the national Prohibition law and considered a victory for the Wets.

The 1924 Democratic platform recognized, "in narcotic addiction, specially the spreading of heroin addiction among the youth, a grave peril to America and the human race" and called for education, control, and suppression. Democrats reaffirmed their "established position in favor of the exclusion of Asiatic immigration." The party frowned on the "maladministration of Alaskan affairs" and promoted improvements of the National Park, the harbors and breakwaters, and the Federal roads, of the Territory of Hawaii. The party also condemned betrayal of

"Armenia for the Chester Oil Concession." And it welcomed Greece "to the sisterhood of Republics."

Under the leadership of William J. Bryan, who had refused to remain as Wilson's Secretary of State when the nation went into the Great War, the 1924 Democracy denounced war as "a relic of barbarism," and said war was, "justifiable only as a measure of defense. We demand a strict and sweeping reduction of armaments by land and sea, so that there shall be no competitive military program or naval building. Our Government should secure a joint agreement with all nations for world disarmament. . . ." And the Democratic Party proclaimed that war was unacceptable except, "in case of attack or threatened attack."

The Resolutions Committee had been unanimous on these issues. But it had failed to endorse the Child Labor Amendment to the Constitution that Mrs. Roosevelt and other women had been lobbying to endorse. (The Child Labor Amendment was submitted to the states for ratification in June 1924.) And Miss Alice Paul, vice president of the National Woman's Party, denounced Democrats and Republicans alike for failure to endorse an Equal Rights Amendment.

Two particularly divisive planks then were taken to the open floor of the Convention for debate: the future of the League of Nations, and the plank on Freedom of Religion, Freedom of Speech, and Freedom of Press. The Majority Plank on the League of Nations read, in part, "The Democratic Party pledges all its energies to the outlawing of the whole war system. We refuse to believe that the wholesale slaughter of human beings on the battlefield is any more necessary to man's highest development than is killing by individuals. The only hope for world peace and for economic recovery lies in the organized efforts of sovereign nations cooperating to remove the causes of war and to substitute law and order for violence.

"It is of supreme importance," the plank went on, "to civilization and to mankind that America be placed and kept on the right side of the greatest moral question of all time; and, therefore, the Democratic Party renews its declarations of confidence in the ideal of world peace, the League of Nations, and the World Court of Justice as together constituting the supreme effort of the statesmanship and religious conviction of our time to organize the world for peace."

How? "It is desirable, wise, and necessary to lift this question out of party politics, and to that end to take the sense of the American people at a referendum election, advisory to the Government, to be held officially under an Act of Congress, free from all other questions and candidates, after ample time for full consideration and discussion through the Country . . ." whether the U. S. should become a member of the League of Nations, "under such reservations or amendment to the

Covenant of the League as the President and the Senate of the United States may agree upon.''

Rhetorically, the Majority Plank seemed like a strong reaffirmation of the position the party had taken with Wilson, and that candidate James Cox defended in 1920, and the nation had rejected by choosing President Harding who was less committed to the League. At any rate, four years later, the United States was still outside the organization. What would the Democracy do? The debate began, with each side limited to an hour.

For the Majority Plank, Homer Cummings, the Resolution Committee's Chairman, yielded twenty minutes to Alfred Lucking, of Michigan, who was chief counsel to Henry Ford. ''The only differences between these two reports are, first that the Committee report is very short and the other is very long,'' he received applause. ''The other one provides that we shall plunge this question into the party political contest of this year, commingled and confused with forty or fifty other questions . . .'' as had been the case in the election of 1920. The crowd liked his logic and applauded.

Then he related the story of Wilson's efforts upon leaving Paris to negotiate a treaty. He recalled Wilson's own promise, perhaps metaphorical, to take ''a solemn referendum to the American people on this question.'' During his speech there was turmoil on the floor. Lucking forged on. ''I think it would be most unwise, both in the interest of the League itself, and in the interest of the Democratic Party, to make the issue of joining the League so direct in this campaign that America's attitude would be irrevocably determined by the result of it.''

Senator A. A. Jones, of New Mexico, joined in defense of the Majority Position. He pointed out that the vote in the Resolutions Committee was thirty-four in favor of the Majority Plank and sixteen for the Minority Plank. ''I believed it then, I believe it now, that it is the tragedy of this generation that the United States failed to become a member of the League of Nations.'' He projected his sentiments across the vast Garden audience. Senator Jones told the delegates how he had worked for the League night and day against a pamphlet campaign of misrepresentation in the rural areas of his state. He reminded the crowd that it took a two-thirds Senate vote to enact the Treaty and that the Democracy was in the minority on this issue. ''I have never felt that our foreign relations should become a question of partisan politics.'' His position was rewarded with applause.

Newton D. Baker, of Ohio, Wilson's Secretary of War, then came to the rostrum to argue the Minority Plank. Baker was one of Wilson's closest political and personal friends and had been at Wilson's side throughout the great conflict and was a passionate League advocate. He spoke for nearly an hour, offering a substitute plank that made entry into the League of Nations an immediate commitment of the Democratic Party, without any delaying referendum, but as the avowed principle upon which the party would run in 1924.

"I respect my associates on this committee," the once powerful Federal executive said of the Senators whom he now faced, but quickly went on the offensive. "I venture to say that in no Convention of a political character in the United States . . . has so fantastical a proposition ever been proposed with regard to American constitutional practice as is proposed by the revolutionary report of the Majority," Baker charged, seeking to get the strict constitutionalists on his side. "What does the Majority Report do? With praiseful and perfumed voice it lauds the League of Nations as a lover would describe his sweetheart . . . . Hear these praises . . ." he mocked them as he read them again. "Confidence in the ideals of world peace, . . ." and so on.

But what did it mean? "After having said that there is no substitution for the League of Nations, that the world will be a wreck unless war is prevented after having said all of these things, there is not one syllable in the Majority Report that proposed that the United States shall go into the League until after a fanciful, irregular, unconstitutional, revolutionary referendum shall have been held, operated either by postal-cards, through the Census Bureau, or some other way, . . . " Baker exploded.

"I know what my associates on this committee thought as they sat over there and drew this. They said to themselves: 'We must speak well enough of it to satisfy their devotional affection for it.' " Then he belittled their scheme of referendum and the inordinate time it would take for "full consideration." The Convention laughed as he ridiculed the Majority plan point by point. "Ah, my fellow men and women, I am not talking to Democrats. I am talking to lovers of mankind." There was loud applause. "I sat in that room across the street for five days and nights and heard talk about 'expediency' and 'votes' until I am sick. I am talking about life and death and love and duty. . . .

"What becomes of men when they are afraid to say what they think? What becomes of parties when they abandon their ideals?" Baker asked beseechingly. "My plank is to go into the League the way the Constitution says we may go in. Their plank is one more Mount Everest to climb. . . . I am a middle-aged man and I shall never be called upon again for any useful service in any other war. . . . But I have memories. On the battlefields in Europe I closed the eyes of soldiers in American uniform who were dying and who whispered to me messages to bring to their mothers," said the former Secretary of War.

"I talked with them about death in battle, and, oh, they were superb and splendid; never a complaint; never a regret; willing to go if only two things might be: one that mother know that they had died

174

bravely; and the other, that somebody would pick up their sacrifice and build on the earth a permanent temple of peace in which the triumphant intellect and spirit of men would forever dwell in harmony, taking away from the children of other generations the curse and menace of that bloody fight.'' Applause rang through the hall. ''And I swore an obligation to the dead that in season and out, by day and by night, in church, in political meeting, in the marketplace, I intended to lift up my voice always and ever, until their sacrifice was really perfected.''

The *Times* observed that, ''to a man, the delegates arose and cheered.'' From the floor flew a cry, ''Three cheers for Newton D. Baker,'' and the Convention complied while the band played ''The Battle Hymn of the Republic'' and then ''Onward Christian Soldiers.'' The delegates and guests sang along in one of the most genuine demonstrations since the Convention had begun. The noise finally died down after Newton Baker came forward one more time to acknowledge the loud acclaim.

Senator Key Pittman, of Nevada, took up the argument in favor of the Majority position on the League. ''I have had the pleasure to serve in the same Government with my friend, the great orator who has just preceded me,'' he began sarcastically. ''I witnessed the great work that he did as Secretary of War. I remember that he was one of the closest advisers to the President. And when I think of those things I cannot help but think of some of the other men who were standing back of Woodrow Wilson in every fight that he was in. I look at the Chairman on this very Platform Committee, Mr. Cummings. I know that there was no man in public life who stood any closer to the President than Mr. Cummings.

''And there was Jones of New Mexico. And there was Hitchcock, of Nebraska. Senator Hitchcock sacrificed himself on the altar of loyalty to Woodrow Wilson.'' (In 1922, Hitchcock lost re-election over the League issue.) ''And that is more than the gentleman from Ohio has ever taken any chances on. . . . I do not mind any criticism that my opponent might make with regard to the plank . . . that is legitimate. But when he, by insinuations, attempts to say that those men who signed this report are guilty of a treachery to the Democratic Party, to the memory of Woodrow Wilson, he is saying something that no intelligent man or woman who knows the circumstances should believe.''

Senator Pittman again reviewed the history of the League and how Republican Senator Henry Cabot Lodge had torpedoed it. A group of friends had told Wilson that he could not get the two-thirds of the Senate to endorse his treaty. ''It was the advisers that surrounded him such as the fanatical orator that stands here today that said to him: 'Go to the Country. Fight it to the death and you shall win.' He fought it to the death, and he owes his death today to the misguided advice of these men. . . .'' A voice from the crowd angrily shouted, ''No more of that.''

Pittman presented the political reality that he saw before them. "There are today forty-three Democratic Senators, fifty-one Republicans, two Non-Partisan Leaguers. It takes two-thirds of the United States Senate to ratify this Treaty. We cannot elect over six Democrats at this coming election to save our lives . . . . That will give us forty-nine votes . . . . Don't you see . . . . You have got to take it out of politics or you cannot win. There are over one hundred great non-partisan peace societies in this County, and they are all fighting to bring about the necessary two-thirds . . . The only question is as to how to bring it about. That is the question."

The Nevada Senator had won back the audience to the Majority. "Those who love world peace more than they do the pride of their own position, those who would rather accomplish than defend some failures of the past, let them get behind this committee and do something that will bring about a non-partisan spirit on the League of Nations question." The applause affirmed him. Then he turned to repay the grudge he felt: "The speaker who spoke before here, with tears in his eyes and his broken-down, slobbering body across this rail, is trying to appeal to your sympathies, not to your judgment." Suddenly Pittman was rebuffed with jeers and boos. "Don't say it again," someone warned.

Pittman concluded, "He must know that the thirty-four delegations represented on that committee are just as honest as he is. He has got to learn that you cannot have your own way all the time on all things." Then Pittman warned that the electoral defeat of 1920 was awaiting them again if they repeated their strategy. "There is but one chance on earth to win the League of Nations . . . a non-partisan election."

The delegations were given five minutes to deliberate before the Roll Call on the future of the League. A vote in the affirmative was to substitute the Minority Plank. Alabama split 12½ Ayes, 11½ Nos. So did most of the states until Georgia threw all its 28 against, Illinois cast 48 Nos, Indiana 30, Iowa 26, Kansas 20, Louisiana 20, Mississippi, Missouri, Montana, Nevada, New Jersey, all voted against the Minority. New York was split 55 No's, 35 Ayes. In the end, the Minority Plank was trounced 742½ to 353½. The Democracy would try to survive the 1924 election by cutting its link to Wilson's legacy, abandoning its principal of support for the League of Nations. The damage from the debate would be measured in November.

The next day the nation's papers were filled with passionate reaction. The *New York Herald-Tribune* called the League vote "Cowardly and Dangerous." The *Chattanooga Times* proclaimed, "League is Killed at Last." The *Omaha Bee* concluded, "Party Sold its Soul to Hearst." The *Washington Post* complained the League referendum idea was, "A Vicious Precedent."

The Convention had debated into the evening and was exhausted, but without break Chairman Walsh, standing under the glare of sputtering Klieg lights, launched into a mighty struggle over the Religious Liberty Plank and the Minority replacement that had been brought to the floor. The atmosphere was tense and the Garden was packed to capacity with the largest crowd yet to witness the oratorical battle that had been building all week. The Anti-McAdoo forces had raised the issue as a way to divert the Californian's momentum.

McAdoo pointed out to reporters that, "It has been the history of American politics that whenever special privilege has been challenged by a popular outburst of public indignation, it sets up straw man issues to divert the people's attention from the real problems of the day; that deceit is being attempted now. Congress during the past year has exposed the looting of the public domain by private interests, aided by corrupt political officials."

But the Klan problem the Convention was about to debate had become the dominant focus of delegates. Norman E. Mack, the National Committeeman from New York, told the press, "This subject, unless cool heads prevail in the Convention when it considers the platform, may cause a schism in the party not unlike slavery. Whatever the Convention does will cause bitterness and defections. We started the Convention with bright hopes and now dire troubles overshadow our deliberations."

The crowds had increased so that the aisles were clogged, the galleries filled to the brim, every seat in the house occupied by perhaps the largest crowd in the old Garden's long and varied history. Headlines in the local papers warned of a possible riot on the Convention floor. The debate had become an unintended centerpiece in the Convention's agenda, having taken on a life that overshadowed the nomination itself. Many saw it as an early showdown between Smith and McAdoo. Certainly it had been launched by Smith and Underwood supporters as a way to put McAdoo on the defensive. Many thought Smith's chances now rested with the success of the anti-Klan effort.

But immediately before the vote, both Smith and McAdoo passed the word through their floor managers that all their delegates were free to vote their conscience. While McAdoo was opposed to the Klan, the Klan had adopted him. The *Times* reported that the issue "seems to have created considerable uneasiness among some of those devoted to the fortunes of the California candidate. McAdoo has been accused of being the candidate of the Klan." He was not, but needed their votes.

Governor Smith followed the titanic debate from his room in the Manhattan Club across the street from the Convention. Rumors were spreading that he would drop out of contention for the nomination if the anti-Klan plank was defeated. "There is not a word of truth in it," Norman E. Mack retorted. "The Governor is not mixing in this matter in any way. It would be most unseemly. . . ." Judge Alton Brooks Parker, the Democratic nominee for President in 1904, added, "The fact that Governor Smith has a religion and tries to live up to it is said in some quarters to be a source of weakness. It would be a great misfortune to our beloved country if we should ever take a hostile political action against any man by reason of his religion."

The Majority Plank on Freedom of Religion—Freedom of Speech—Freedom of Press asserted, "The Democratic Party reaffirms its adherence and devotion to those cardinal principles contained in the Constitution . . . that Congress shall make no laws respecting the establishment of religion, or prohibiting the free exercise thereof, or abridging the Freedom of Speech or of the Press, or the Right of the people peaceably to assemble and to petition the Government for a redress of grievances, that the Church and the state shall be and remain separate. . . . We insist at all times upon obedience to the orderly processes of the law, and deplore and condemn any effort to arouse religious or racial dissention."

Senator Robert L. Owen, of Oklahoma, came to the rostrum in defense of this Majority Plank. "This is a matter upon which emotion has been aroused. It is a subject of the most delicate and critical character," he began. "First, this is not a question as to the Ku Klux Klan winning or losing," he tried to reassure everyone. "This is a difference of judgment between the large majority of the members of your Committee on Resolutions and a minority of the same committee. The Majority members present you with a plank declaring in the strongest possible terms for Freedom of Religion, Freedom of Speech, Freedom of the Press, freedom of the Right of every individual citizen to the enjoyment and to the protection of the laws.

"The only difference," Owen asserted, "is whether or not the Democratic National Convention shall stigmatize the Ku Klux Klan by name as being guilty of interfering with the religious Liberty and with the political Rights of their fellow citizens." A roar went up from the galleries. "Make no mistake about the issue. There is not anybody anywhere in America that I know of in any responsible position that would for a moment defend any organization, Ku Klux Klan or not, in violating the principles of the Constitution.

"Shall we now allow the Democratic Party, which has the greatest opportunity in history, to be divided upon this question of Jew or Gentile, or Klan or anti-Klan?" Owen asked. "No, no, no," answered the crowd. "Are we not marching to battle now to defend the liberties of the great producers of this Country?" Owen claimed that there was an estimated one million members of the Klan in the U. S. (In actuality, there were closer to five million Klansman, North and South, in the mid-1920s.) "I do not defend the Ku Klux Klan. I think there are some brilliant rascals among them. But I know, too, that there is a large number of good citizens among them who believed, in joining the order, that the order was committed to obey and observe and protect the Constitution and the laws of this Country." Owen's defense of some Klan members was booed and hissed as the Oklahoma Senator stepped away from the microphones.

In his place stepped forward Governor William R. Pattangall, of Maine, to defend the Minority Plank. He read the Minority amendment: "We condemn political secret societies," he said, "does anybody object to that?" Cries of "No, no," answered his query, "of all kinds as opposed to the exercise of free Government and contrary to the spirit of the Declaration of Independence and the Constitution of the United States. Does anybody object to that?" Again the negative cries supported him as he read the Minority plank. "We pledge the Democratic Party to oppose any effort on the part of the Ku Klux Klan or any organization to interfere with religious Liberty or political freedom of any citizen, or to limit the Civil Rights or to limit the Civic Rights of any citizen or body of citizens because of religion, birthplace, or racial origin." His Amendment elicited strong applause from half the delegates and most of the spectators.

Pattangall continued: "Is there anybody who is an attendant on this Convention as a delegate or an alternate who is so ignorant of what is going on in American life today that he does not know that that secret society that we mean lays down as part of its fundamental principles that no man who is of the Catholic or the Jewish religion, no man who is colored, no man who is not native-born, is eligible to office? Is there any denial of that?" he asked. "No, no, no," the galleries and many delegates shouted back.

"I want the gospel of Democracy to be preached alike in Maine, in Colorado, in Texas, and in Pennsylvania . . . ." A voice shouted, "Attaboy." Another, "That's good." Pattangall resumed, "There is more in this matter than the mere naming of a secret organization. There has crept into American life so strong an influence in certain states that United States Senators told me last night that if the Klan was opposed by them they could not be reelected to their seats in the Senate. . . . I have in my pocket a card issued by this organization, whose methods, not whose membership, I condemn, with questions written on it: 'Are you a Protestant?' 'Are you white?' 'Are you native born?'

"Well, I am reasonably white," he heard laughter, "I am native born; my ancestors have lived in the state I live in for 200 years. I am a Protestant. I am a Knight Templar Mason. So I am eligible to join that order if I want to join it. . . . But I wonder if its leaders, when questionnaires were being prepared in 1917 to send the youth of America," he was interrupted with loud applause, "I wonder if Senator

Owen . . . or anybody else suggested that we should only draft to defend our Country the boys who were 'white,' 'Protestant,' and 'native born.' " Loud applause echoed through the hall. "On the battlefields of France, Catholic, Jew, Protestant, Negro and naturalized citizen fought side by side to maintain the institutions that mean so much to you and me."

Governor Pattangall concluded his defense of the Minority Plank: "I am a Democrat because I was taught to believe that the basic, fundamental creed of the Democratic Party was that all Americans, living in every section, children of every race, members of every church, stood equal on the Democratic platform. I do not want to believe anything else. And I say to you that there is need to be sent over the whole wide United States a message from Democracy that our party hates bigotry, hates intolerance . . . and therefore calls bigotry and intolerance and hypocrisy by their right names when it speaks of them." As Pattangall stepped away from the microphone, hurrahs swept through Madison Square Garden as though a champion had knocked out his despised opponent.

Next, Mrs. Carroll Miller, of Pennsylvania, added to the Minority argument. "It is an issue between free Americans on the one side and a vicious un-American organization on the other, the members of which, regardless of their professed religious views, are in no conceivable sense Christians," she preached. "What would you, my friends, think of a home in America where the little children shuddered nightly in terrorizing fear of the hooded Ku Klux Klan?" she asked. "Oh, there are such places, hundreds of them . . . where the foreign born is discriminated against by the shopkeeper, where the wife waiting for her husband to return from the mine, the field, or the factory, never feels sure that he will not be mobbed or beaten to death before he returns to her and his family . . . . Since when has the Democratic Party ever knelt before the god of political expediency?"

Senator Cummings, who was managing time for the Majority Plank, yielded ten minutes to Governor Cameron Morrison, of North Carolina. "I have not arisen to speak in defense of the Ku Klux Klan, but I do desire to say something of the Rights of the men who mistakenly belong to the Ku Klux Klan." Half of the Convention applauded. "Who are they?" Someone yelled. A voice answered, "Nobody knows." The Governor answered his own question. "About one million men who profess the Protestant form of the Christian religion. That is not a preliminary to thuggism in American life. Are we, without trial and without evidence, in political Convention where only basic principles should be dealt with, to try, condemn, and execute more than a million men who are professed followers of the Lord Jesus Christ? What do we mean by religious Liberty in the United States?" A voice answered, "Thou shall not kill." The North Carolina Governor continued. "When they said the Ku Klux committed an outrage in North Carolina—and there have only been a few instances—we offered rewards, and we found, arrested and tried them, and we put three of the professing Ku Klux on the chain gang. . . ." He added, "The suggestion of the Minority will make a half million Ku Klux in the next ten days, in my judgment."

The Honorable Bainbridge Colby, of New York, Woodrow Wilson's third Secretary of State, next spoke for the Minority Plank. "I am somewhat accustomed to the cowardice that evades the issue of the Ku Klux Klan, but I confess to my surprise that, seated on this platform, I am obliged to witness the hardihood, or shall I say effrontery, of its open defense . . . . I am opposed to the Majority Report because it is an obvious stuttering, stammering, and falling failure . . . It does not satisfy my manhood. It is no credit to . . . the indomitable Democracy. . . . The Ku Klux Klan is composed of either vicious or foolish people. . . . It is bound to disintegrate. There is not a man here who would not regard the accusation that he was a member of the Ku Klux Klan as a reflection upon his character. That is why they cover up. That is why they go at night . . . . The man that is ashamed will skulk away. . . ."

Senator David I. Walsh, of Massachusetts, also took up the Minority cause. "We are Democrats . . . In and through our party Catholic and Jew and foreign born have found asylum, have been elevated to high public office, have participated in the councils and the works and the benefits of its principles in the fullest possible measure. It has been the party in America of the downtrodden and the poor, and in every great popular Government issue and on every great economic question it has unfailingly stood for the Rights of the oppressed and for those least able to speak for themselves. It has defended their cause against selfish and predatory interests, the enemies alike of Christian and non-Christian. It has ungrudgingly championed the cause of millions in their desperate struggle for Justice and for a fair deal in the mad clamor of Republican materialism.

"We ask you to cut out of the body politic with the sharpest instrument at your command this malignant growth which, injected, means the destruction of everything which has made America gloriously immortal. If you can denounce Republicanism, you can denounce Ku Kluxism. If you can denounce Bolshevism, you can denounce Ku Kluxism."

Edmund H. Moore, of Ohio, also rushed to the Minority's defense with an appeal to Thomas Jefferson. "Less than a hundred years after that great spirit took its flight to Him who gave it, we, his followers, are confronted with the proposition that an organization founded upon religious bigotry and intolerance undertakes to control a Democratic Convention. The Imperial Kleagle—oh, I guess I don't just know their nomenclature, I guess it is the Imperial Wizard," he heard laughter in the hall, "has been here laboring throughout this Convention, and with him is the Imperial Dragon, a Republican from my own hometown," again there was laughter, "who boasts that he has obtained twenty members of my own delegation to vote against this Minority Plank. I do not believe it. [When the vote came, 15½ of the Ohio votes went against the Minority.]

"But think of the proposition when religious bigots, Republican bigots, can come into a Democratic Convention and attempt to control its action. . . . If 343 members of the Klan who are members of this Convention can control the action of the other 800, if the Imperial Wizard has got us all in his pocket, I for one, am going to crawl out." He was buoyed by cheers and applause.

"What is the situation?" Moore asked. "We have before this Convention as one of the Candidates a Democrat who, for the reason alone that I prefer another, I hope will not be nominated. If that man had not learned his faith at his mother's knee, a faith different from that of mine and of a majority of this Convention, nine-tenths of you would admit in conversation that it would not be five ballots until, on account of his power as a vote-getter, because of his distinguished public service, his unspotted public record and his private virtues, he would be the nominee of this Convention." Applause affirmed his position.

"This, gentlemen of the Convention, is the most momentous question that has faced the Democratic Party since 1860," Moore asserted. "You all know that if we do not denounce the Ku Klux Klan, there is no ambitious politician in that great Southland to which the Democratic Party must look for a large bunch of Electoral votes but must go home and align himself with the Klan. A score of them have told me in private conversation . . . they pray to God that I would win it, because they said when they go home they would either have to cut out of politics or join the Klan." Voices from Klan-controlled delegations shouted out, "Oh shut up," and "Sit down." Moore finally did.

Andrew C. Erwin, a tall, young, World War veteran and McAdoo delegate, joined the Minority chorus. "I am a delegate from Georgia. I am proud of it. To my mind, the Ku Klux issue is the most vital one which the Democratic Party has to determine. You can, by adopting the report of the Majority, evade the issue, which would, in effect, give your approval to the activities of this organization." Many delegates objected with cries of "No, no," and "Sit down."

Erwin bolstered Underwood's Southern assault on the Klan. "Follow this course and you may prepare for an ignominious defeat at the polls in November." Some were comparing the Klan to the Masons or Elks. "I have not heard of the Masons or Elks," Erwin retorted, "moving from state Convention to state Convention, regardless of party, a highly paid staff of officials, lobbyists, and spying investigators, with a view of controlling the acts of the delegates chosen to represent the people of this Country. And just as soon as they do, then I favor a plank denouncing them, or any other secret society.

"The Ku Klux Klan makes a direct attack on these vital principles of our fundamental law," Erwin proclaimed. "Its insidious activities have spread discord and distrust throughout this land of peace and harmony. However worthy the motives of its adherents may be, it constitutes the most destructive element in America today. . . . They challenge every citizen who cherishes and respects the Constitution." He then challenged his delegation to stand up, "against the hooded menace, which prowls in the darkness, that dares not show its face, that is not worthy of his ancestry. . . ."

Erwin pleaded, "I call upon you, my fellow delegates from the South, in the name of that hallowed Roman Catholic priest, Father Ryan, the Poet Laureate of the Southern Confederacy, whose deathless verse you learned at your mother's knee . . . from the entire Country I invoke the memory of those Americans of other races than your own who died with your own kindred on the fields of France . . . and to Georgia to erase the stigma that has been placed upon your state."

His speech thrilled and angered his audience and was judged to be the climax of the debate. One half of the Convention was on its feet cheering. The other half remained bitterly seething. New York policemen pushed their way down the side aisles in lines of blue to prevent any violence from breaking out. As Erwin stepped down from the platform, he was lifted upon the shoulders of delegates and paraded around the hall to the tune of "While We Go Marching Through Georgia." A woman from Rhode Island, Mrs. Isabella Ahearn O'Neill, rushed up to kiss Erwin on the lips. The Convention "packed with humanity" then followed the band with voices strong into a rendition of "The Star Spangled Banner." Turmoil prevailed.

Former Governor Jared Y. Sanders, of Louisiana, tried to stem the rapids of the Minority position. "Louisiana has voted the Democratic ticket for more than a hundred years," be began, "It will vote the Democratic ticket a hundred years more." He said in Louisiana of late, voters had stood up to the Klan, "and the politicians were confounded. The new Governor [Henry Fugua] had passed laws making every member of secret societies register with the Secretary of State, and any crime committed with a mask, a felony." Laws were signed within twenty-one days after the Governor took office. "Oh, my fellow Democrats, no matter where you come from, remember all the bigots do not belong to one church, nor do the rascals belong to one section. You cannot fight intolerance with intolerance. You cannot fight the devil with fire. He is an expert in that line. . . . We are for the Majority Report because we want the issue to be the Green House on K Street, not the Three K's."

C. M. Bryan, of Tennessee, added to the Minority case. "I am not skilled in the subtle arts of buying votes by the sacrifice of principle. I do not know the gentle science of trying to deceive people with words, of trying to lead them astray by old-time platitudes . . . I come from the state of Old Hickory, where they were always ready to meet any issue face to face, sometimes maybe, with an oath, but never with a trace of fear. I do not know how the Democratic Party can condemn the Republicans for corruption and make a bargain with iniquity.

"I come from where the Ku Klux Klan are," Tennessee's Bryan recounted. "I have seen six thousand of them in a public square. I have seen them denounce all of the things that thousands of people have been taught to hold sacred; and if the Ku Klux Klan want to leave the Democratic Party and go with the Republican Party, we shall have the delicious satisfaction of knowing that we can walk safely abroad, because all those who violate the law will be on the same side." He finished to cheers.

Then Francis X. Busch, of Illinois, concluded the Minority argument. "This is not a religious question. This is a political question. It was Thomas Jefferson who said: 'A frequent recurrence to fundamental principles is essential to the preservation of Liberty.' It is adherence to these principles which has brought about the unprecedented development of this Country until it is today the richest Country in its material prosperity in the entire world. Of these fundamental principles, none is more clearly written into the Declaration of Independence and the Constitution of the United States than the principle of the equality of all men and the Right of every man to worship God by the practice of his own faith in the light of his own conscience.

"Today," Busch charged, "a secret organization, recruiting its membership from the unthinking, the deluded, and the weak-minded," he was halted with laughter from the delegates, "who, although calling themselves 100 percent American, realize absolutely nothing about the beginnings or the development of the structure of America, is seeking to arouse racial and religious prejudice against large elements of our population . . . . The activities of these organizations are undemocratic and un-American.

"I say that the platform, and I think it is a splendid, forward-looking Progressive platform that you have listened to today, did not hesitate to denounce Newberryism by name, it did not hesitate to refer to a Republican ex-Secretary of the Interior or to a Republican ex-Secretary of the Navy, or to a Republican ex-Attorney General, and call things by their names. I say that it is the part not only of wisdom but it is the part of courage in view of the traditions of America. It is a part of the courage of this Convention." Busch finished his remarks to loud applause throughout the Garden.

The last address in defense of the Majority Report was made by the man who had created the modern Progressive Democratic Party, starring in his last platform debate. William Jennings Bryan, no longer of Nebraska but of Florida, which had been his home since his service in the Spanish American War. Now 64 years of age, Bryan was a year away from his prosecutorial role in the famous Scopes Monkey Trial and a little farther away from his own death. Cheers rose from all parts of Madison Square Garden for the most popular man in the Democratic Party.

It was already after midnight in the sweltering Garden when Bryan began addressing the large, hot and agitated crowd. "It is now twenty-eight years since Democratic Conventions became gracious enough to invite me and patient enough to listen to me, and I have not words in which to express my gratitude for the love and loyalty of millions of Democrats who have been my co-laborers for more than a quarter century." The whole Convention gave the man the Democracy had first nominated in 1896, and again in 1900 and 1908, his due with a surge of applause.

"I have spoken to you on many themes, never on themes more important than today," the "Commoner" boomed. "Let us eliminate the things that are not in this issue and come down to the three words that these, our good friends, as honest, as patriotic, and as anxious for the welfare of the party as we are, take out of the language and exalt above any other three words that will be used in this campaign. . . . We said 'strike out these three words and there will be no objection.' But three words were more to them than the welfare of a party in a great campaign." Bryan was applauded in some quarters. "We have heard pleas pathetic for people in distress, but none of our principles, none of our pleas stirred the hearts of these men like the words, 'Ku Klux Klan.' "

Suddenly, the old warrior of Democracy was showered with long and continuous hisses, boos, and jeers. Some one on the floor shouted, "Clear the galleries of the hoodlums." But Bryan could defend himself. "Citizens of New York, you show your appreciation of the honor we did you in holding our Convention here." The galleries and the floor were in chaos. Permanent Chairman Walsh banged his gavel relentlessly. "If the speaker is again interrupted by the galleries they will be cleared . . . . I warn the delegates that this speaker is to continue, and without interruptions from them."

Bryan then submitted five reasons for the Majority Report. "First, this plank, these three words, are not necessary." He pointed out that all states had laws in support of religious Liberty. "Second, it is not necessary to protect any Church. I, my friends, have such confidence in the Catholic Church, which was for over a thousand years my mother church as well as yours. . . . The Catholic Church, with its legacy of martyred blood and with all the testimony of its missionaries who went into every land, does not need a great party to protect it from a million men.

"The Jews do not need this resolution. They have Moses. They have Elijah, who was able to draw back the curtain and show upon the mountain tops an invisible host greater than a thousand Ku Klux Klans." Bryan's allies cheered his eloquence and scriptural erudition. "The Ku Klux Klan does not deserve the advertisement you give them." The applause turned to cheers. "The Minority, the fourteen members . . . have raised the Ku Klux Klan to a higher altitude than the Ku Klux themselves ever raised their fiery crosses."

Bryan's third reason was that, "We have no moral Right to let them divert us from as great a mission as our party ever had." Much of the Convention agreed. "My friends, it requires more courage to fight the Republican Party than it does to fight the Ku Klux Klan. Here we have farmers driven into bankruptcy, a million driven from the farms in a single year. We find monopoly spreading. We find nearly every great line of industry in control of gigantic combinations of capital. . . . Only the Democratic Party can stand between the common people and their oppressors in this land."

Then Bryan appealed to pragmatics. "My friends, if the Democratic Party will lose a considerable number because it insists on being what it has been, how many will it lose if it tries to be what it has never been. The Democratic Party has never been a religious organization . . . has never taken the side of one church against the other. The Democratic party must remain true.

"I have left for the last what I regard as the greatest argument," added the party's greatest orator. "If the Democratic Party is diverted from its duty, some other party will take up its task." He referred to Senator LaFollette and his Progressives. "No, no," the delegates shouted back. "But no party that takes up a noble task will find its leaders in the gallery today," Bryan chided, to the laughter of the delegates.

"And now I want to tell you my last and strongest objection, and let the galleries scoff if they dare: I say I am not willing to divide the Christian Church when we would stand together to fight the battles of religion in this land." He paused for the applause. "I have tried to defend the Democratic Party because of all I owe to it. It took me up when I was ten years younger than any other man had been when he was nominated by a great party, and it found me in a western state, farther West than it had ever gone before, and it gave me a million more votes than it had ever given any Democrat before, and it nominated me twice afterward, and I never had to use any money, and I had no organization. The Democratic Party has done more for me than any other living man, my friends, and I am grateful," Bryan tried to tighten the common bond with his audience.

"But, my friends, much as I owe to my party, I owe more to the Christian Religion. If my party has given me the foundations of my political faith, my *Bible* has given me the foundations of a faith that has enabled me to stand on the Right without stopping to count how many stood to take their share with me." The Convention cheered the old political evangelist. "I believe the World needs now not so much to get into a fight between denominations as it does to get back to God and a sense of responsibility to God. Burglars stole sixty-five millions in a year and pickpockets stole nearly as much, and bank robbers and bandits took large sums; but swindlers took two billions, ten times as much as all the people in the penitentiary too. Isn't it worth while, my friends, to unite the Christian Church in behalf of the Ten Commandments and the Sermon on the Mount, instead of dividing them into warring factions?" Bryan inquired.

"The world is coming out of the war, the bloodiest ever known. Thirty millions of human lives were lost, three hundred billion of property was destroyed, and the debts of the world are more than six times as great as they were when the first gun was fired. My friends, how are you going to stop war?" He rebutted appeals to commerce or education as solutions, and took on science. "It was science that made war so hellish that civilization was about to commit suicide. . . . There is only one thing that can bring peace to the world, and that is the Prince of Peace." His pronouncement was applauded. After a brief religious sermon, Bryan concluded, "My friends, we can exterminate Ku Kluxism better by recognizing their honesty and teaching them that they are wrong." The applause for Bryan's somewhat contradictory appeal was overtaken by prolonged hissing as the Commoner retreated on the platform.

Chairman Walsh banged his gavel and gave the delegations five minutes before voting on whether to adopt the Minority Plank. The floor was in frenzy as the delegations submitted their tallies amid challenges and charges of intimidation. In the massive crowd on the floor were several Klansman, including Walter Bossert, head of the Indiana Klan, and Texas Senator Mayfield, said to be a Klansman. Under the guidance of Senator Underwood, Alabama cast all its 24 votes in favor of including the Klan denunciation as stipulated by the Minority Plank. California cast 19 of its 26 against the Minority; Georgia failed to listen to the appeal of its fellow delegate, and cast 17 against the Minority, 2½ in favor, with 8½ abstaining. Illinois cast 45 in favor of condemning the Klan, and 13 against the Minority; Indiana went 25 to 5 against the Minority; Louisiana cast all of its 20 against; Mississippi voted its 20 the same way; Massachusetts affirmed the Minority 35½ to ½. New York proudly cast all of its 90 votes in favor of the Minority position. Texas threw all 40 of its votes against the Minority.

Hundreds of voices were screaming at once and wild disorder reigned under the hisses and boos coming from the galleries. After all the challenges and recounts in delegation after delegation that took over an hour to count and whose totals were almost impossible to collect amid the turmoil, the final vote on whether to denounce the Ku Klux Klan by name failed. With 1,083 6/20th votes cast, those in favor of the Minority plank were 541 3/20th; those voting no, 542 3/20th. The 1924 Democratic National Convention's effort to condemn the Ku Klux Klan had failed by just one vote.

Shouts for reconsideration filled the air. The Chair called on Franklin D. Roosevelt, of New York. "It is now nearly two o'clock of the morning of the Sabbath Day. I move, Mr. Chairman that the Convention do now adjourn until 9:30 o'clock Monday morning." After a mighty struggle of eleven hours of continuous debate, his motion passed amid shouts of "No" by those seeking a recount.

In the wake of the Klan debate came fears of a shattered party. Some called the way the issue was handled, "one of the worst bungles in the history of the party." Klansmen on the Convention's floor predicted the debate would help swell their ranks with thousands of new members from all parts of the Union. They also said the Republicans would be the main political beneficiaries of the debate. The *New York Herald-Tribune* wrote that the vote was "portentous of disintegration." The *Washington Post* opined, "The Ku Klux Klan should be singled out for condemnation. . . . The question then arises, can a Catholic be nominated? It seems impossible." The Springfield, Massachusetts, *Republican* affirmed, "Bryan was right."

The *St. Paul Pioneer Press* pointed its finger at the Convention. "There was no doubt in the minds of the delegates as to the issue with which they were confronted in the matter of the Klan. The question was saving the soul of the party at the expense of offending the solid and Klannish South, of being true to the ideals of Democracy at the cost of rending the party from within, or of lining itself up on the side of religious and racial oppression, of intolerance, violence, and terrorism and of defiance to American Liberty, for the gain of Klan votes . . ." which seemed to sum up the political situation.

In Albany, the *Knickerbocker Press* charged, "The vote of a woman, frightened by the Klan whip of Georgia . . . changes the tide of political history." The woman later said it was a message from the McAdoo camp that convinced her to change her vote in favor of the Majority. And she disputed the charge that all of the Georgia delegation was Klan-invested. She really was against the Klan, she said. The *Times* reported that the fact the Klan was in the majority at the Convention, "was one of the biggest political surprises in the history of the Klan." Meanwhile, followers of Senator LaFollette predicted the Democratic platform would drive voters to their third party campaign which was ready to kick off on July Fourth at Cleveland. There had rarely been a day like this in Convention history. The two debates ominously marked the party's future.

On Sunday, Mayor Hylan took five thousand Democratic visitors on a trip to Coney Island to witness the sights. Other groups rode the Day Line streamer *Hendrick Hudson* up the great river on a cruise trying unsuccessfully to escape the heat of the city. Meanwhile, efforts on the part of the various candidates intensified in the hot hotels as the balloting neared.

That night McAdoo gave a rousing pep speech to a thousand followers at the Park Avenue Hotel urging them not to be intimidated by the "packed galleries," the "bootleggers," the representatives of "big business," or the "corrupt press." He charged, "We know the evil influences we have to fight. We ask no quarter and will give none. The corrupt forces of a subsidized and debased press can't alter this result . . . . My friends, we defy them all and give them notice that their days are numbered."

The Sixth Day, Seventh Session, of what was becoming the longest political party Convention in U. S. history opened at 10:29 a.m., Monday June 30, 1924, when Permanent Chairman Thomas J. Walsh, of Montana, pounded his gavel. The prayer by the Reverend Gustav A. Carstensen, of New York, asked: "Help us in all that we say and do, and in such measure as Thou doest make the world safe for democracy, help us to show unto Thee that democracy is the salvation of the world."

"McAdoo Managers Predict Swift Victory," read the front-page headline of the *Times*. "Governor Smith is so confident he will win the Democratic nomination that he doesn't want further delay," read another *Times* story. "The delegates are beginning to realize that a man of the Governor's religion is the only candidate the Convention can logically select if the party would show to the nation that it is not dominated by the Ku Klux Klan." Smith himself said that he could stand on the platform as passed. "It is all the expression of the supreme body of our party. It has got to be accepted by every Democrat and that includes me."

Finally, after a week of contentious wrangling, the Convention arrived at its main purpose. "The next order of business," the Chairman declared, is the Roll Call of the States for the vote for the nomination for President. Mr. Lawrence F. Quigley, the 29-year-old mayor of Chelsea, Massachusetts, preferred not. "I want to know the action or what would be the result of the ruling of the Chair, if it be known to the Chair that a delegate who voted on Saturday last because of intimidation . . ." his voice was lost in a chorus of shouts to "Sit down," "Out of Order," arousing a high pitch of conflict and anger. Walsh answered: "The Chair knows of no way by which the question proposed by the delegate from Massachusetts can be inquired into." He was applauded. "I call for the regular order," shouted Franklin Roosevelt. And the Chair so ordered.

Even though most party professionals could see that the McAdoo and Stop-McAdoo forces were poised to block each other, the Roll Call began with a hopeful air that the Convention might soon complete its business. With 1,098 votes, and two-thirds of all of them necessary for nomination, the winning candidate would need 732 votes to secure the party's top spot.

On the First Ballot, the early trends were set. Twenty names received votes, most of them favorite sons. Not all states abided by the Unit Rule, with some delegates casting individual votes. Alabama led the way with 24 votes for Senator Oscar Underwood, who received a scattering of additional votes from Arizona, Maine, Minnesota, Pennsylvania, Alaska, Hawaii, and Porto Rico for a total of 42½; Senator Robinson received 18 from his home of Arkansas, plus a scattering from Minnesota, and Hawaii for a total of 21.

On the First Ballot, William Gibbs McAdoo, the pre-Convention favorite, attracted 431½ from Arizona, California, Florida, Georgia, Idaho, Illinois, Iowa, Kansas, Maine, Minnesota, Missouri, Montana, Nevada, New Mexico, North Carolina, North Dakota, Oklahoma, Oregon, Pennsylvania, South Carolina, South Dakota, Texas, Utah, Vermont, Virginia, West Virginia, Wyoming, Alaska, the District of Columbia, the Philippines, and Panama Canal Zone. His managers were holding back votes for subsequent ballots.

Governor Al Smith, of New York, McAdoo's closest competitor, received a total of 241 votes on the First Ballot, from Connecticut, Illinois, Maine, Massachusetts, Minnesota, Montana, 90 from New York, 35 from Pennsylvania, Rhode Island, and Vermont, 23 from Wisconsin, Alaska, Hawaii, and the Philippines. Governor Saulsbury received 7 from Delaware and Pennsylvania; Senator Ralston started with 30 from Indiana; Governor Jonathan M. Davis corralled his 20 votes from his home State of Kansas; Governor Ritchie received 16 of his 22½ from Maryland; Senator Ferris attracted all 30 of his votes from his home State of Michigan.

James M. Cox, the Democrat's 1920 nominee, attracted 10 from Illinois and all 48 of Ohio's for 59; Governor Charles Bryan got 2 votes from Illinois, 15 from his home of Nebraska, and 1 from Minnesota; Governor Brown received 8 from Connecticut, 1 from Massachusetts, and 8 from New Hampshire; Governor Silzer totaled 38, with 10 from Illinois and 28 from his home State of New Jersey; Senator Carter Glass received all 24 of his native State of Virginia, plus 1 from Pennsylvania.

190

Ambassador John W. Davis started with 5 from Porto Rico, 1 from Hawaii, 4 from Pennsylvania, 4 from Illinois, 1 from Minnesota, 16 from his home State of West Virginia for a total of 31; Governor Sweet received 12 from his home State of Colorado; Senator Pat Harrison collected all 20 from his State of Mississippi, 1 from Pennsylvania, 2 from Illinois, 20 from Louisiana, ½ from Massachusetts, for a total of 43 ½; Huston Thompson, of Colorado, received 1 from Pennsylvania; and former Governor John Benjamin Kendrick, who would serve as a three-term Senator, received 6 from Wyoming.

At the end of the First Ballot, William G. McAdoo posted a large lead with 431½, but was 300 delegates short of the nomination. Al Smith's 241 delegates weren't going anywhere, but he had an even higher hill to climb. James Cox was a distant third with 59. Thus, the 1924 Democratic nomination began as a two-man race between factions that had come to bitterly regard each other during the course of the Convention's first week and who were little willing to compromise, and much willing to deny their opponents.

That meant one thing: Stalemate. And that is what happened throughout the Sixth Day of the Convention and into the Evening Session. Through the Second Ballot, the Third, the Fourth, the Fifth, the Sixth, the Seventh, the Eighth, the Ninth, the Tenth Ballots, the numbers changed only slightly and the relative strength of the candidates not at all. The favorite sons seemed reluctant to yield for a leader.

By the end of the Tenth Ballot, McAdoo had risen to 471.6; Smith to 299.5; Cox was at 60; John W. Davis, Wilson's Solicitor General, recorded 57.5. Amidst confusion on the floor and boredom in the galleries, the Eleventh Ballot, was followed by the Twelfth, the Thirteenth, the Fourteenth, and the Fifteenth Ballot. As the Convention adjourned after midnight, McAdoo stood at 479 and Smith at 305.5, with John W. Davis inching into third place with 61.

The Seventh Day, Ninth Session of the Convention, opened at 10:50 a.m. on July 1, 1924. Bishop Luther B. Wilson, of the Methodist Episcopal Church, of New York, noted, "The eyes of our fellow citizens are upon us. The very ends of the earth are looking this way." What they witnessed was resumption of the stalemate and the repetition of ballots.

The morning *Times* reported that David Ladd Rockwell, McAdoo's manager, admitted his schedule had miscarried, but predicted victory by Wednesday. But the Wall Street gamblers had their eye on the headline reading, "Coolidge Says Taxes Must Be Cut More, Expenses Lessened." The President called the "surplus too small" and ordered an $83 million cut. Another front-page story wasn't such good news for the President or McAdoo. Coolidge's former Secretary of the Interior, Albert B. Fall, the Dohenys, father and son, of the Pan American Oil and Transport Company, and Harry F. Sinclair, president of the Mammoth Oil

Company, had been indicted for a $100,000 bribe and conspiracy in the Teapot Dome scandal.

As the Roll Call of the States continued, challenges began appearing in the delegations. Dissenters in the Missouri delegates charged that McAdoo money was controlling decisions. Individual delegates no longer wanted to be bound by their delegation's original choice. Chairman Walsh ruled, "It is easily conceivable that every state in the Union might adopt a preferential primary, and in many cases, would declare its preference for its favorite son. If, then, the delegation were bound by its preference so that they could vote for no one else, it is perfectly obvious that there could never be a choice by the Convention, whether by a majority or otherwise." He ruled that delegates were not bound by their state primary or state Convention. But the Unit Rule still applied in most delegations.

At the end of the Twentieth Ballot, Senator Claude A. Swanson, the Acting Permanent Chairman, announced that McAdoo had fallen to 432 and Smith had edged forward to 307½, while John W. Davis jumped to 122. The balloting continued through the Twenty-First Ballot, the Twenty-Second, with a dispute in the Kentucky delegation, the Twenty-Third, and the Twenty-Fourth.

The Convention adjourned until that evening at 8 p.m. By the Twenty-Fifth Ballot the field had narrowed to ten candidates: Oscar W. Underwood was holding with 39½, Joseph T. Robinson had 23, John W. Davis 126, Samuel M. Ralston 31, James M. Cox 59, Carter Glass 29, Jonathan M. Davis 5, Albert Cabell Ritchie 17½, Thomas J. Walsh 16, Willard Saulsbury 6. The leaders were still Alfred E. Smith with 308½ and William Gibbs McAdoo back to 436½. The Roll Call of States resumed with the Twenty-Sixth Ballot, the Twenty-Seventh, the Twenty-Eighth, on through to the Thirtieth Ballot, the last before the Convention adjourned at 11:40 that evening with little change in strength of the contenders.

On July 2, 1924, the Convention's Eighth Day, the meeting came to order at 10:58 p.m. with a prayer by Rabbi Louis I. Newman, of New York. "Step by step we are marching forward to the consummation of our labors," he optimistically estimated. "We shall need concord to master our common adversaries of deceit, hypocrisy, and betrayal."

The *Times*, in the hand of delegates reading the morning paper, announced "Drama Unfolds At Garden, Two Large Audiences See 'The Decline of William G. McAdoo.' " "McAdoo on 30th Ballot Sags to 415½; Smith Up To 323½; J. W. Davis Spurts to 126½." "Bryan's Hostility Arouses Davis Men." "McAdoo Sees A Conspiracy, His Manager Charges 'Big Business' is at Work Behind West Virginian." Bryan was quoted: "Gentlemen, You are throwing Democratic chances to the wind by voting for Davis. His clients and his connections in the

East make him desirable there, but he can command no following in the Northwest where the election will be decided." The morning papers also noted that Coolidge had opened his national campaign office at Chicago and the President and General Dawes already were receiving an, "extraordinary number of requests from all parts of the country" to appear as speakers.

Governor Smith had predicted, "I believe I will be nominated when the delegates get down to selecting the real man after distributing the complimentary votes." But when would the favorite sons fade? The Thirty-First Ballot was called with little progress in the results: McAdoo 415½, Smith 322½, Davis 127½. Robert L. Owen, of Oklahoma, showed up with 25 votes. The Thirty-Second Ballot yielded few changes. McAdoo, Smith, and Davis all slightly slipped on the Thirty-Third Ballot. To get closer to the action, McAdoo moved his operation to the Madison Square Garden Hotel as his supporters on the floor became more downcast.

And so it went through the Thirty-Fourth, the Thirty-Fifth, the Thirty-Sixth, and the Thirty-Seventh. The Chair then recognized William Jennings Bryan, who insisted, "I have only one desire, and that is that we shall win this next election. . . . We have a man in Florida. He is President of our state university." There was laughter in the hall. "His name is Dr. A. A. Murphree." The gallery began to chant, "We want Smith. We want Smith." Bryan continued, "He is a Democratic scholar." The chants turned to hisses and boos. "I mention him as first on the list." Bryan had other alternates in mind as well to break the stalemate, including Josephus Daniels, of North Carolina, Wilson's Secretary of the Navy. Voices in the gallery chanted "Smith," in response.

Bryan also recommended Joseph Robinson, of Arkansas, the Minority leader in the Senate. "Here are three men from the South," Bryan announced. "Some people have said that you cannot nominate a man from the South. I remind you that we have had two wars since the Civil War, and the sons of those who wore gray and the sons of those who wore the blue marched side by side and were ready to die together on the battlefield. . . . It is time we hush forever the voice that excludes the South from full participation. . . . What this nation wants is a man whose heart beats in sympathy with the common people, and we don't care where he was born or where he lives."

Then Bryan suggested three Northern men he could back, Senator Samuel M. Ralston, of Indiana, a Progressive Democrat; Edwin T. Meredith, of Iowa, Wilson's second Secretary of Agriculture and future publisher of what became *Better Homes & Gardens* magazine; and Bryan's own brother, Governor Charles W. Bryan, of Nebraska. Then the Commoner added Thomas J. Walsh, of Montana, "As a lawyer, he has no superior; as a statesman, he has few equals; as an investigator, he is above them all."

Even though Bryan had tipped the 1912 Democratic Convention in Baltimore for Woodrow Wilson in much the same way he was trying to do now, the audience was getting restless. "What's the matter with Smith?" someone yelled out. Other voices chanted, "McAdoo, McAdoo, McAdoo!" Then, after outlining the work of Progressive Democrats along with Progressive Republicans in the last Congress, Bryan named his real choice. "The man who is credited with making a victory this year possible, whether you like him or not, whether you nominate him or not—the man who has made possible the nomination and election of a Progressive is William Gibbs McAdoo, of California." Bryan finished to a chorus of boos. Cheers went up for Smith.

A voice demanded, "Tell us about Doheny and McAdoo and oil," and then the cries of "Oil, oil, oil." Another voice demanded, "Have the galleries cleared." The Permanent Chairman had had enough. "The Sergeant-at-Arms will clear the galleries. Clear those people out of the galleries."

Mr. Fitzpatrick, of New Jersey, rose to address Bryan. "You have said that Senator Walsh has been the greatest investigator in the United States. Senator Walsh has exposed the fact that McAdoo has accepted oil retainers." After objections from all corners and calls for "Regular Order," Bryan replied: "The gentleman asks about Mr. McAdoo's retainers from Mr. Doheny . . . . Mr. McAdoo's retainers had to do with oil in Mexico . . . . But I will go farther than that. If any oil has ever touched William G. McAdoo, the intense, persistent, virulent opposition of Wall Street washes all the oil away." Bryan was booed. Delegates were wildly shouting from the chairs upon which they stood.

Mr. D. F. Dunlavy, of Ohio, yelled: "May I inquire if Youngstown, Ohio, is in Mexico, where he got $200,000 for getting $2,000,000." There were tremendous cheers and cries. Bryan retorted, "The gentlemen who find fault with Mr. McAdoo"s fees have a Right to present their complaint to the bar associations and disbar him if his conduct has not been ethical." The floor was in chaos again with shouting, boos, cat-calls. Tammany's James J. Hoey, of New York, shouted, "How about the coal contracts?" Others shouted that Bryan had exceeded his time.

Then Bryan launched into a long defense of the Progressive Democracy and its mission in overcoming problems the nation faced. "My friends, the Republican Party has been granting privileges and favors. It gave one hundred millions to Doheny, about one hundred millions to Sinclair. It tried to give ninety millions in relief from taxation to less than five thousand of the biggest taxpayers. . . . Thank you for your attention," he finally concluded to a mix of applause and boos. The

Times reported the next day that Bryan had "provoked more pugnacity, ill-feeling, bad blood and un-Christian ferocity than is ever seen in the Garden in a whole boxing season."

The Roll Call of the States resumed for the Thirty-Eighth Ballot. McAdoo accumulated 444 votes, Smith 321, Davis 105, Ralston 32, Underwood 39½, Robinson 24, Glass 24, Cox 55, Ritchie 17½, Saulsbury 6, Walsh 1½, Jonathan Davis 4, Robert L. Owen 24. Bryan's appeal had fallen on deaf ears. The Convention recessed at 4:05 in the afternoon.

That evening witnessed more horse trading. On the Thirty-Ninth Ballot, McAdoo jumped to 499, Smith fell to 320½, Davis tumbled to 71. On the Fortieth Ballot, McAdoo topped 500 for the first time, at 506.4, Smith fell further to 315.1 These results set off a parade of banners for McAdoo that lasted ten minutes, while others in the hall yelled, "Smith, Smith, Smith." The Forty-First Ballot saw no follow-up for McAdoo, nor did the Forty-Second Ballot, after which the deadlocked Convention adjourned until Thursday morning.

At 10:30 a.m. July 3, 1924, the Convention went at its duty again. The *Times* proclaimed that "Convention In Uproar as M'Adoo Pushes His Vote to 505½, But Fails In Fierce Night Drive To Gain A Majority." "Bryan Wages Furious Afternoon Battle With Hecklers." "More Ralston Talk Amid The Deadlock." The *Times* also reported that William McAdoo had taken personal charge of his drive from Suite 203 of the Madison Square Hotel, working side-by-side with the financiers Bernard Baruch and Thomas Chadbourne. Floor managers William F. O'Connell, of Chicago, E. T. Meredith, of Iowa, Colonel Thomas B. Love, of Texas, rushed in and out of his room with new instructions. Their strategy was to gain a majority and then leverage it to gain the two-thirds vote. McAdoo was working to persuade Senator Robinson to drop out as a favorite son.

Meanwhile, Indiana boss Thomas Taggart was pushing Senator Ralston. "He is Progressive. He is honest and open and everyone knows it. . . . And as a vote getter he is not excelled by any man thus far mentioned for the nomination." The odds on Wall Street had become 3½ to 1 against either Smith or Davis.

The fight resumed. On the Forty-Third Ballot, McAdoo tailed off to 483.4 and Smith edged up to 319.1. There was little difference in the Forty-Fourth, the Forty-Fifth, the Forty-Sixth, the Forty-Seventh, or the Forty-Eighth Ballots. McAdoo fell another 20 points to 463½ on the Forty-Ninth Ballot, but Smith gained little. John W. Davis was at 63½ and Samuel M. Ralston edged forward to 57. The Fiftieth Ballot offered no new light. On the Fifty-First Ballot, McAdoo slid to 442½, Smith climbed to 328. On the Fifty-Second try, McAdoo fell further to 413½, Ralston advanced to 93. George Gordon Battle attracted 20. On the Fifty-Third tally, McAdoo edged forward again to 432½, Smith was a little more than 100 behind at 320½. Franklin D. Roosevelt attracted 1 vote on the Fifty-Fourth Ballot. The Conventioneers, exhausted, frustrated, and angry, then adjourned until the evening. Many of the female delegates moved into the homes of New York women, having depleted their funds to pay for hotels and meals.

That evening, the Chair continued the relentless Roll Call of the States and after the Fifty-Fifth Ballot, there was little movement. The Fifty-Sixth Ballot saw McAdoo increase his standing to 430 again. Smith remained at 320½. The Fifty-Seventh Ballot produced the same results. The Chair read an invitation to delegates from the Society of Tammany inviting them to attend its One Hundred and Thirty-Sixth Fourth of July celebration the next morning. On the Fifty-Eighth Ballot, McAdoo climbed to 495, Smith rose to 331½. On the Fifty-Ninth Ballot, McAdoo slid back to 473½. The Sixtieth Ballot saw no breakthrough, nor did the Sixty-First.

At 1 a.m., Edmund H. Moore, of Ohio, expressed the exasperation of all. "It is evident we are getting nowhere with this monotonous Roll Call, and that we need some little time not only for sleep but for consultation. I move we now adjourn." The Convention complied.

The Twenty-Fourth Democratic National Convention's Tenth Day, July 4, 1924, began with a prayer by the Reverend Paul Mansfield Spencer, of the Church of the Strangers, in New York City. On the nation's anniversary, he observed, "Empires have come and gone, thrones with centuries of glorious history back of them have fallen into decay, while America, this Divine experiment, has advanced with amazing glory until the luster of her free institutions has become the model of nations reaching out after the new ideals."

Mrs. William E. Mills sang "The Star Spangled Banner," and the Democratic assembly heard a reading of The Declaration of Independence by New York delegate Augustus Thomas, who noted that "a million people are listening on radio." Afterwards, Mr. Hollins Randolph, a delegate from Georgia, and the great-grandson of Thomas Jefferson, read his First Inaugural Address.

The *Times* summarized the situation: "Democrats Take 61 Fruitless Ballots, Breaking Record, Smith Gain of 10 Over-Matched By Swing of 65 To M'Adoo, Raltson Up To 97, Then Drops." "Garden Show Livens Up." "Crowds Hoot Bryan Again." "McAdoo Hits Favorite Sons, Lays Deadlock To Them."

Meanwhile, at Cleveland, the Conference for Progressive Political Action was meeting to nominate Wisconsin Senator Robert M. LaFollette to run against Coolidge and whomever the Democrats nominated. Its leaders were saying that LaFollette could win twelve states. Montana Senator Burton K. Wheeler was nominated to run with LaFollette. His supporters were fervently hoping that John W. Davis or "some other conservative" Democrat would be nominated to help the Progressive cause. And the Progressives had forged an alliance with the non-communist Socialist Party. LaFollette fired away at the monopoly control of Government and industry by private wealth. Among the party's platform planks were calls for the direct election of the President, a national referendum before any declaration of war, and reduced military spending.

The Democratic Convention in New York City returned to its arduous task of finding a candidate for President of the United States. The Sixty-Second Ballot offered no solution. On the Sixty-Third Ballot, the favorite sons were still supported by states holding out for a deal or a better name. The Sixty-Fourth Ballot showed the stalemate tightened. Henry Goeke, of Ohio, then read a telegram from the party's 1920 nominee, James M. Cox, sent from Dayton, in which he withdrew his name to "promote harmony and bring the existing deadlock to an end. . . . I have no personal ambition that rises above my devotion to the Democracy. . . ."

But instead of breaking the deadlock, Ohio added the name of Newton D. Baker to the mix, and he attracted 48 of Cox's 59 votes. The deadlock resumed on the Sixty-Fifth Ballot with McAdoo at 492 and Smith with 336½. Baker climbed to 55 votes on the Sixty-Sixth Ballot, while John Davis retained his third position with 74½. The situation was getting desperate. A vote to go into Executive Session while all the nominees addressed the executive body was defeated.

Franklin D. Roosevelt then took the floor with a resolution to suspend the rules so Governor Alfred E. Smith might address the Convention. By this time, Roosevelt himself was becoming known as the "Happy Warrior," the phrase he had used to describe Governor Smith. He had spent most of the Convention on the aisle of the second or third row of the New York section smiling and shaking hands and exchanging words with a constant stream of visitors. He had been overheard telling Newton D. Baker that "The first hundred ballots are the hardest." His resolution failed. The Convention recessed until that evening at 8:30 p.m.

That night, the Convention was read a telegram from the Vanderbilt Hotel in which William Gibbs McAdoo urged the body to "grant unanimous consent" to Governor Smith to address the body. Cries of "No, no," echoed in response. A resolution to that affect was voted down and the Roll Call of the States resumed with the Sixty-Seventh Ballot, which saw relatively no movement for McAdoo or Smith. On the Sixty-Eighth Ballot, which saw no improvement for the leaders, humorist Will Rogers, who was covering the Convention for several papers, received a single vote, which sparked laughter and applause.

On the Sixty-Ninth Ballot, McAdoo shot higher with 530 to 335 for Smith, 64 for John Davis, 56 for Baker, and 2½ for Josephus Daniels. The Seventieth Ballot saw West Virginia, Ohio, Alabama, Arkansas, Virginia, Maryland, and a few other states holding on to their favorite sons. A resolution by Edward Frensdorf, of Michigan, to have both McAdoo and Smith step aside was defeated, and the Convention adjourned until its Eleventh Day.

On July 5, 1924, delegates gathered at 10:48 in the morning for another round of voting. The headlines noted ''M'Adoo In Night Spurt Reaches 530;'' ''Ralston And Cox Out;'' ''Convention Rejects Pleas to Hear Smith;'' ''Governor's Friends Angry Over Rebuff.'' Other headlines told of ''A Day Of Frayed Tempers.'' ''M'Adoo Leaders Ask Smith To Withdraw.'' ''Resolution Calling Upon Two Leaders to Withdraw Only Amuses the Floor.'' ''Delegates Feel Need Of A 'Boss.' ''

Another headline was more ominous: ''Calvin Coolidge, Jr. Is Seriously Ill; Father and Mother at Bedside of their Younger Son, Who Has Septic Poisoning, Blistered Heel The Cause.'' The problem had resulted from a game with his brother on the White House tennis court. Another headline held election consequences: ''LaFollette Accepts Call.'' Meanwhile, another story noted, ''10,000 In Klan Parade At Little Rock.''

On the Seventy-First Ballot, there was no resolution of the deadlock. The same was the case with the Seventy-Second Ballot. Edward M. Semans, of Oklahoma, presented a resolution calling for the favorite son candidate with the lowest vote total of each ballot to withdraw his name. It failed. The Seventy-Third Ballot produced no winner and none of the favorite sons withdrew. Resolutions to suspend the Convention and reconvene later were defeated. The delegates felt the agony of trench warfare as both leading sides locked in for a long siege.

By the Seventy-Fourth Ballot, Newton D. Baker's support had evaporated to 5 votes, McAdoo registered 510, Smith 364. On the Seventy-Fifth Ballot, James M. Cox reappeared with a single vote. The Seventy-Sixth produced no change. Franklin D. Roosevelt reappeared with a single vote on the Seventy-Seventh Ballot. Former Senator Thomas Taggart, Indiana's Democratic boss, introduced a resolution calling for a conference of the leading candidates. That passed by voice vote, and then the Convention adjourned at 4 p.m. Saturday afternoon until Monday morning.

Over the weekend, the nation watched as surgeons operated on the President's son. As most of the delegates rested, a four-hour conference tried to break the deadlock, but each side was holding tight. Each failure brought a new round of groans. Delegates were beginning to demand that the leaders quit, but McAdoo asserted that he ''had just begun to fight.''

On Monday, July 7, 1924, the Twelfth Day and Eighteenth

Session of the Convention, the body took a moment to pass a resolution expressing sympathy to the President and Mrs. Coolidge on the critical illness of their son, Calvin Jr. The Convention as one voice rose in support. A report was filed from the Conference Committee that had met over the weekend trying to resolve the deadlock. At a Waldorf conference, Smith had given George E. Brennan authority to act on his behalf. The *Times* reported, "The Governor believes there is nothing he or his representatives can do now to break the deadlock, since control of his delegates is almost entirely out of his hands." At least one hundred of his supporters were locked up in McAdoo delegations that were still observing the Unit Rule.

New Yorkers were also saying that the nomination would be useless now no matter who got it. Another headline noted, "Dark Horses Ready For New Contest." But the night before, McAdoo, speaking to a fervent crowd of a thousand supporters at the Hotel Commodore, said he would never quit. "I don't know how those rumors get started. . . . Let's stop kidding. . . . Let's go on with the dance, with the music of victory in our hearts and triumph inevitable. I am trying to do what I can to bring this unfortunate deadlock to an end."

The day before at the conference, a document had been signed by all the candidates, except Mr. McAdoo, to "hereby release each and every delegate from any pledge, instruction, or obligation" to vote for any candidate. McAdoo sent his own letter saying such a release did not, "offer a solution of the unfortunate deadlock in the Convention." He called for the abrogation of the Unit Rule, and "that a majority rule be substituted for the Two-Thirds Rule in nominating a candidate. . . ." McAdoo suggested that in each succeeding ballot, those with the lowest vote total be eliminated. His resolution did not pass.

By the Eighty-First Ballot, things had changed little. McAdoo held at 432, Smith gained to 365, John W. Davis was stuck at third with 70½, and the favorite sons were still drawing support. On the Eighty-Second ballot, Senator Carter Glass, of Virginia, moved to the third spot. Albert W. Gilchrist, of Florida, then stood and asked once more to suspend the rules to release all delegates from any pledges or instructions. This time the resolution passed 985 to 105.

But the Chair ruled the resolution did not abrogate the Unit Rule, so every delegation would still vote together. Before the balloting began, the Chair read a letter of thanks from President Coolidge for the Convention's concern over the illness of his son, which he "profoundly appreciated." The Roll Call of the States resumed and again McAdoo collected 418, Smith 368, Carter Glass 76, and John W. Davis 72½. The Convention then recessed at 3:55 in the afternoon until that evening. Consultations between the leading candidates continued without a break.

At 8:40 p.m., July 7, 1924, the Democratic National Convention reconvened for its Nineteenth Session. Then on the Eighty-Fourth Ballot, the contest suddenly tightened with McAdoo falling to 388½. Governor Smith was just 23 votes behind at 365, Senator Ralston with 86, Carter Glass 72½, John W. Davis 66, Senator Underwood 40½, Senator Robinson 25, Ritchie 16½, Saulsbury 6, Thomas J. Walsh 1½, Governor Bryan 6½, Franklin Roosevelt 1, Senator Owen 20, and William Coyne 1. The Convention immediately proceeded to the Eighty-Fifth Ballot with similar results.

Finally, on the Eighty-Sixth Ballot, New York Governor Al Smith took a slim lead for the first time in what had become the nation's longest Convention with 360 to McAdoo's 353½. Edwin T. Meredith, of Iowa, showed up with 26 votes. The Eighty-Seventh Ballot saw McAdoo fade further to 336½, while Smith picked up only 1, and Mrs. Emma Guffey Miller, sister of the leader of the Pennsylvania delegation, received 1 vote, the first Democratic woman to receive a vote for the Democratic presidential nomination.

Another resolution was offered to reassemble a Conference Committee with representation from each state "for solemn counsel on any suggestion which might tend to bring to a conclusion our deliberations." The Chair put the motion on the table while he made a sad announcement. "With profound grief," Walsh told the vast crowd, "the Chair announces that information has just come to him that Calvin Coolidge, Jr. died at 10:30 this evening." A gasp and then hush passed over the delegates and guests. Walsh announced he would send sympathies to the President's family, and then at 11:48 p.m., he adjourned the Convention until the next morning.

The Convention's Thirteenth Day, Twentieth Session, was called to order at 10:55 ante meridian, July 8, 1924, by Chairman Walsh. After Reverend Francis Potter, of New York, asked that they "perceive, through the accidental, the eternal," Rabbi Stephen S. Wise, of New York, offered a resolution in the name of the New York delegation. "This Convention of the Democratic Party gathers this morning under the shadow of the grief that has come to the home of the Chief Magistrate of our nation. Together with all our fellow Americans, we bow our heads in sympathy and reverence by the side of our President as he and his family pass through the valley of the shadow of death." The resolution passed unanimously. Then Mademoiselle Tamaki Miura, of the San Carlo Grand Opera Company, led the Convention in the "Star Spangled Banner."

The *Times* headlines reflected the new mood of the Convention: "Allied Drive Sends M'Adoo Below Smith On 86th Ballot." "M'Adoo Bloc is Melting, Floating Away, Piece by Piece, Like Ice Jam in a Thaw." "McAdoo Chiefs Undaunted." "Cox Arrives Here For Harmony Move, Disclaims Any Ambitions." "Feeling End of Deadlock is Near."

The papers also were filled with stories recounting the final brave hours of President Coolidge's 16-year-old son. The betting on Wall Street showed the President was now favored 11 to 5 for re-election, perhaps with the sympathy vote.

When the Roll Call resumed with the Eighty-Eighth Ballot, Governor Smith took a large lead at 362 to McAdoo's 315. Smith was still 369 votes short of nomination, with delegates for the favorite sons holding firm. The Eighty-Ninth Ballot put Smith at 357, McAdoo 318½, Senator Ralston, back in the race, was the first candidate beside the two leaders to top 100, by ½ a vote.

On the Ninetieth Ballot, Smith too began to fall back, to 354½, while Ralston jumped to 159½. On the Ninety-First Ballot, Ralston forged forward with 187½, while McAdoo and Smith held steady, and John W. Davis posted 66½. On the Ninety-Second Ballot, Ralston edged forward to 196½, and Homer S. Cummings attracted 8½.

The frustration was overwhelming. Frank C. Davis, of Texas, rose and moved that, "the National Executive Committee be authorized to fix a time and place, and that this Convention adjourn to such a time and place . . . for further deliberations." The Chair ruled the motion out of order and called for the Ninety-Third Ballot and there was no relative movement. Davis, of Texas, then moved to hold further proceedings of the Convention in executive session. His motion was defeated.

Chicago boss George E. Brennan rose: "This Convention has been in session now for more than two weeks," he complained. "The Democratic folk at home expect us to make a nomination. With the hope that the men with the interests of the party at heart will in the meantime take action towards that end, I move now that we take a recess until 9 o'clock this evening."

Charles M. Hay, of Missouri, injected: "Unless some delegations come here prepared to try to help nominate somebody, instead of trying to keep somebody from being nominated, we will never end this Convention." He was applauded. "There has not been today, in my judgment, a good faith effort on the part of delegations, except a limited few, to try to find a candidate for this Convention. I came here supporting Mr. McAdoo. My heart is with him now, for that matter. Others here have been anxious to nominate the great Governor of New York," he was interrupted by cheers. "Others have been supporting their favorite sons. There does not seem to be a willingness on the part of any faction to get together upon an acceptable candidate who can stand four-square upon the platform announced by this Convention. So far as I am concerned, I am unwilling to pull the Democratic Party's house down for the sake of any man." The Convention then voted at 2:50 p.m. to adjourn until 9 p.m.

The Twenty-First Session, July 8, 1924 was called to order by

Chairman Walsh at 9:07 post meridian. Reverend Wythe Leigh Kinsolving, of New York, prayed that, "Thou remove from the minds of the men and the women in this place all bigotry, all intolerance, all racial or sectional or denominational smallness. . . ." He asked, "Build up in the hearts of those men wishing to be chosen a willingness to sacrifice any selfish egoism for party harmony, to sacrifice personal ambition for national good. . . ."

Chairman Walsh then read a letter from Indiana Senator Samuel M. Ralston asking that his name be withdrawn from further consideration by the Convention. "Great as the honor would be I do not want the nomination." (Ralston would die the next year.) The band played "On the Banks of the Wabash" to the cheers of the Convention. The strong contingent of McAdoo women stood on their chairs and sang: "Glory, glory, Halleluiah; Glory, glory, Halleluiah; Glory, glory, Halleluiah, We're All For McAdoo." The Convention then congratulated the U.S. Olympic team in France on its various victories putting it in first place, ahead of Finland.

Then the thrills came fast. Franklin Roosevelt, chairman of the Smith campaign, asked for unanimous consent to address the body: "You have been far too good to me, much better than I deserve," cries of "No, no," followed, "but all the same I want to say to you that this is, I hope, the last time that I shall address a Democratic Convention, until 1928 . . . . The candidate for whom I speak now leads the poll in this Convention. We have advocated his nomination as the representative of great Democratic principles, but the future of the Democratic Party rises far above the success of any candidate. After nearly one hundred ballots it is quite apparent to him and to me that the forces behind Governor Smith, the leader in the race, and those behind Mr. McAdoo, a close second, cannot be amalgamated. For the sake of the party, therefore, Governor Smith authorizes me to say that immediately upon the withdrawal by Mr. McAdoo of his name, Governor Smith will withdraw. . . ." Smith's clever concession linked to his opponent drew loud applause. "I would add only this, that until such withdrawal has been made by Mr. McAdoo, I can say that Governor Smith's supporters will continue to vote for Governor Smith."

The Ninety-Fourth Ballot was called. McAdoo took back the lead with 395 to Smith's 364, John W. Davis moved back into third place with 81¾, and Samuel M. Ralston still received 37 votes. On the Ninety-Fifth Ballot, McAdoo rose to 417½, Smith increased to 367½, Davis jumped to 139¼, and Ralston dropped off the board. Edward M. Semans, of Oklahoma, introduced another resolution to abrogate the Two-Thirds Rule. The Chair over-ruled him. On the Ninety-Sixth Ballot, McAdoo increased to 421, Smith fell to 359½, Davis rose to 171½, and the votes for many of the favorite sons dried up.

Eugene D. O'Sullivan, of Nebraska, introduced another resolution to go into executive session and adopt the Australian (secret) Ballot. "It behooves us to put freedom of choice above compulsion of choice, above the candidate of our choice, and Right above everything." The resolution was voted down and the Ninety-Seventh Ballot was called. Davis advanced to 183¼. Another resolution to abrogate the Two-Thirds Rule failed. A resolution to remain in continuous session until a nomination was made was also voted down. Once more the galleries were packed with an eager crowd in which the *Times* said "the fiery spirit of the opening night blazed again. On the floor there was less evidence of high expectations."

The Ninety-Eighth Ballot put McAdoo at 406½, Smith 354, Davis 194¾, Underwood 38¼, Robinson 25, Glass 36, Charles Bryan 5, Walsh 6, Ritchie 18½, Saulsbury 6, Thomas R. Marshall (Wilson's Vice President) 3, and Owen 1. The Ninety-Ninth Ballot kept McAdoo ahead of Smith by just ½ a vote at 353, with John W. Davis moving up with 210. The crowds in the balconies were detecting a resolution. "The Convention seemed to have come into its second honeymoon," the *Times* commented.

Before the One Hundredth Ballot, Chairman Walsh read a letter from William Gibbs McAdoo. "The Convention has been in session two weeks and appears to be unable to make nominations under the Two-Thirds Rule. This is an unfortunate situation imperiling party success. I feel that if I should withdraw my name from the Convention I should betray the trust confided to me by the people in many states which have sent delegates here to support me. And yet I am unwilling to contribute to a continuation of a hopeless deadlock. Therefore I have determined to leave my friends and supporters free to take such action as, in their judgment, may best serve the interests of the party. I have made this fight for the principles and ideals of Progressive Democracy, for righteousness, and for the defeat of the reactionary and Wet elements in the party which threaten to dominate it."

There was a chorus of hisses and applause reflecting the Dry and Wet Democratic divide over Prohibition. McAdoo's letter continued, "I hope that this Convention will never yield to reaction and privilege, and that the Democratic Party will always hold aloft the torch which was carried to such noble heights by Woodrow Wilson." On the One Hundredth Ballot, McAdoo slipped to 190, Smith stood pat at 351½, John Davis fell to 203½. Then the Convention adjourned to digest the letter from McAdoo.

On July 9, 1924, the Convention gathered for its Fourteenth Day, Twenty-Second Session. After a prayer asking for solace for the President and his family over the death of his son, intoned by the Reverend William Wilkinson, of New York, the Convention resumed. The headlines of the *Times* told the story: "M'Adoo Frees Delegates For Meredith: J. W. Davis Gets 203½ On The 100th Ballot." "Ralston Announces He Will Not Accept."

That word had come as Tom Taggart said he was ready to put him over the top. "Just as things were looking so favorable," Taggart commented with resignation. "Turmoil In McAdoo Camp, Some of His Leaders Opposed His Abandoning Fight." " 'Chief' Calls In Each One." But the *Times* editorial page was disgusted and advised, "Adjourn; Go Elsewhere." It complained, "McAdoo and his moneyed friends, pushed so desperately after the sentiment and the judgment of his party and of the country had turned definitely against him." The paper also noted that "New York Mourns With The President."

Smith and McAdoo had met in an hour-long, secret parley the afternoon before with party chairman Cordell Hull mediating at the Ritz-Carlton in the apartment of Hugh Wallace, former Ambassador to France. "We knew each other in the tube days," Governor Smith said of McAdoo, referring to the Hudson tunnels that they both had championed. "I had no trouble recognizing him." The talks led nowhere. Some Smith delegates had begun switching to Ralston before he pulled out a second time.

Meanwhile, the Convention cost over-runs were causing a crisis. After already spending $800,000, the host committee had turned things back to the Democratic National Committee, which itself was running short of funds and began axing ushers. The Roll Call of the States was taken for the One Hundred and First Ballot. McAdoo dropped to 52 votes, Smith faded to 121, Oscar Underwood surged forward to 229½, and John W. Davis took the lead with 316. Thomas J. Walsh received 98, Edwin T. Meredith attracted 130, mostly McAdoo votes, with a handful of favorite sons receiving scattered votes. The long and hopeless deadlock had been broken.

On the One Hundred and Second Ballot, John W. Davis, Woodrow Wilson's Solicitor General and Ambassador to Great Britain, picked up almost 100 votes to 415½, Oscar Underwood rose to 317, McAdoo fell to 21, and Smith to 44. While other delegations were fading, the *Times* reported, "West Virginia Delegates Alone Showed No Weariness After Long Days of Voting." The paper also noted, "The flag of William J. Bryan had been nailed to the mast of the McAdoo ship and was going down with the craft beyond doubt."

After two long weeks of bickering, the band wagon was beginning to roll. Iowa signaled the break when it switched its votes to Davis. Finally, on the One Hundred and Third Ballot of the 1924 Democratic National Convention, John William Davis, of West Virginia, broke through and won the nomination with 844 votes. Underwood received 102½, McAdoo 11½, Smith 7½, Robinson 20, Walsh 58,

Meredith 58, Glass 23. Thomas Taggart moved that the nomination be tendered "by acclamation." And the Convention agreed. The next morning headlines described the scene: "Davis Put Over In Wild Stampede." "Weary Delegates Jump For Band Wagon and Join the Big Demonstration."

Davis received the news while alone smoking a cigarette at the townhouse of his friend and home-state supporter, Frank L. Polk, at 6 East Sixty-Eighth Street. "You've won!" shouted his wife from the next room where she and his daughter by his first marriage were listening to the radio. Within a few minutes, they were inundated with calls from friends, supporters, reporters, and the curious who filled the street in front of Polk's place. Spontaneous crowds celebrated in Davis' hometown of Clarksburg, West Virginia. Polk, who had started the campaign for Davis five years earlier, revealed that including the effort at the San Francisco Convention in 1920, the Davis campaign had spent only $5,000 nominating its man. And since Davis favored Prohibition, the Anti-Saloon League saw his victory as a win for Drys.

Amid a roar of relief on the Convention floor, Governor W. A. McCorkle, of West Virginia, gratefully addressed the worn-out delegates, asking them to recognize the party's 1920 nominee, James M. Cox, who then spoke: "Historians have said in the past that in the case of Conventions marked by very bitter contests, ofttimes the compromise candidate selected, so called, was a man of minor ability; but in this instance, with the longest and most spirited Convention in all the history of American politics, there emerges from it under harmonious auspices one of the most resplendent statesmen in the last century."

Cox's assertion was met with great applause. "In his brilliant and blameless career, in his intellectual honesty and courage, in his capacity to deal successfully with large problems, in his experience in domestic and international affairs, John W. Davis, our candidate, is a platform in himself."

A rash of resolutions thanking New York, the press, the radio broadcasting companies, the New York Police Department, the Convention itself, followed. Messages of congratulations that poured into Madison Square Garden were also read to the body. Franklin Roosevelt told a reporter that Davis was "a warm personal friend of mine. I have found him to be a man of splendid intellect, clean thinking, and high Progressive ideals. Davis will have my heartiest support."

After a brief rest, the Convention then heard nominations for a number of possible vice presidential candidates including the first woman proposed for that office, Mrs. Leroy Springs, the national committeewoman from Lancaster, South Carolina, who had headed the Committee on Credentials.

But before the final votes for a Vice President were tallied, the

Convention heard from a defeated Governor Al Smith, who was greeted by prolonged applause from all but the Klan delegations. Most of the delegates had never seen him in person and craned their necks to get a look at one of the men who had held them in captivity for two full weeks. Amid laughter. he instructed them, "If you have been annoyed in any way by the various people with whom you have come in contact, in their zeal to explain to you why in their opinion, I am the greatest man in the world, overlook it."

Smith then launched into a defensive listing of New York's accomplishments during his terms, reasons he implied, he should have been nominated; civil service laws, reorganization of government, improved public schools, road construction, water power development, enlightened factory codes and workmen's compensation, prison reform, public health, pension law, agricultural assistance, and tax cuts. "Therefore we feel that the State of New York has done her full share, under Democratic auspices and under Democratic control, to address a National Convention, and promise her support to the candidate of the Convention." His endorsement received thunderous applause.

Smith. confided, "I want to make just a passing reference to my own situation as far as the nomination for the presidency is concerned. If I were to tell anybody in this hall that I was disappointed, it would not be true; I am not. I have gotten as far in the public life of this Country and of this state as I ever expected to get, and even further. I have nothing in my heart but real gratitude, and entertain no harsh or ill feelings." He received great applause, but few believed that the bitter and bigoted opposition to his candidacy had not damaged his natural optimism. Smith concluded, "the very instant that this Convention is finished, I shall take off my coat and vest, and do what we can to improve conditions in the United States of America by the election of the ticket that is going to come from this Convention," said the man who would win the nomination four years hence, only to encounter the same bigotry in the Country at-large.

Then, after more resolutions of thanks, the new candidate himself, John William Davis, of West Virginia, briefly addressed the Convention. The man who stood in front of them had a distinguished public service record which began as a West Virginia state legislator. Davis had been elected to two terms in Congress, but served only from 1911 to 1913. He then was appointed Solicitor General by Woodrow Wilson, serving from 1913 to 1918, and was Ambassador to Great Britain from 1918 to 1921, where he helped Wilson write the Treaty of Versailles. He had served as president of the American Bar Association from 1922 to 1924.

Davis began, the first-ever Convention acceptance speech: "You will not be surprised if I say to you at this moment, grateful as I am for this great honor, I think even more of the burdens and the duties you have given me to bear and perform. But I take heart of grace, for I realize that, whatever may be said of the wisdom of your selection, no one, I think, in all this land will contend that this Convention has acted in haste and without deliberation." The assembly laughed heartily at its own stubbornness.

"The great principles of the Democratic Party are: Honesty in Government; all public office is a public trust; Equal Rights to all men, and special privilege to none." (Davis would go further than the platform and denounce the Klan during his campaign.) He continued. "Fair and equal taxation; an open door of opportunity to the humblest citizen in all the land; loyalty at home, courage and honor and helpfulness abroad.

"These principles are as dear to the American of the East as to the American of the West, as highly revered by the American of the North as they are by the American of the South. And in the name of this truly national creed, this truly national party, it is ready again to do battle with all those who challenge this creed. . . . On this platform all Progressives in this Country can stand; to this banner all liberals can rally; and in this cause all Democrats can, aye, all Democrats will unite." Davis received great applause. The Convention was satisfied with its Dark Horse selection.

Davis concluded, "As a more or less interested bystander, I cannot be ignorant of the fact that this Convention has had its debates and its differences, and in the truly Democratic fashion has fought out its conflicts of opinion; and all these things, as disturbing as they have seemed at the moment, were but the thunder storm that has cleared the clouds away and left shining on us the sun of a coming victory and success." Davis was showered with a thunderous ovation.

The next day, papers around the country generally praised the Davis nomination and condemned the Convention that made it. Will Rogers wrote, "Who said miracles don't happen? Didn't the Democratic National Convention nominate a man at last?" He added Davis was "the class of the race." And he sarcastically added that W. J. Bryan's record of influencing every Convention since 1896 was still intact. "When he came out against Davis, Davis was a nominated man."

The *Omaha World-Herald* called Davis, "an eminent lawyer, a true liberal, one of the greatest and ablest men ever nominated by either party." The *Texas American* commented, "The least that can be said for Davis is that he is a match for Coolidge." The *Chattanooga Times* wrote, "business enterprise and industry may now feel safe. . . ." The *Savannah Morning News* concluded, "He is presidential caliber, with international training." But Hearst's *New York American* charged that Davis was, "the personal choice of the House of Morgan." The *Boston Globe* rebutted, "Mr. Davis has had a good deal of other clients, and among them were Eugene V. Debs and Mother Jones."

The Buffalo *Express* called Davis, "the closest to the Woodrow Wilson type and best qualified to represent Mr. Wilson's ideals and to make the League of Nations the leading issue." The *Portland Press-Herald* said his triumph was "a triumph for the conservative forces of the Democratic Party." The *New York Times* editorialized, "Both the Democratic Party and the country will experience a great sense of relief at the nomination of Mr. Davis, coming as the unexpected issue of depressing days of senseless strife. . . ." The papers also announced that William Gibbs McAdoo was "going abroad" with his family for several weeks in Europe.

The 1924 Democratic National Convention nominated Nebraska Governor Charles W. Bryan for Vice President at 2:23 in the morning of July 10, 1924. He was pre-selected by a room filled with party bosses, in part to bring his brother William Jennings Bryan along with the ticket. His victory was met with boos from the Garden galleries. The nominations finally done, the Convention adjourned sine die, to the uncertainties of the coming campaign and election.

Wall Street set the early odds at 2 to 1 for Coolidge. A peacetime election during a period of prosperity favored the incumbent. "Keep Cool with Coolidge," Republicans advised. The President didn"t even bother to campaign until the last week of the contest. Davis countered with charges of corruption and international neglect. In addition to attacking the Klan, Davis was a forceful advocate for the League of Nations. The voters were not buying the idea in 1924 any more than they did in 1920. Bryan, true to his word, stumped for the ticket, but to no avail.

In the end, though, William Jennings Bryan proved partially right. Davis, perceived as a front for Wall Street, had no chance of winning the Northwest or the West. But it wasn't the Progressives who prevailed there. On Election Day, November 4, 1924, the first ever to use voting machines, Coolidge swept to victory and his first elected term, with 382 Electoral votes to 136 for Davis and just 13 for LaFollette. Davis won the twelve states of the South, but did not take his home State of West Virginia, losing 49.5 to 44 percent. LaFollette only won his home State of Wisconsin with 54 percent of the vote. Coolidge won thirty-five states, including the Midwest and all of the Northeast.

Although LaFollette hurt Davis in several states that might have gone Democratic, President Calvin Coolidge drew 15,719,921 votes, or 54 percent of the popular total. Davis attracted just 8,386,704 votes, or 28.8 percent of the popular vote. LaFollette received 4,832,532, or 16.6 percent.

The United States settled in for five more years of economic speculation before the collapse leading to the Great Depression. And for the next fifty-two years, New York did not host another National Presidential Nominating Convention until 1976, when the Democrats returned to nominate Jimmy Carter, who became the nation's Thirty-Ninth President. Millions in the United States and around the world watched the event on television. A new era of closely-scripted Conventions, with little spontaneity, few real debates, or dramatic nomination fights, had already begun. The exciting era of New York's pre-TV Conventions had come to an end.

New York Presidential Conventions, The TV Era (1976-2004)

Year	Party	Location	Nominee	No. of Ballots
1976	Democrat	Madison Square Garden	Jimmy Carter	1
1980	Democrat	Madison Square Garden	Jimmy Carter	1
1992	Democrat	Madison Square Garden	William Jefferson Clinton	1
2004	Republican	Madison Square Garden	George Walker Bush	1

Bibliography

Adams, John Quincy. *Memoirs of John Quincy Adams, vol. 12.* Philadelphia: J. P. Lippincott & Co., 1877.

Allen, Frederick Lewis. *Only Yesterday: An Informal History of the 1920's.* New York: Harper & Row, 1931.

Allen, Oliver E. *The Tiger: The Rise and Fall of Tammany Hall.* Boston: Addison-Wesley Publishing Company, 1993.

Bagby, Wesley M. *The Road to Normalcy: The Presidential Campaign and Election of 1920.* Baltimore: The Johns Hopkins Press, 1962.

Bancroft, George. *Martin Van Buren. New York: Harper & Brothers, 1889.*

Bain, Richard C. and Judith H. Parris. Convention Decisions and Voting Records: Studies in Presidential Selection. Washington D. C.: The Brookings Institution. 1973.

Biographical Directory of the United States Congress, 1774-1989, Bicentennial Edition. Washington, D.C.: U.S. Government Printing Office, 1989.

Black, Mary. *Old New York in Early Photographs.* New York: Dover Publications, Inc., 1973.

Burnham, Walter Dean. *Presidential Ballots, 1836-1892*

Carman, Syrett, and Wishy. A History of the American People, vol. 1. New York: Alfred A. Knopf, 1960.

Chance, Joseph E., ed. *Mexico Under Fire.* Fort Worth: Texas Christian University Press, 1994.

Chaplin, Jeremiah and J. D. Chaplin. *The Life of Charles Sumner.* Boston: D. Lathrop & Company, 1874.

Congressional Quarterly. *National Party Conventions, 1831-2000.* Washington, D.C.: 2000.

Cramer, C. H. *Newton D. Baker: A Biography.* Cleveland and New York: The World Publishing Company, 1961.

Crawford, John E., compiler. *Millard Fillmore: A Bibliography.* Westport and London: Greenwood Press, 2002.

DeGrecorio, William A. *The Complete Book of U.S. Presidents.* New York: Gramercy Books, 2001.

Democratic National Convention. *Official Report of the Proceedings Held in Madison Square Garden, New York City, June 24-July 9, 1924.* Indianapolis: Bookwalter-Ball-Greathouse Printing Co., 1924.

Dillon, Merton. *The Abolitionists: Growth of a Dissenting Minority.* DeKalb: Northern Illinois University Press, 1974.

Duberman, Martin, B. *Charles Francis Adams 1807-1886.* Boston: Houghton Mifflin Company, 1961.

Dyer, Oliver. *Phonographic Report, 1848;* National Era, Aug. 17, 24, 31, 1848.

Elson, Henry W. *Side Lights on American History.* London: The MacMillan Company, 1902.

Ferrell, Robert H. *The Strange Deaths of President Harding,* Columbia and London: University of Missouri Press, 1996.

Fladeland, Betty. *James Gillespie Birney: Slaveholder to Abolitionist.* Ithaca, New York: Cornell University Press, 1955.

Foner, Eric. *Free Soil, Free Labor, Free Men: The Ideology of the Republican Party Before the Civil War.* New York: Oxford University Press, 1970.

Goodell, William. *Slavery and Anti-Slavery: A History of the Great Struggle in Both Hemispheres.* New York: Negro Universities Press, 1852.

Hamilton, Holman. *Zachary Taylor.* New York and Indianapolis: The Bobbs-Merrill Company, 1941.

Hart, Albert Bushnell. *Salmon Portland Chase.* Boston and New York: Houghton, Mifflin and Company, 1899.

Hart, Albert Bushnell. *Slavery and Abolition 1831-1841.* New York: Harper Brothers, 1906.

Hesseltine, William B. *The Rise and Fall of Third Parties.* Washington, D.C.: Public Affairs Press, 1948.

Hofstadter, Richard. *Great Issues in American History, vol. 1 1765-1865.* New York: Vintage Books, 1958.

Holt, Michael F. *The Rise and Fall of the American Whig Party: Jacksonian Politics and the Onset of the Civil War.* Oxford and New York: Oxford University Press, 1999.

Horton, John Theodore. *History of Northwest New York, Erie, Niagara, Wyoming, Genesee and Orleans Counties.* Lewis Historical Publishing Company, Inc., 1947.

Hoyt, Edwin P. Jr. *Jumbos and Jackasses.* Garden City, New York: Doubleday & Company, Inc., 1960.

Jackson, Kenneth T. ed. *The Encyclopedia of New York City.* New Haven and London: Yale University Press, 1995.

Josephy, Alvin M. Jr. *500 Nations: An Illustrated History of North American Indians.* New York: Alfred A. Knopf, 1994.

Josephson, Matthew and Hannah. *Al Smith, Hero of the Cities: A Political Portrait Drawing on the Papers of Frances Perkins.* London: Thames and Hudson, 1969.

Johnston, Alexander. *American Political History, 1763-1876.* New York and London: G. P. Putnam's Sons, 1905.

Katz, Irving. *August Belmont: A Political Biography*. New York and London: Columbia University Press, 1968.

Lambert, Oscar Doane. *Presidential Politics in the United States, 1841-1844*. Durham, North Carolina: Duke University Press, 1936.

Lowance, Mason. *Against Slavery: An Abolitionist Reader*. New York: Penguin Books, 2000.

McCabe, James D., Jr. *The Life and Public Service of Horatio Seymour Together with a Complete and Authentic Life of Francis P. Blair, Jr.* New York, Cincinnati, Chicago, St. Louis, Atlanta, and San Francisco: United States Publishing Company, 1868.

McCormac, Eugene Irving. *James K. Polk: A Political Biography*. New York: Russell & Russell, Inc., 1965.

McKivigen, John R. *The War Against Proslavery Religion, Abolitionism and the Northern Churches, 1830-1865*. Ithaca and London: Cornell University Press, 1984.

McPerson, Edward. ed. *The Political History of the United States of America during the Period of Reconstruction*. New York: DaCapo Press, 1972.

Mandelbaum, Seymour J. *Boss Tweed's New York*. New York, London, and Sydney: John Wiley & Sons, 1965.

Who Was Who in America: Historical Volume, 1607-1896. Chicago: A.N. Marquis Co., 1963.

Martin, Michael and Leonard Gelber. *The New Dictionary of American History*. New York: Philosophical Library, 1952.

Menken, H. L. *A Carnival of Buncombe*. Baltimore: The Johns Hopkins University Press, 1956.

Mitchell, Stewart. *Horatio Seymour of New York*. Cambridge, Massachusetts: Harvard University Press, 1938.

Murray, Robert K. *The Harding Era*. Minneapolis: University of Minnesota Press, 1969.

Mushkat, Jerome. *Tammany: The Evolution of a Political Machine, 1789-1865.* Syracuse, New York: Syracuse University Press, 1971.

Mushkat, Jerome and Joesph G. Rayback. *Martin Van Buren.* DeKalb: Northern Illinois University Press, 1997.

New York Evening Post, August 24, 1848.

New York Times, The, July 3-November 5, 1868.

New York Times, The. June 19-July 10, 1924.

Peterson, Norma Lois. *The Presidencies of William Henry Harrison and John Tyler.* Lawrence: University Press of Kansas, 1989.

Presidential Elections 1789-2000, Congressional Quarterly Press, 2002.

Rayback, Joseph G. *Free Soil: The Election of 1848.* Lexington, 1970.

Rayback, Robert J. *Millard Fillmore: Biography of a President.* Buffalo, New York: Henry Stewart, Inc., 1959.

Ripley, C. Peter. ed. *The Black Abolitionist Papers, vol. III, U.S., 1830-1846.* Chapel Hill: University of North Carolina Press, 1991.

Roseboom, Eugene H. *A History of Presidential Elections.* London: The MacMillan Company, 1957.

Sautter, R. Craig, and Burke, Edward M. *Inside The Wigwam: Chicago Presidential Conventions 1860-1996.* Chicago: Loyola Press/Wild Onion Books, 1996.

Sautter, R. Craig. *Philadelphia Presidential Conventions (1856-2000).* Highland Park, Ill: december press, 2000.

Schlesinger, Arthur M. *History of U.S. Political Parties, vol. I, 1789-1860, vol. II, 1860-1910, vol. III, 1910-1945.* New York: Chelsea House Publishers, 1973.

Sellers, Charles Grier. *James K. Polk: Jacksonian.* Princeton, New

Jersey: Princeton University Press, 1957.

Sewell, Richard H. *Ballots for Freedom: Antislavery Politics in the United States 1837-1860.*

Shepard, Edward M. *Martin Van Buren.* Boston and New York: Houghton Mifflin Co., 1888.

Shotwell, Walter G. *The Life of Charles Sumner.* New York: Thomas Y. Crowell & Company, 1910.

Silbey, Joel H. *Political Ideology and Voting Behavior in the Age of Jackson.* Englewood Cliffs, New Jersey: Prentice-Hall, Inc., 1973.

Silver, Nathan. *Lost New York.* New York: Schocken Books, 1972.

Smith, Elbert B. *The Death of Slavery in the United States.* Chicago: University of Chicago Press, 1967.

Smith, William Ernest. *The Francis Preston Blair Family in Politics, vols. I & II.* New York, Boston, Chicago, Dallas, Atlanta, and San Francisco: The MacMillan Company, 1933.

Smith, James Morton, and Murphy, Paul L. ed. *Liberty and Justice: A Historical Record of American Constitutional Development.* New York: Alfred A. Knopf, 1958.

Southwick, Leslie H. *Presidential Also-Rans and Running Mates, 1788-1980.* Jefferson, North Carolina and London: McFarland & Company, Inc., 1984.

Stegmaier, Mark J. *Texas, New Mexico, and the Compromise of 1850.* Kent, Ohio, London, England: Kent University Press, 1996.

Steiner, Bernard C. *The Life of Reverdy Johnson.* Baltimore: The Norman, Remington Company, 1914.

Stone, Irving. *They Also Ran: The Story of the Men Who Were Defeated for the Presidency.* Garden City and New York: Doubleday, Doran and Company, Inc., 1945.

Strong, Douglas M. *Perfectionist Politics: Abolitionism and the Religious Tensions of American Democracy.* Syracuse, N.Y.: Syracuse University Press, 1999.

Storey, Moorfield. *Charles Sumner: American Statesman.* Boston and New York: Houghton, Mifflin and Company, 1900.

Swanberg, W. A. *Citizen Hearst.* New York: Charles Scribner's Sons, 1961.

Van Deusen, Glyndon G. *Thurlow Weed: Wizard of the Lobby.* Boston: Little, Brown and Company, 1947.

Van Deusen, Glyndon G. *Horace Greeley: Nineteenth Century Crusader.* Philadelphia: University of Pennsylvania Press, 1953.

Van Doren, Charles. ed. *American Biographies.* Springfield, Massachusetts: Merriam-Webster, 1975.

Wakeman, George. official reporter. *Official Proceedings of the National Democratic Convention held at New York, July 4-9, 1868.* Boston: Rockwell & Rollins, Printers, 1868.

Weymouth, Lally. *1876: The Way We Were.* New York: Random House, 1976.

Wilson, Henry. *The Rise and Fall of the Slave Power in America. vol. I.* New York: Negro Universities Press, 1872.

Wilson, Major L. *The Presidency of Martin Van Buren.* Lawrence: University Press of Kansas, 1984.